Amsterdam

ALSO BY RUSSELL SHORTO

Descartes' Bones
The Island at the Center of the World
Saints and Madmen
Gospel Truth

Amsterdam

A HISTORY OF
THE WORLD'S MOST LIBERAL CITY

Russell Shorto

Little, Brown

LITTLE, BROWN

First published in the United States in 2013 by Doubleday,
a division of Random House
First published in Great Britain in 2014 by Little, Brown

Book design by Maria Carella
Jacket design by Michael J. Windsor
Front of jacket: middle painting © Patrick Hughes/Art agency Vieleers;
tiles © Christopher Elwell/Shutterstock; windmill © Canicula/
Shutterstock; map © Encyclopaedia Britannica/UIG/Universal Images
Group/Getty Images; top image of Blue bridge and the Amstel River
photomechanical courtesy of the Library of Congress Prints and Photographs Division
Back of jacket: tulips melis © Shutterstock; Rembrandt © Rijksmuseum,
Amsterdam; bike © Hein Nouwens/Shutterstock; John Lennon and Yoko
Ono courtesy of the National Archief

A CIP catalogue record for this book
is available from the British Library.

Hardback: ISBN 978-1-4087-0347-2
C Format: ISBN 978-1-4087-0348-9

Printed and bound in Great Britain by
Clays Ltd, St Ives plc

Papers used by Little, Brown are from well-managed forests
and other responsible sources.

MIX
Paper from
responsible sources
FSC® C104740

Little, Brown
An imprint of
Little, Brown Book Group
100 Victoria Embankment
London EC4Y 0DY

An Hachette UK Company
www.hachette.co.uk

www.littlebrown.co.uk

For
Pamela, Anna, Eva, Anthony, Reinier, Hector, and Benjamin

Contents

Amsterdam

Part One

A BICYCLE TRIP

A day in Amsterdam begins with me leaving my apartment with my toddler son in my arms, strapping him into his seat between the handlebars of my bicycle, working his blocky little sneakered feet into the footpads, then setting off through the quiet, generally breezy streets of our neighborhood, which is called Oud Zuid: Old South. You could look at the work of any Dutch master for an idea of the morning light we cycle through. There is a white cleanness to it, a rinsed quality. It's a sober light, without, for example, any of the orange particulate glow you get from the Mediterranean sun. The houses of the neighborhood are three- or four-story brick buildings, all constructed in the first two decades of the twentieth century, when what was then a vigorously working-class city, one that still smelled of herring and roasting coffee beans, expanded rapidly around its central core of canals.

We cycle past street-level apartments, some of which, following a Dutch tradition that I like to think has to do with an ingrained commitment to openness, feature a central uncurtained window that puts the living room on public display, as if the family who lives there thinks its life is worthy of a museum. For a while I didn't understand why, when we reach the part of the route that has us riding alongside a canal, my son would break out in a series of high screeches. Then I realized Anthony was imitating the gulls that squeal as they do their crazy arcs and dives above the water.

We pass a few businesses. The bakery is usually scenting the morning air with cinnamon as we ride by. The display windows of the corner bicycle shop exhibit sturdy, gleaming new models, lately in an array of pastel tones, by Gazelle and Batavus, factories that have been turning out Dutch bicycles for a century. An open door to the right of the windows leads down to the basement, and the repair shop, whose interior I know too well. The grooves in the concrete at both sides of the stairway leading below are meant for bicycle tires.

Once in a while I will vary the route and turn down along the Hobbemakade, where on our right is a slightly forlorn-looking stretch of canal, with weeds growing up through the quayside where rickety houseboats are moored, and on the left are the remnants of one of the smallest and least noticeable of the city's several red light districts. De Wallen—Amsterdam's central red light district—is a sort of alternate-universe Disneyland, noisy and with a certain ragged cheer, visited not only by drunken male tourists but also by couples strolling arm in arm and even families. Here, by contrast, there are only three or four of the display windows that the city's licensed prostitutes sit in to exhibit themselves, in the midst of what is otherwise a residential street. I never get how customers would know to find them. Nevertheless, even in the morning there is often at least one woman on duty, wearing a swimsuit, sitting on a stool, smoking, or listlessly punching the keys of a cell phone. Sometimes she will wave at Anthony and give him a little smile. The other window might be empty save for a stool with a towel folded on the seat that is crumpled in a way that looks like it has been sat on. Such details—the crumpled towel, the bored look of the woman facing a long day of staring into the street, punctuated by short intervals of sex with strangers—bring the city's infamous tolerance of vice out of the realms of sensationalism and idealism and into the realm of the deeply mundane. As with any other place, living here for a time causes the exotic to collapse under the weight of ordinariness. Two doors down is another storefront business, an advertising agency whose name—Strangelove—you might think is intended as a wry commentary on the neighbors, but I would bet not. I'll bet they don't even notice.

Amsterdam School is the name given to the style of architecture that was pioneered in my neighborhood as it was coming into being. The style has a formal aesthetic, which has its technical descriptors and philosophical (socialist) underpinnings, but to me it simply embodies a reasonably pleasant combination of whimsy and stolidness. Brick (what could be more stolid?) is the medium, yet there is an infinity of playful variations: rounded turretlike corners, embedded deco-ish sculptures that seem to mock the hardness of the material (a girl surrounded by rabbits, a baby holding up a doorway), block-long apartment buildings that could have had an ocean liner as their inspiration, or a wedding cake.

The neighborhood is no more than five minutes by bike from the canal belt and the storied seventeenth-century heart of Amsterdam, but when developers were laying it out a hundred years ago they must have felt a need to connect the new area to the city's history. If Rembrandt visited the immediate area around my home he might feel some familiarity, for even though this was swamp and fields in his time the streets bear the names of many of the artists whom he groomed in his workshop or competed with for commissions: Frans van Mieris, who wrought exquisite small portraits of the wealthy class; Nicolaas Maes, who often painted ordinary people at prayer and at meals and gave the same loving attention to a glistening loaf of bread or an earthen pitcher on a table as he did to the faces of his subjects; Philips Wouwerman, who specialized in hunting scenes and was known to paint a mean horse.

At the time my neighborhood came into being, all of those were figures of the grand past, so that the names Nicolaas Maesstraat and Frans van Mierisstraat instantly gave the new neighborhood some of the luster of Amsterdam's age of glory, when it was—briefly

and improbably—the greatest city in the world. To this day the
houses on those streets have dignified presence. But as you go farther away from the center, as we do on our morning trip, the houses
get plainer. It seems the city fathers of a century ago did not want to
dilute the grandeur of the golden age by spreading its names too far.
On the other hand, in 1905, right at the time that the more distant
part of the neighborhood was being laid out, the nearby Stedelijk
Museum, the city's modern art museum, mounted the first exhibi-
tion in the country devoted to Vincent van Gogh. The Dutch artist
had died only fifteen years before; his home country had done its
best to ignore him, but it was now obvious that they would have
to pay attention. Yet at the same time, his name didn't carry bourgeois heft—and who knew if those thick swirls of bright color would
withstand the test of time? As a result of what I imagine were con-
siderations such as these, Vincent van Goghstraat—the only street
in the area whose name is instantly, globally recognizable today—is
among the humblest: a single block of monotone dwellings.

That street also signals the end of our little journey. As Anthony
and I pass it, I hop off the bicycle, unstrap him, and set him on
the sidewalk. While I ring the doorbell, he opens the mailbox flap,
which is on his level, and hollers into it. The door is opened by a
Moroccan woman in her thirties, wearing a head scarf, floor-length
robe, and sandals. She has a kind face and smiles at Anthony as she
tells him he's grown over the weekend: "Nou, wat een grote jongen
ben je!" He plays a game, trying to scramble up the stairs to the
next floor instead of going into her apartment. Iman and her husband have lived in Amsterdam for ten years. They have two young
daughters. Her husband drives a city bus; she is a licensed gastouder:
literally, "guest parent," what in the United States would be called
a day care provider. Her four-year-old, Marwa, emerges from behind
her, with a tangle of curls and big deep eyes, and says hello over and
over, very loudly. Then she tells me Anthony is ugly. Then she gives
him a hug and hauls him into the apartment.

Iman and I chat for a few minutes. Some weeks before she asked

if Anthony's mother and I would sign an immigration document in
support of her sister, who wanted to come to Amsterdam to visit. I
was confused at first: I thought one was required to get such statements of support for people who intended to emigrate, not who
merely wanted to visit family. I subsequently learned that it was now
necessary in the Netherlands for people from certain countries (read
poor countries—or, to be more precise, Muslim countries) to file
extensive applications, including having residents vouch for them,
even if all they wanted to do was see the canals and tulips. We
signed the form. Then a few weeks later Iman said her sister's application had been denied. The reason given: she was "*onbetrouwbaar*"–
untrustworthy. When Iman asked, through an immigration lawyer,
for clarification, she was told that because of "ties" in the country it
was feared that her sister might stay in the Netherlands. Iman was
confused by this. She and her husband were legal residents of the
Netherlands. They paid taxes. The family spoke Dutch at home.
They were, as they say, playing by the rules. Yet their legal residence
itself was deemed a reason for untrustworthiness. Much later, the
decision was reversed, and Iman's sister was allowed to visit, but such
is a conundrum of our era: a city famed historically for championing
the notion of tolerance now seemed to be charting odd new frontiers
of intolerance.

Once a week, after I've left Anthony in Iman's care, I don't return
directly home but spend the morning exploring another, quite different frontier of intolerance. Taking another route, I pull up at a corner of the Beethovenstraat (now having reentered the tonier part of
the district, whose precincts are suited to grand names—nearby are
Rubenstraat and Bachstraat), peruse the street corner florist's kiosk,
buy a bunch of variegated tulips or mauve roses, and ring a doorbell
a few steps away. Upstairs, I am met by an elderly woman with short
steel-gray hair, a sharply angled jawline, and darting, birdlike eyes.
Her name is Frieda Menco. We exchange the standard Dutch greet-
ing of three kisses, I hand the flowers to her, she protests mildly
that I shouldn't have, then we enter her apartment. The living and

dining rooms are wide, very bright, and sparsely filled with modernist furniture. A spread is laid out on the coffee table: cookies, chocolate, a pot of coffee and two cups, a jug of water, a vase of flowers.

We sit. I turn on my recorder. We exchange small talk. Then she turns her face toward the watery sunlight pouring in through the windows and says, "Now, where was I?"

Someone outside is shouting—no, a lot of people, confused voices. The train lurches suddenly; the packed bodies sway; people scream. Frieda is sixteen and for two days and nights has sat scrunched on the lap of a middle-aged man whom she doesn't know. The cattle car is so crammed with people that the atmosphere would seem to be one of horror, but instead the press of inexorable power brings on a wave of colossal deadness. The air is clotted with the reek of their waste—a barrel in the corner has been the communal open toilet. It sits perversely high, so in order to relieve herself she not only has to endure the public nature of a private act but must balance herself on its rim and try not to knock it over. There are no windows in the car, and when the door is slid shut there is no virtually no light; the air is dark and stifling as death. Occasionally she catches a glimpse of her parents where they sit wedged on the other side of the car—their eyes frightened but still holding the hard, almost uncrushable nugget of hope in them. She is their only child.

Finally, she is outside, standing on the ground. More shouts—real chaos in the distance. And there—a gallows, a human body, hanging, swaying in space. People over there are running now, screaming. Here, they are being jostled into lines. Now some are pushing into them—they are Jews like them but who know the routine, everyone wearing blue-and-white-striped prison uniforms—whispering hard into their faces: *If you have anything of value, give it to me, because they will take it from you.* Some of the newcomers hand over their jewelry; she gives nothing because she has nothing. They are formed into four lines: two of women and girls, two of men and boys. She and her mother are in one line, to the far right, then comes the other female line—though she doesn't know it yet, this second line, holding people who were quickly deemed not fit for work, is headed directly into the gas chamber—and she spots her father in the third line. Soldiers and dogs keep people in place: those uniforms, the *Stahlhelm*, the helmet with its infamously and menacingly scooped curve. But no, these things didn't register that way yet, didn't have the heavy meaning they would take on.

A grim geometry problem is on display, taunting her to find a solution: as the people lurch forward, the space between where her father stands in his line and where she and her mother are in their line grows wider.

Then, improbably, out of character, she sees her father seem to calculate, reach a rash decision. He has lunged—he is moving across that open space, obliterating that vacuum, passing through the second line of women that stands between his line and hers, defying the gray-uniformed soldiers with their helmets and guns. He is here, breathing, his face—a soft, round, gentle face—close to her. His is an artistic soul, bent by necessity toward commerce. Joël Brommet is a professional window dresser, who also gives correspondence courses in graphic design. Frieda is his joy. She helps him with his work, cranks the mimeograph machine that occupies a corner of their Amsterdam living room, running off the inky-smelling sheets, each with a carefully typed lesson, each beginning, "Worthy student," folds the packets, and stuffs them into brown envelopes to be sent to towns and villages around the country, to young people who hope to escape farming or fishing for a life with a touch more glamour. She would sometimes make trips with her father to stores to observe his latest work. He showed her how he crafted every detail of a window display: the price tags, the signs ("*Speciale prijs! 13 ct.*"), mannequins posed just so. Frieda's earliest memory is of him. She is maybe three years old, happy and sleepy in her bed in their comfortable middle-class apartment. "Will you catch the moon for me, and put it on the cupboard?" She still remembers that cupboard and what a nice ornament she thought the silver disc of the moon would make sitting on top. He answers: "If you sleep like a sweet little girl, I'll fetch a long ladder and get the moon for you."

A wind blows on the Polish plain. Someone is barking a command: an SS guard has spotted her father out of line and is moving toward him. Joël Brommet wraps his arms around his wife and sweeps her up in a kiss: good-bye. Then, obedient as everyone else, following the weight of this new logic, the window dresser runs back to his place. Frieda will never see him again.

Someone grasps her arm. A young man, German. He has her hold it out, palm extended. She feels a jab. A pen marks a rough tattoo in the soft flesh of the underside of her left forearm: A25080.

Into a wide hall the line extends. Then, things moving fast, the women and girls are undressing, standing naked, clothes on the floor, staring down, arms across breasts, and now she feels a wholly new kind of terror grip her as she bends her head and her hair is shaved off and she watches it drop in clumps onto the floor. Another sick shock as gasoline comes raining down on her head. Then they are standing still, naked, shivering, dripping, some ugly, flat suspense building inside them. "We were broken . . ."

Frieda stops talking and gives me an apologetic look. Her eyes show two kinds of pain: one the past horror, the other a small annoyance, but magnified because it is in the present. The weak sunlight strokes her silvery skin. "No, we did this already . . ."

I tell her it's all right, that every time we go over a piece of her story again I learn something new. But I have realized that Frieda is hard on herself. She is eighty-six, suffers from intestinal problems that began with typhoid and dysentery she contracted at Auschwitz, from back and neck pain that stems from torture the prisoners were put through as punishment whenever there was an escape attempt (at an earlier meeting I was on my knees on her living room floor as she directed me into the posture they were forced to keep for hours at a time, holding heavy blocks above their heads), as well as a variety of normal age-related ailments, yet her mind is very sharp—sharp enough that she worries constantly about losing her sharpness. Lapses of memory irritate her. She labors to be proficient at Internet browsing; she takes her car out regularly to keep herself familiar with the streets of the neighborhood where she has spent her life. She will send me an e-mail with a small mistake in it, then later send a follow-up correcting the error.

She was born nearby. Oud Zuid was then a center of Jewish Amsterdam. It still is to some extent, but the war ripped the heart out of it (there were 80,000 Jews in the city in 1940; today there are about 15,000). Frieda's childhood home was an apartment on a wide boulevard that was then called Zuider Amstellaan but that after the war was renamed Rooseveltlaan. The apartment was on the second floor, facing the street. On my computer I have a scanned copy of one of Frieda's most cherished possessions: a photograph, taken at the dining room table in that apartment, of her extended family, seated for a meal in celebration of her grandfather's seventy-fifth birthday. Of the seventeen people at the table, twelve died soon after, most of them at Auschwitz. The very furniture that filled the room—except for a bureau that stands behind the chair where Frieda normally sits as we hold our weekly chats, which her mother managed to track down after the war—was ground under the wheels of history.

Before the war, Frieda knew her neighborhood with the intimacy of childhood: nooks that adults ignored, who came and went. And she knew everyone. Just around the corner from her childhood home is a triangular park rimmed by small apartment buildings. On the second floor of one of these—at 37 Merwedeplein—lived a Jewish couple and their two daughters. She remembers the family as rather *chique mensen*, stylish people, perhaps because they had emigrated from Germany some years earlier and so seemed slightly exotic. The elder girl, Margot, was two years younger than Frieda. The younger, who was four years her junior, would eventually become the most famous girl in the world, Anne Frank. Frieda remembers Margot as quiet and Anne as a neighborhood scamp bristling with intelligence. But mostly they were "just normal girls."

She jumped rope with them. Her most vivid memory of the Franks is of being invited by Anne up to their apartment. In the stairwell, Anne scolded Frieda to be quiet because her mother was taking her afternoon nap. The scene lodged in Frieda's mind because the idea seemed somehow extravagant; her own mother never took naps.

It might make sense to freeze the narrative here and to say something about why I was moved to write a book about the city I have lived in for more than five years: to begin to explain, anyway, why an American who grew up in western Pennsylvania and spent his more recent life in New York City should come to find this European city so fascinating—or necessary, even. If we stand back far enough from that scene, it's possible to see the two Jewish girls whispering in an Amsterdam stairwell, circa 1938, with no worldly notion that the weight of their century was about to collapse onto them, as representing something larger than even the vast fame that one of them would achieve. The threat both girls were about to face—and they would meet up again, in Auschwitz, where through a twist of fate the one who was closest to death would end up living a rich, full, complex life—was against a way of life that is commonplace to most of us and that is under a variety of new threats today. As it happens, the origins of that way of life—the origins of much that we think of as "modern"—are intimately associated with my adopted city.

That association is not immediately apparent. Mention to someone that you live in Amsterdam, and you may receive a low chuckle in response. The eyes may dart to one side as your friend peers through a haze of memory for recollections of a student-era trip to the city. Amsterdam, you will be told, is a crazy place.

That is not only true, it's more or less official policy. Job Cohen, who was mayor of the city from 2001 to 2010, told me one evening as I interviewed him in the eighteenth-century mayor's residence on the grand Herengracht ("Gentlemen's Canal"), "In Amsterdam, craziness is a value." He meant it as a good thing, though many would dispute that, including some of its residents. The squatting of buildings—forcing your way into a place that isn't yours and inhabiting it—was legalized in 1971, provided the building has been unoccupied for one year, and though the law was changed in 2010 it is still relatively common to see dilapidated facades hung with banners proclaiming the inhabitants' defiance of authority. The city has between 5,000 and 7,500 licensed prostitutes in a given year, most working in streetside windows, the rest in authorized brothels, and if you are nervous and confused as to how to engage a prostitute in the red light district you can ask one of the police officers on the beat for help. At a coffee shop (as opposed to a café), you order marijuana and hashish from a menu, where products may be divided into categories such as Indoor, Outdoor, and Foreign, and from there into varieties with names like Shiva, White Widow, and Elephant. While prostitution is legal and regulated (only EU citizens can prostitute themselves, since, as with any other job, a work permit is required), the marijuana trade falls under the curious Dutch classification *gedogen*, which means "technically illegal but officially tolerated."

So yes: a crazy place, where you might think the sky would be perennially in danger of falling from the sheer weight of mayhem. And yet, most parts of the city have such a blanket of conventional calm on them, such an utter paucity of craziness, that one might think the only drug consumption in the vicinity was some kind of middle-class sedative. The secret truth about the Dutch is that they are a deeply conservative people, from their relentlessly (and, it must be said, rather tastelessly) manicured gardens to their seemingly insatiable need in the workplace to hold meetings, including meetings whose purpose is to schedule further meetings. The craziness fits into such a culture in a couple of ways: the city is proud of its tradition of tolerance, and there is the logic that says it is better to legalize and regulate activity that will happen anyway. No one claims that the approach has been entirely successful. In the case of both the sex and the soft drug trades, it has long been recognized that being essentially the only place where such products are officially tolerated leads more or less inevitably to the city's becoming something of a global headquarters for black marketeers.

But if the craziness is true, so is this: Amsterdam is the same size as Columbus, Ohio (that is to say, modest, at 800,000 inhabitants), and it lies on the same latitude as Saskatoon, Saskatchewan (that is to say, remote), yet it has influenced the modern world to a degree that perhaps no other city has, and its imprint on the United States in particular goes to the core of the American identity.

Both of these observations are true for the same reason. Amsterdam is famous for one thing (besides canals, and cannabis cafés, and prostitutes): the tattered, ancient, much-misunderstood word *liberalism*. Amsterdam is, by most accounts, the most liberal place on earth. It is often laughably liberal or shake-your-head-in-disbelief liberal. In saying this I am using the definition of liberal as synonymous with free, open, and permissive. But the word has another, deeper and higher meaning, which is in fact related to the other.

Liberal, of course, comes from *liber*, the Latin word for free, which also underlies *liberty*, *libertarian*, and *libertine*. *Liberal* is one of those words that through history have been mercilessly pulled in various directions. Its first known appearance in written English is in the Wycliffe translation of the Bible, circa 1384, where a passage from 2 Maccabees (part of the biblical Apocrypha in many traditions) says the people of Tyre were "most liberal" in permitting the burial of men who had been unjustly put to death. Here, John Wycliffe, the medieval Church reformer who prefigured the movement to make the Bible available in common tongues, translated dutifully from the Latin *liberalissimi*, but the word was already in English at the time. Chaucer uses it repeatedly, generally to mean abundant, as in "youre liberal grace & mercy."

From early on it had both low and high associations. In *Othello*, Shakespeare's Emilia, defying her husband, Iago, who has ordered her to be silent (and who is about to murder her), cries, "No, I will speak as liberal as the north," that is, with wildness and abandon, the way the north wind blows. In *Henry VI, Part 3*, Shakespeare uses the word to mean generous:

> *In them I trust; for they are soldiers,*
> *Witty, courteous, liberal, full of spirit.*

And he even referred to "the liberal arts," using the term in something like the way we would today. It also came to mean physically large, as in "her liberall brest" or "One big fat man, with a stack of chins on his shirt front and a pair of *pince-nez* eye-glasses awry on his liberal nose."

A difficulty that the word suffers from today is that it has seemingly opposite meanings in the United States and in Europe. That is because its root meaning—free—can apply to very different things. The nineteenth-century Europeans who took to using *liberalism* as a term for their politics were businessmen who wanted freedom from tariffs—that is, limited government involvement in public affairs. In the United States, it was more vigorously and specifically applied to social causes and individual freedoms and so meant more government involvement to enforce those freedoms. The free-market platform of the Dutch Liberal Party would thus be considered more or less the opposite of liberal in an American context.

Add the *-ism* to the word and it becomes something broader still, an umbrella of grand ideas each of which ties to other, no less grand concepts. The pedigree of *liberalism* in English is not so ancient. It first pops up in 1816 in the *Morning Chronicle* (the London newspaper best remembered for publishing Charles Dickens's early works), in an article about the King of Spain's condemning "fifteen persons accused of the crime of liberalism" to "hard labour, banishment, &c." The King of Spain's usage relates to the political sense of the word and the idea of individuals being free to choose their government. So liberalism is closely associated with democracy. It also has an economic meaning, according to which capitalists claim that a basic component of individual rights is the right to own property.

What all uses of *liberalism* go back to is the centrality of the individual. In this sense—the sense I will employ in this book—the word describes a fault line between the modern and the medieval: it represents our break with the Middle Ages and from the philosophy that has knowledge and power centered on received wisdom from the Church and the monarchy.

Historically, then, liberalism involves a commitment to individual freedom and individual rights, and not just for oneself but for everyone, every human being who breathes the air. And liberalism's roots are intertwined with those of Amsterdam. It might be possible to go further, and say that liberalism was born in Amsterdam. Of course, a statement like that can be attacked. I'll attack it myself. Liberalism is a diffuse concept comprising a number of equally diffuse ideas—about justice, ethics, private property, and so on. It can no more be pinpointed to a particular place than oxygen can. A list of the indisputably great theoreticians of liberalism would include John Locke, Jean-Jacques Rousseau, Voltaire, Adam Smith, John Stuart Mill, and Thomas Jefferson. If we were to be serious about assigning geographic medals, we could give them to Paris, London, and Jefferson's Monticello estate in the Virginia hills.

All of this is true. Yet ideas have histories and origins; they are embedded in people and their struggles, their bodies, their physical or emotional turmoil, their hunger for new fashions and flavors, their yearnings to be free from whatever they may feel bound by. Psychoanalysis came into being in the genteel drawing rooms of fin de siècle Vienna; jazz was born in the early years of the twentieth century, when waves of black southerners, descendants of slaves, fled Jim Crow oppression and took up new lives in the vigorously industrial cities of the northern United States. Likewise, a remarkable number of forces came together in Amsterdam in the century or so beginning in the late 1500s that would spawn a new way of thinking about people and their relationship to one another and to the state. The story of the city's golden age is one of history's classics, on the same level of vividness and import as the story of the American Civil War or the classical period of ancient Greece. The city's rise was so sudden it startled even those living through it. The elements and individuals that constituted it are iconic, but more than that they are linked: there are natural tendons connecting the founding of the world's first stock market, the development of secular art with Rembrandt and his contemporaries, the crafting of a groundbreaking official policy of tolerance, the fostering of an atmosphere of intellectual freedom that brought thinkers from all over Europe and that created the world's most dynamic publishing center, and the physical transformation of the city: the digging of Amsterdam's famous canals. There is even a case to be made that our modern idea of "home" as an intimate personal space goes back to the Dutch canal houses of this period.

Underlying all these various breakthroughs—conceptual or physical—is the unleashing of the individual, which has its origins in the Protestant Reformation and the first wave of scientific experimentation and which relates too to Amsterdam's geographic and social conditions. These ingredients went to make up a new kind of place: a breeding ground for liberalism.

These forces coalesced in the mind of a young Amsterdam Jew of the seventeenth century. Probably more than any other major philosopher, Baruch Spinoza is looked to as a guide by serious thinkers today: theologians, computer scientists, philosophers, people who dare to grapple with the really big questions. I think one reason has to do with his being at the epicenter of modernity as the forces of liberalism, and the worldview of thinkers of today, came into being. Just as Shakespeare could only have emerged at his time—after the English language had absorbed the Latin of the High Middle Ages, the medieval French of the Norman invasion, and other influences that made it so richly expressive—so too Spinoza's revolutionary philosophy, which has influenced modern political thought, ethics, and theology, could arise only in the Amsterdam of the late seventeenth century, after the city had forged its principles of tolerance, of the placement of secular powers over church powers, and of the first truly modern free-trading culture. Spinoza took part in the philosophical debates that raged in coffee shops and bookstores; he was fascinated by public anatomical demonstrations, by the sight of the bending lines of fluyts and yachts beating sail from the harbor toward all points of the globe, by the idea of popular representation. All of this—the fruits of Amsterdam's fecund, nutritionally rich heyday—was boiled, condensed, and distilled into his philosophy. And from there—as well as from many other sources—it made its way into the wider world.

So while this is a book about a city, it is also about an idea. Amsterdam's history belongs to all of us, for those of us who live in Western democratic societies—wherever we place ourselves on the political spectrum—are all liberals, who depend on liberalism as a foundation of our lives.

Yet while liberalism is one of our most precious cultural possessions, it can also be overstretched, belittled, squandered. For liberalism is a delicate thing. It encompasses so much—constitutional government, democratic elections, freedom of worship, civil rights, free trade—that we think of it as timeless and universal. But liberalism came into being in a real place and time, like a flame it has wavered in various eras, and it can be snuffed out.

My weekly bicycle trip in my Amsterdam neighborhood bears out James Baldwin's observation that "people are trapped in history, and history is trapped in them." Frieda Menco's life is remarkable in part because she survived the greatest overt threat to liberal values that we have ever faced. There was actually a time when people wanted to give Hitler the benefit of the doubt as to his intentions (in 1935, Winston Churchill thought it possible that Hitler might "go down in history as the man who restored honour and peace of mind to the Great Germanic nation"). Eventually, the overwhelming nature of Hitler's threat brought the liberal heritage more sharply into focus. And victory, the triumph of liberal ideals over totalitarianism, resulted in the world we have inherited. In the postwar period, Amsterdam blossomed in a new, exuberant expression of those ideals—a celebration of them, even—as it became a center both of late-twentieth-century progressivism and of global finance. Indeed, the decades from the 1950s through the 1990s were what some think of as a new golden age, when the city threw off the vestiges of the Dutch Reformed Church and other conservative structures and developed into the twentieth-century version of a liberal capital. It became a laboratory for new ideas, from gay rights to gay marriage, from free love to free bicycles.

My other regular morning routine—bringing my son to his Moroccan Dutch caregiver and experiencing some of the difficulties her family faces—touches on another side of Amsterdam's liberal heritage, and another threat to it. But where the Nazi threat to liberalism was clear, this one—which much of the world is facing today—is harder to grapple with. The concept of a mixed society has for a long time been part of the terrain of liberalism. The idea of multiculturalism—meaning a belief that society should actively accommodate and support its cultural minorities—came into being in the 1970s, and the Netherlands, and Amsterdam in particular, led the way. The city not only welcomed non-Western immigrants but paid them to keep up their languages and traditions. Multiculturalism proved to be a failure. It was leading not to a mixed society but to a multiplicity of ghettoized communities living next to but cut off from one another: the very opposite of a "society." So how, in an increasingly interconnected world, do we integrate and still keep our values? The debate about tolerance relates to the theme of this book: what is the status of liberalism now, how has it been misconstrued or overextended, in what sense is it elemental to Western values, and what is its future?

This may sound like a political essay, but I don't want it to be.

Liberalism is an abstraction but its roots, some of them anyway, can be located in a real place—the city in which I happen to live. The past impresses itself on you in all sorts of ways as you move through Amsterdam. There is the inexpressible, soft-heavy sadness that the sight of gulls careening above a medieval canal in gray weather can summon. There is the mysterious pleasure you feel climbing into the attic of the former West India Company warehouse, where clotted old beams still mildly reek of the tobacco leaves that were packed into the space four centuries ago, an odor that evokes the exploitation and unfathomable adventure that brought our world into being.

But the deepest roots are not to be found in city streets. Liberalism comes down to individual freedom and thus to the importance of the individual human being. So this book is about people. Some of the personalities who fill its pages—Rembrandt, Spinoza, Anne Frank—are world famous. The lives of these world-historic individuals revolve around the theme; *liberal* is what they all have in common—that, and Amsterdam. Other people whose lives are central to this book are not so famous. The names Wouter Jacobszoon, Catalina Trico, Geertje Dircx, and Frieda Menco may not be well known, but the lives of these people are also bound up with Amsterdam and its liberalisms. And because I couldn't seem to avoid it, in a small way the book also traces the path of an American writer who came to call this city home.

THE WATER PROBLEM

It was May 1971, and the sun was shining on the oily green surface of the Oudezijds Voorburgwal, one of the most ancient canals in Amsterdam's medieval center. Kiki Amsberg, a thirty-two-year-old journalist for Dutch public radio, was walking, bell-bottomed and tie-dyed, along the canal with her husband. They paused before a grand four-story brick house that dated from the early seventeenth century. Upstairs was an apartment for rent.

It was, of course, a time of freedom: of expression, from authority. In many ways it was a time of fallout from battles over freedom and the excesses of freedom—fallout from the sixties. Janis Joplin and Jimi Hendrix had recently died. The *New York Times*, citing the principles of freedom of information and society's right to know what its government was doing, was about to publish the Pentagon Papers, the U.S. military's secret history of the war in Vietnam. Antiwar demonstrations were unfurling across college campuses in the United States and around the world.

Amsterdam in 1971 was two cities. Its bones and its guts were still of the postwar era: it was a conservative, religious (Catholic, Protestant, and Jewish), working-class, keep-your-head-down kind of place. Much of the city center had remained as it had been during

World War II, its ancient canal houses boarded up and unused. At
the same time the postwar fever for freedom had hit Amsterdam
with unique force, and Kiki Amsberg had been in the middle of
things: miniskirts, peace signs, antinuclear rallies. The city's role in
it all seemed to be cemented when John Lennon and Yoko Ono held
their "bed-in" at the Amsterdam Hilton Hotel, which so captivated
Kiki and her husband that they staged their own bed-in. The philosophical center was the Provo movement (as in "provoke"), which
used nonviolent means to taunt the authorities. Its magazine outlined the Provo demographic in a way that gives a toothsome feel for
the city's counterculture. The magazine's first issue proclaimed that
it was for "anarchists, provos, beatniks, pleiners, scissors-grinders,
jailbirds, simple simon stylites, magicians, pacifists, charlatans, philosophers, germ-carriers, grand masters of the queen's horse, happen-
ers, vegetarians, syndicalists, hustlers, pyromaniacs, santy clauses,
kindergarten teachers, and don't forget the secret police."

Shortly after Kiki Amsberg and her husband, Nic Brink, a drama
teacher, moved into their apartment, they learned the building had
been put up for sale. They were upset because they had just put
money into it: they had installed heating, relocated the toilet, which
had been placed, tenement style, right beside the kitchen, and added
an attic window. When the real estate broker suggested they buy the
place, they scoffed. "We were leftists," she said. "We were against
authority and ownership. Buying real estate was for *patsers*." (The
word doesn't translate well, but "establishment assholes" gets close.)

On reflection, though, they decided that their reason for being
there was to be part of the takeover and revitalization of the city
center, so having a stake in it made sense. Besides, real estate was
cheap; even with their small salaries they were able to get a loan
to buy both the large town house and the small *achterhuis*, or back
house, that adjoined it, in which a family was already living.

Kiki's life played out in the building. Her daughter was born a
year later. She joined in antiwar demonstrations and protests to stop

the city's planned demolition of much of the city center. She campaigned for urban greenery and won a battle to have a small dock, with two park benches, placed along the canal in front of the house.

As a journalist, she covered the story of the evolution of liberalism in her city. There was the "white bicycle" experiment, in which the city provided free bicycles to be used by anyone, without restrictions. There was the *actie tomaat* ("tomato action"), in which students threw tomatoes at actors during plays as a way to call for a more socially engaged theater. Kiki began interviewing feminist leaders from the United States and around Europe (Nancy Friday, Kate Millett, Nancy Chodorow, and others) and in 1982 coauthored a book, *Thinking About Love and Power*, that was the top nonfiction best seller in the Netherlands for six months. It shook up what had been (and in many ways remains) a very traditional society when it comes to the role of women. Meanwhile Kiki's personal thoughts on love and power played a part in the breakup of her marriage.

As the 1980s and 1990s rolled along, the city center gentrified. The fires of leftist liberalism dimmed. Pleasure boats became commonplace on the canals. And real estate prices shot up dramatically. Kiki took to renting out the first two floors of her house.

In 2008, when I was beginning research on this book, I became one of her tenants. I needed a transitional home, one that would serve as a refuge and pondering point, for I was in the middle of a divorce and my wife was planning to return to the United States with our two daughters. So while I spent a great deal of time pacing the ancient floorboards of the second-floor apartment of Kiki's house, more of that time involved marveling at the ridiculousness of my own life than considering the history of Amsterdam. It was, however, an excellent locale for either activity. The apartment overlooked the canal; a snapshot taken from the living room window would make a salable postcard. It was a view that contained several of the classic elements of the city's charm. There was the trough of languid water, the little boats moored to the quay, the row of tilting gabled buildings on the opposite bank, and, on any given day, a couple dozen bicycles chained to the railing of the humpbacked bridge.

One day, while researching a sixteenth-century Augustinian prior named Wouter Jacobszoon, who wrote one of the first diaries in the Dutch language, in which he chronicled the pivotal moment in Amsterdam's rise to greatness, I suddenly realized that Brother Jacobszoon's home had been the Sint-Agnieten Convent. Next door to Kiki Amsberg's house is the Sint-Agnieten Chapel, which is all that remains of a religious complex that dates to 1397. Or not quite all that remains: the convent, at its height, encompassed much of the block, including the land on which Kiki's house now stood. While the convent was disbanded after 1578, and Kiki's house dates to about 1620, dendrochronology tests reveal that some of her house's beams were cut in the early 1500s, so that they were most likely recycled from the convent. That is to say, what I realized was that Brother Jacobszoon had lived right next door. He had looked out in the same direction across the same canal as me. From this same vantage, then, Kiki Amsberg witnessed the high (and low) point of liberal expression, late-twentieth-century style, and, four centuries earlier, Brother Jacobszoon experienced the beginning stage of liberalism in its broader and deeper meaning. I was living at a place where Amsterdam's—and for that matter the world's—two liberalisms converge.

———

It was not an auspicious beginning to the city's rise that the monk observed. He witnessed such horror he was convinced the maw of hell was opening up to swallow the city. The spiraling chaos compelled him to put quill to paper. His journal is remarkable in being unusually personal for writings of its time; it gives an intimate perspective on what it felt like to be caught between the tectonic plates of shifting historical forces.

Mostly, the monk felt terror. He was not a native of Amsterdam—

in fact, he had only arrived in the city a month before, traveling through a landscape of war. He was a man of fifty who had spent most of his life in the Augustinian monastery of Stein, near the little cheese-making city of Gouda. He had become the prior of that monastery twenty-two years earlier. His long service in that post, and the style of his diary, suggests that he was a man of duty and routine—not a great thinker or visionary, and certainly not an adventurer, though he was an acute observer. His diary seems to have been written as part of the practice of Augustinian monks to record their observations during meditation.

War—sharply sectarian war—had reached Gouda the month before, making the city unsafe for those in Catholic orders, and the monk had made his way to Amsterdam, where he found refuge among the nuns of the Sint-Agnieten Convent and began serving as assistant to the rector.

But mayhem followed him into the city. Brother Jacobszoon spent his nights in his new home lying awake in his cell. He worried over the ominous reverberations of what sounded like distant drums but were in fact the thrum of artillery. From the window he saw fires burning on the horizon. People with nowhere else to go took to living in the streets; as winter set in, they froze to death. A woman was found dead in a ditch with her baby still suckling at her breast. "We only hear talk of robbing, murder, arson, and hangings," Brother Jacobszoon wrote. He believed that Judgment Day was near.

The pitch of terror rose. Young men roved in gangs. People were impaled, drowned, beheaded. Marauders targeted priests and nuns in particular: stripped them naked, paraded and humiliated them, tortured them, killed them. The body of a priest was found with the genitals hacked off. "Who wouldn't be reduced to screaming, crying, and howling?" the monk wrote, perhaps in commiseration with his Catholic brethren or maybe to excuse his own behavior.

If we could pull up and away from the Sint-Agnieten Convent in the year 1572, we would see masses of people, desperate to escape, thronging around the Regulierspoort, the nearby gate in the medieval city wall (the gatehouse still exists in my Amsterdam, and houses a pretty shop selling blue-and-white delftware). As we traveled over and beyond the city wall, we would see corpses swinging from trees along the main roads. Farther afield, the marauding patrols would give way to phalanxes of soldiers in proper armor, wearing the distinctively curved helmets of the Spanish army and shouldering pikes and matchlock muskets.

Pulling back farther still would reveal events unfolding as if on a war-gaming map. For Europe in 1572 was indeed a battlefield, the Dutch provinces were central pieces in a geopolitical power struggle, and the city of Amsterdam was a fulcrum on which an age would ultimately turn.

To appreciate the fulcrum and the monk's horror—the horror of the Catholic citizens of Amsterdam in the late sixteenth century—requires taking another step back in time.

In the family of European capitals, Amsterdam is one of the younger siblings. Even if we set aside Romulus and Remus, archaeological evidence suggests that Rome started with herders and farmers settling the cluster of hills along the Tiber around 900 BC. Athens goes back staggeringly farther than that, into the Neolithic predawn. Amsterdam, by contrast, with its inhospitable geographic position discouraging human settlement, began life circa AD 1100, when, in an effort to stop the sea from remaking the shoreline every year, a few hundred farmers set to heaping up earthen dikes along the edge of the marshy wilderness they had chosen to call home.

Indeed, early humans, in their migratory roaming, sensibly stepped around the whole corner of Europe known as the Low Countries. Looking at the planet not from the perspective of human beings but merely in terms of its own processes, one might say that this region was meant to be purely for drainage purposes, for what is today the Netherlands is one vast river delta. Three of northern Europe's largest rivers—the Rhine, the Meuse, or Maas, and the Scheldt—having variously swept down from the Swiss Alps, rolled across German plains, and twisted through northern France and the forests of the Ardennes in Belgium, reach here to meet the sea. In its natural course, this drainage is a complex process that keeps the boundary between land and sea constantly shifting. Starting around AD 1000, the early inhabitants of what became the province of Holland began to interfere with nature. The peaty land was good for farming, provided the peat—which is essentially spongy decayed plant material—could be drained. The inhabitants built up dikes to keep out the sea, then cut channels in the peat bogs, which allowed the water contained in them to flow down into rivers. That strategy led to further difficulties, since once the peat loses its water it begins to sink. Eventually the peat level falls below the water level, whereupon the land is once again in danger of flooding, which necessitates more dikes as well as pumps. Medieval Hollanders—and their neighbors in Zeeland to the south and Friesland to the north—thus set off a never-ending struggle against nature, one that continues today. This—the water, the perils, the bravery, the absurdity of the geographic position, and the development of complex communal organizations to cope with the situation—explains much of Amsterdam's history and provides as well a backdrop to the development of liberalism.

The Dutch writer Matthijs van Boxsel gives his perspective on this history in an idiosyncratic book called *The Encyclopedia of Stupidity*, in which he characterizes the historical predicament of the Dutch and their battle with water in terms he makes clear in the title. I don't exactly agree that "stupidity" is the right word, but I do find it compelling that he and other Dutch writers see the historic struggle against water as formative to a cultural ethic of cooperation that created a society strong enough for it to impel, curiously, a commitment to value the individual.

But I wouldn't stop there. I think we can see the position of the Dutch—and of Amsterdam in particular—as mirroring the wider situation of the Western world. We have all by now mirrored this "stupidity": we've used up resources, jerry-rigged our environment, gotten ourselves into a place where we value individualism and yet need vitally to cooperate. We demand our personal freedom but we have to work together. So perhaps this is a working hypothesis to keep in mind as we explore the foundations of liberalism: individualism, as a theory and an ideal, is related to extreme conditions and, seemingly paradoxically, to the need to band together.

Sometime after the year 1200, then, in order to control flooding, the inhabitants of a region of marshy soil at a juncture of two bodies of water—the spot where a river flowed into a vast bay that connected with the North Sea, fifty-odd miles away—built a dam on the Amstel River. The dam would ever after mark the center of the city, and it gave the community a name: Amstelredamme.

Perched on the far northwestern flank of the Continent, soaked by rains, beaten by winds, ravaged by tidal currents, it was destined to remain a distinctly minor urban hub, home to farmers who grew barley and rye to make their porridge and bread and to fishermen who caught pike, eel, and carp in the marshy inlets, all of them living in wooden huts with straw roofs and clay floors sloped to let rainwater flow through rather than puddle. Even among other cities of the Dutch provinces it was a, well, backwater. In part because of the rivers connecting Germany and central Europe to the North Sea, other cities had long held a certain strategic importance. Utrecht was the bishopric of the region; Nijmegen and Maastricht to the east had been population centers since the Roman era.

But in the year 1345 a miraculous change overtook Amsterdam. The adjective should be taken literally, for on a frigid Tuesday night before Palm Sunday in that year, the ordinary circumstance of an old man quietly dying at home took a strange turn. Shortly after the man was given the sacrament of Holy Communion, he vomited, and the women who were attending him were confounded to see that the Eucharist reemerged from his mouth whole. They threw the vomit on the fire, presumably reasoning that flames offered the least sacrilegious way of disposing of its holy contents, but, lo, the host did not burn. The town's clergymen processed to the church bearing the wondrous wafer—which seemingly behaved with a supernaturalness akin to the body of Christ that Catholics believed the Eucharist to be—and a miracle was declared. An imposing church was built on the site of the man's house, and when it later burned to the ground, not once but twice, and each time the host survived the fire, the "miracle of Amsterdam" became a medieval phenomenon.

If you were to look at a typical map of Europe circa 1400, you would probably find it traversed by inexplicable meandering lines, which in turn would probably be the most intelligible thing about the map to a person of the time—for holy pilgrimages held more meaning than latitude and longitude (the latter of which of course did not exist then). People did not do the Grand Tour; they didn't see the sights or travel for the experience of foreignness. They sought out holy places in search of relief for their suffering and forgiveness of their sins. The rocky hillocks of Wales were dotted with markers guiding the way to Shrewsbury and Llandderfel. The shrine of the murdered saint Thomas Becket at Canterbury was the obvious goal of English pilgrims. People believed that walking prescribed routes to Jerusalem and the holy city of Santiago de Compostela absolved virtually any sin.

The miracle of Amsterdam put the city on the map. The miracle became the subject of religious art, with all the elements—the berobed old man ejecting the contents of his stomach into a vessel, the attendant women, angels gathered around the fire, the glowing host—committed to paint, ink, and bronze. According to one story, the city's popularity ratcheted up to another level following a celebrity cure: Maximilian of Austria, the ailing son of the Holy Roman emperor and himself a future emperor, arrived at the shrine as a pilgrim in 1489 and was healed.

Thousands came from all over the Continent, bearing their sick. Into the city they streamed, via a street that became known as the Holy Way. Today the outer portion of the street, called Overtoom, is a gritty, Broadway-like stretch of drab shops and rental car outlets, but the final block still bears the name Heiligeweg, despite being chockablock with an unholy assembly of jewelry stores and designer shoe shops. The pilgrims turned left onto Kalverstraat (whose name preserves the memory of a cattle market that was held there—today it is the city's central pedestrian shopping street) and so came to a stop at the shrine that housed the host that had defied the flames. In one of those odd twists of history that defy fiction, the site of the miracle—what was once one of Europe's holiest spots—is today the home of a hypercheesy tourist attraction called the Amsterdam Dungeon. The pilgrimage itself—after being banned when the city officially converted to Calvinism in 1578—was reinstated in the late nineteenth century, and now every March several thousand devout Dutch Catholics make an all-night procession around central Amsterdam.

Amsterdam grew up around its miracle. Its first canals were dug—to control the ever-shifting waters, channeling them into navigable courses, turning a threat to advantage. The still-tiny city, hemmed in from the forbidding sea by its dikes and dams, filled with religious professionals. The city's original, modest church, dating from 1306, was rebuilt in 1369 as a lavish, three-aisled Gothic structure and named for St. Nicholas. Just four decades later, with the population growing and the numbers of religious tourists continuing to swell, another parish church was built on the dam in the city center. It was called, with Dutch practicality, the New Church, whereupon the St. Nicholas Church was called (and today is formally known as) the Old Church.

That was only the beginning. A certified miracle in medieval Europe brought on the equivalent of a gold rush. Religious professionals of every stripe flocked to Amsterdam. In little more than a century no fewer than nineteen monasteries and convents set up shop inside the city, with two others just outside the walls. Followers of several orders took vows of silence, but that only went so far. The narrow streets—lined with tall, gabled wooden houses—reverberated with backbiting and intrigue. The Holy Place—the shrine built over the site of the miracle—became a power center in its own right and the locus of a vigorous trade in holy trinkets (medals depicting the woman snatching the host out of the fire or bearing two angels praying over it, the earliest dating from about 1400, have been dug up around the city), arousing the envy and ire of the two parish churches. Meanwhile, the monasteries and convents were mini-fiefdoms, walled off from the rest of the city, that vied with one another for wealthy patrons. The two parish churches fought against these incursions into their monopoly on sanctity by demanding annual payment from the other religious institutions in exchange for the right to offer mass, hear confessions, or maintain their own cemeteries.

With monasteries, convents, and churches standing cheek by jowl, monks and nuns, priests and penitents became medieval Amsterdam's core constituents. While fights broke out among the various orders and institutions, the greater tension was between the religious orders collectively and the city residents, who objected to the monasteries' having taken large swaths of land along the canals.

What is today the oldest part of the city—Kiki Amsberg's neighborhood, the densely packed, low-skied, high-walled center of the center of Amsterdam—preserves the memory of its rise on the waves of Catholic piety mostly in names (Monk Street, Paternoster Alley, a tiny lane called Gebed Zonder End, or Prayer Without End) that are often jarringly incongruous given that this also happens to be the location of the red light district. So the "blood" in Blood Street refers not to street crime but to the blood of Jesus. Surely few patrons of the prostitute windows of the area realize (or care) that the name of the little alley called Kreupelsteeg refers to the crippled pilgrims who came this way, their hearts filled with hope and desperation and prayer—looking for, you might say, a different kind of transcendence.

Meanwhile, another industry coincided with the rise of religious worship, contributed equally to the city's growth, and arguably plays a greater role in its culture today than does religion. By and large, Dutch cuisine deserves its mournful reputation, but if a visitor to Amsterdam asked me to name the finest traditional culinary experience on offer I would lead him or her to one of the street stands that are still fairly common, and where the main product is typically served with onions and sweet pickles. For centuries prior to the miracle of Amsterdam, Dutch fishermen had plied coastal waters for the rich, oily, strongly flavored fish of the species *harengus* and genus *Clupea*, aka herring. The fish were caught, hauled ashore, gutted, and packed in brine to preserve them. The Dutch had no monopoly on the herring trade—it was a common activity in many northern European lands, and the Dutch for a time were regular customers of Swedish-caught herring.

But roughly around the time that the miracle of the fire-retardant host took place in Amsterdam, Dutch fishermen developed an innovation that would transform Europe and, in particular, play a role in the rise of Amsterdam. It was the tiniest of things, and it was probably discovered by accident. Fish such as herring have little pouches in their stomachs called pyloric caeca, which contain enzymes that aid digestion. If, instead of gutting the fish entirely, you leave these pouches, as well as the pancreas, in the brine mixture, the result is fish that keeps for a much longer period of time and, as a bonus, has more flavor.

This discovery gave Dutch fishermen—theoretically, at least— the ability to move away from the coastlines and into the deep, icy, impetuously heaving waters of the North Sea. More or less in the middle of that body of water lay Dogger Bank, a broad and relatively shallow region of sea that held a motherlode, for it was thick with the muscular, silvery bodies of shoaling herring.

But such a journey required a new kind of vessel. In 1416, shipbuilders in the town of Hoorn, to the north of Amsterdam, developed a long, stout, eminently seaworthy boat with bulging sides and a cavernous interior. Along with it came modifications that made it possible to do the gibbing (the technique of gutting and curing herring) aboard ship. Thus the herring buss—essentially a factory that could plow through rolling seas—came into being. Instead of immediately needing to get caught fish ashore, where they then had to be quickly processed and shipped off, the Dutch boats were able to stay at sea for five weeks or more at a stretch, fishing, gibbing, and fishing some more, and when they returned to port their hulls were packed with market-ready barrels of cured herring—lightly salted, or "soused," in the terminology of the Elizabethan period—that would last for a year and that, to boot, were tastier than fish that had been cured in the old manner.

Within a few decades the Dutch had cornered the market. They shipped tons of herring to Poland, to France, up the Rhine into Germany, even as far afield as Russia. Dutch artists made etchings of herrings wearing crowns and writers spoke of "our noble herring."

Transforming the herring industry could happen only if there was an unusual degree of cooperation among different people. Here Amsterdam's tradition of water management—which already had a couple of centuries of history behind it—served the city well. Building up dikes and dredging canals were massive communal activities in which everyone concerned had to see a common as well as an individual interest in order to take part. Fishing the coastline required little more than a father and son and a few hands, but moving into deep waters meant a commitment of capital and a complex support infrastructure. The ships were larger, and they had teams of specialized workers: sailors, gutters (a skilled team of gutters could process 2,000 herring an hour), packers, officers. Since a herring fleet had such a recognizably valuable cargo, it needed a naval escort for defense. Ship chandlers had to supply linen, hemp, tar, tallow, netting, barrels, salt, and other products.

To make all of this work, herring merchants pushed for local government to get involved. The government sent warships to protect the fleet, and over time it developed regulations covering every aspect of the netting, processing, and sale of herring. This was done with one purpose in mind: to keep the quality high. As more money came into the province of Holland, the provincial government required that herring casks be of regulation size and manufacture and that they be stamped not just as Dutch but as Holland Herring—a very early and stunningly successful instance of branding.

At the high point of the industry, fishermen of the province of Holland caught about 200 million herring per year. New wealth came to Amsterdam. And dominance in one field led to success in others. In order to build herring busses, Amsterdam bought timber from Germany and processed it into planks. The city's sawyers (and later saw mills, after a farmer from nearby Uitgeest patented a crankshaft, which turned the circular motion of a windmill into the back-and-forth motion of a sawing blade) produced so efficiently that England's burgeoning shipbuilding industry bought processed wood from Amsterdam and the surrounding area. Meanwhile, the city's own shipyards expanded, producing barges for working the region's rivers as well as seagoing vessels. And the city's merchants in turn became savvy international traders; they paid top dollar for information about faraway events that they could earn money on and adjusted their cargo accordingly. When harvests in southern Europe failed, the city's vessels returned from their herring runs to the Baltic port of Danzig laden with rye and wheat, so that Dutch vessels provided Polish grain for tables in Spain and Italy. The ships likewise carried wine from France to the Baltic and brought beer from Germany for Dutch consumption.

All the while, merchants kept alert for new business opportunities. When they discovered that rapeseed, hempseed, and potash—the main ingredients of soap—could all be got cheaply in the Baltic ports their ships frequented, they carted the raw material home and created an industry. At one point there were twenty-one soap works along Amsterdam's canals. Once again branding became part of marketing: Amsterdam's unique "green soap" became famous throughout Renaissance Europe and for all we know could have been the preferred brand of Leonardo da Vinci or Queen Elizabeth.

Thus, while the cities of Antwerp, Ghent, and Bruges in the so-called southern Netherlands (today Belgium) were among Europe's glittering jewels, cornering the refined trades in spices and rare fabrics, their great artists—from Jan van Eyck to Hieronymus Bosch—as fully a part of the Renaissance as Italian masters, Amsterdam came of age by pursuing an altogether rougher market. The IJ—the city's great inland harbor (it's not a typo: the Dutch syllable is pronounced something like *aey*)—was later famously characterized as a "forest of masts," as busses, buyscarveels, boyers, fluyts, vlieboots, and other vessels offering variations on the theme of durable bulk seagoing transport rode at anchor before the city walls, taking on sailors and supplies before making their way out into the heaving North Sea.

Wealth came, and something else: sailors and traders from faraway places. They presaged what Amsterdam would become: a place of mixed languages and backgrounds. But where the city that was to come would have a high gloss of luxury to it—with its markets of fine goods, its children coddled by loving parents, paintings decorating the walls of ordinary homes that would in later centuries be considered some of humanity's masterpieces—this Amsterdam, the late-medieval city, was still one of rough wooden houses swirling with the acrid smoke of open-pit fireplaces.

Circa 1500, then, at the high point of the Renaissance—as Michelangelo was beginning work on his David statue and Copernicus was getting serious about astronomy—Amsterdam was both a lively shipping center and one of the most intensely Catholic cities in Europe: a grittily holy place of fish guts and church incense, of bilge, tar, dung, and sour beer; a town of narrow alleys and slanting rainfall, of cursing seamen and scheming abbots. And the two main enterprises alternately clashed with and enriched each other, creating a late-medieval frisson of sweat and strife and energy.

He was a smart boy, alone in the world. He had been born forty miles south of Amsterdam, and if one were to create a fictional character who would come to alter the course of Christianity and Western history by contributing to a grand schism in the Catholic Church, one might devise circumstances of birth and upbringing that mirrored his. His father was a priest, his mother the daughter of a local physician. He had to endure the secrecy and shame of his illegitimacy and then, after the plague swept in, the simultaneous deaths of both his parents. Whereupon he was given to the local monastery to be raised. While we can't be sure of the precise nature of the abuse and suffering he endured there, his graphic descriptions later of what went on in monasteries—monks "whipping boys to death every day" and creating an atmosphere in comparison to which there was "more innocence in a brothel"—certainly explain his lifelong hatred of Catholic monasteries and foreshadowed the imminent avalanche that would become known as the Reformation in terms that echo even to our time.

He is known to history as Erasmus of Rotterdam, though he spent only his first four years in that Dutch city. Remarkably enough, the monastery in which he grew up was the very same one where, half a century later, the diarist Wouter Jacobszoon would serve as prior. But unlike Brother Jacobszoon, Erasmus got out of its cloisters as soon as he could, studied in France, Italy, and England, and became the great Latin stylist of the Renaissance Church. His fame, however, came from substance, not style. While he remained an obedient Catholic all his life, Erasmus mounted a sustained assault on the structures of the Catholic Church, insisting that the essence of Christianity was not to be found in observance of the sacraments, or in the power of the Vatican, or even in the person of the pope but in the individual: in the study and awareness of holy scripture.

His brand of Christian humanism—a learned, honest, individual approach to faith—became a sensation in his homeland. The Dutch were, and are, a practical, no-nonsense people—traits that Dutch writers have linked to their involvement with water and the need for a society in which strong individuals cooperate with one another to get things done on their own, as opposed to the medieval model that prevailed elsewhere in Europe, in which a nobleman ruled an estate and serfs. Examples of the down-to-earth sensibility are everywhere in Dutch history. In the seventeenth century, a French naval commander, on visiting a Dutch sea captain, was shocked to find him sweeping out his own quarters. I used to run into the mayor of Amsterdam in the local supermarket—and he wasn't engaged in a populist stunt (Dutch mayors are not elected but appointed); he was doing the family shopping. This sensibility accounts in part for the depth with which the Dutch people took to Erasmus and his writings as his work gained fame around Europe: he was one of them, and they responded. Erasmus despised the "superstition of ceremonies" to which the Church chained its people. He condemned the trade in indulgences, which saw Catholic clergy selling dying people a kind of insurance policy that guaranteed that on their death their sins would be forgiven. He questioned the very structures of Church life—the religious art, the vestments of the priests, the grandeur of the cathedral—as so many excuses to suck money out of ordinary believing people and bind them to the will of the Church.

What struck Dutch Christians most deeply was Erasmus's focus on the application of individual human reason. The Dutch were among the earliest adopters of a new technology—the printed book—and it proved to be an ideal instrument for advancing this new focus on the individual. Dutch editions of Erasmus's works—his translation of the New Testament and also his *Handbook for the Christian Soldier*, in which he excoriated the trappings of piety and called on Christians to use their brains as well as their spirits—were best sellers at bookshops in Amsterdam, Leiden, Antwerp, and other cities and became the basis for a whole new curriculum in Dutch schools.

Erasmus himself had a term for this new approach to learning. He called it "liberal studies." He never intended it to be anything but a means for correcting faults within the Church. But other people felt differently. In 1517, when the German monk Martin Luther nailed his Ninety-Five Theses to the door of All Saints' Church in the city of Wittenberg, he set off a tidal wave that rolled four hundred miles due west and crashed head-on into the medieval town walls of Amsterdam. It was the era in which popes issued business licenses to brothels (from which they then received revenues), openly fathered illegitimate children, and were so flagrant in manipulating their power that Sixtus IV appointed an eight-year-old as bishop of Lisbon. As a major center of Catholic worship, Amsterdam was as steeped in the excesses and corruption that Erasmus railed against as anyplace. It was common in the city for "celibate" priests to have mistresses. And whether at the Carthusian monastery to the east or in the headquarters of the Canons Regular just outside the city walls to the south, for a young novitiate to enter orders he had to "donate" sufficiently. You rose in power by buying higher offices, so that the families that had grown rich on trade and shipping were able to place their sons as heads of the orders. As Church leaders gained more power, they collected official titles, each of which came with its own salary. It was not physically possible for one man to perform all the fuctions of each office, but that was the idea: a leader collected these offices in order to subcontract the work to others, at lower salaries.

Like other Europeans, Amsterdammers had become fed up with such activity. If Erasmus, the great Dutch theologian who had inspired them, was not willing to take the full step and sever ties with Rome, his German colleague was. Great numbers of Dutch Christians were ready to follow Luther in breaking away from the Church. It all happened in the course of a few years. Erasmus watched in horror as people deserted the Church and declared themselves followers not only of Luther but of Erasmus as well. Dutiful as he remained to his faith, he found it unbearable to hear a Catholic official in the Dutch city of Dordrecht vividly pair the two theologians, saying, "Luther is pestilential, but Erasmus more so, for Luther sucked all his poison from Erasmus' teats."

As did Erasmus, Luther appealed to ordinary Christians. They did not need the Church structure—priests and sacraments—to know the word of God. It was written in the Bible and available for all to read. The printed book had existed for less than seventy-five years, and it became a medium by which ordinary people could both express their exasperation and rechannel their spiritual longings. Two Amsterdam printers, Johannes Pelt and Doen Pieterszoon, began producing editions of Luther's writings and of translations into Dutch of the New Testament.

The Church moved quickly to combat the challenge to its authority. Luther was excommunicated in 1521. That same year, Church officials in the Dutch provinces issued a proclamation that "books made by a certain Brother Luther are not to be read, sold or otherwise dealt with, since these smack of heresy." On November 18, 1525, a messenger arrived in Amsterdam with instructions that city leaders were to burn books published by the local printer Doen Pieterszoon and that singled out "certain books of St. Paul's epistles."

It must have caused a stir when another messenger, representing the Holy Roman emperor himself, appeared in town and flamboyantly decreed: "My lords of the righteous areas, all printers and publishers who produce matter shall first have it inspected and approved by the sheriffs and mayors." The atmosphere in the city was restive, almost festive, with strange energy. No one had ever heard or conceived of anything as outlandishly earthshaking as what some of their own friends and neighbors were doing: rebelling against the faith that had grounded their lives and society. The historian Jonathan Israel puts what was taking place in the Dutch provinces in grand historic context: "Alienation of a society from its own religious culture, on such a scale, was a phenomenon without precedent or parallel." The Catholic Church had provided their moral code, and not only that but the guidelines for everything from how to have babies to how to bury corpses. And now what were otherwise ordinary Amsterdammers doing and saying?

Strange things. Silly-sounding things. Jan Goessens, a card maker (who manufactured the combs used in making cloth), wondered aloud one day whether, if the Virgin Mary was so holy, that meant that the donkey she had ridden was a holy ass. Jacob Klaaszoon, a baker, stood in front of a holy procession that was taking place outside the Old Church and blocked it. A cobbler named Jan Ijsbrandszoon interrupted mass by standing up in midsermon and shouting, "I'm going home! I've heard the seducers of God's word long enough!" Someone called Hillebrand van Zwol announced his opinion that the Eucharist—the sacrament in which the host not merely represents but actually becomes the body of Christ, which was to become a defining tension between Protestantism and Catholicism—was only "ordinary bread." A man named Peter Vetgen publicly compared the Virgin Mary to Ytje, the town crazy woman.

The official reaction in the city of Amsterdam to the orders from the Holy Roman Emperor to crack down on dissent speaks volumes about how the city saw itself even then. Yes, of course we will do as you say and deal with the heretics, the mayors of the city in effect told their superiors (at the time the city had a panel of four mayors, or *burgemeesters*). Whereupon the city's law enforcement officer (the office of *schout* encompassed the duties of both sheriff and prosecutor), a man named Jan Huybertszoon, rounded up a group of eight people who had attended a Lutheran church service and sentenced them: to walk in a procession carrying lighted candles. Other people who had been especially flamboyant in their protestations against the Catholic Church had to spend a month in jail. A man who had gotten drunk and said nasty things about the communion host was made to crawl to the tavern where he had said his piece and ask the landlord for forgiveness. The phrase "slap on the wrist" might have been invented to describe the Catholic city's official crackdown on Protestant dissent. For perspective: at this same time, in 1523, in Brussels, two Augustinian monks who had followed Luther's teaching that forgiveness of sin is a power not of the church but of God were burned at the stake—the first of what would be a long line of Protestant martyrs. Indeed, in some cases Amsterdam dealt more aggressively with Catholics who complained too noisily about Lutheran upstarts than they did with the upstarts. A woman named Marike Meinouwe who made a fuss about Lutherans assembling in their own church services, crying "Heretics! Heretics!" in public, was sentenced to a year in prison for disturbing public order.

Why was Amsterdam so lenient in dealing with purveyors of outlandish new ideas? The simplest answer is that it was a trading city. This meant both that it was used to things foreign—accents, tastes, beliefs—and that its leaders did not want to let nonstandard notions disrupt the flow of business. But that isn't a full enough explanation. Other places in Europe were also trading centers, where exotic people and exotic ideas passed through. Amsterdam was unusual in the brazenness with which its municipal leaders paid lip service to the commands of higher authority to punish dissent and continued to tolerate a wide variety of nonstandard behaviors in its streets—including behaviors that directly challenged the authority of church and monarchy.

Understanding why Amsterdam's municipal leaders preferred to walk such a dangerous path of tolerance requires first getting a picture of the larger power relationships at play. The Dutch provinces were part of the Holy Roman Empire, which at its height encompassed nearly all of central Europe, from eastern France to western Poland and as far south as Tuscany. As the name suggests, it traced its lineage to ancient Rome and its ultimate justification for power to the Catholic faith, though Voltaire was largely on target in his famous quip that it was neither holy, nor Roman, nor an empire: Rome itself was never part of it, and emperors variously waged war with the Vatican. That said, the many divisions within the Catholic Church—the papacy and bishoprics, the monastic orders, and organizations such as orphanages and almshouses—exerted tremendous power on everyone from peasants to princes, so that the successive emperors knew that a considerable part of their own power derived from the perceived legitimacy of their Catholic affiliation. The emperor, in other words, was a Catholic warlord, who used Catholicism as a force for control and for expanding his own power.

The Dutch provinces were for a long time relatively complacent components of the empire. Dutch people had no national identity as such—they related not to a sense of "being Dutch" but rather to their province, seeing themselves as Hollanders or Zeelanders or Friesians. They were pious and hardworking; they contributed a large percentage of the taxes that kept the empire afloat, and in return they received protection.

In another sense, however, the situation of the Low Countries ensured that they would develop in a crucially different way from the rest of Europe—a difference that would lead eventually to violent and world-historic upheaval. One of the defining elements of medieval Europe was the top-down structure of society, called the manorial system, which had a lord who oversaw an estate and peasants who worked the land and paid rent in the form of labor or produce. The lord provided protection and served as the court of law for his peasants, so that the manor was a complete economic and political unit. And the lord, in turn, owed fealty to both a greater lord and to the Church.

The Dutch provinces did not become manorial, and the reason, as with nearly everything else, related to water. Since much of the land was reclaimed from the sea or bogs, neither Church nor nobility could claim to own it. It was created by communities (hence the Dutch saying "God made the earth, but the Dutch made Holland"). Residents banded together to form water boards that were responsible for the complex, nonstop task of maintaining polders (reclaimed lands), dams, dikes, and water mills to keep the water at bay. The boards—*waterschappen*—are still very much a part of Dutch life and have exerted an enormous influence on the culture, in particular on the peculiar combination of individualism and communalism that helps define Dutchness.

In this system, people bought and sold their own plots of land.

Many Amsterdammers owned land just outside the city, which they farmed or rented out for extra income. The striking feature of this is that it was individuals, of all levels of society, who were invested in the land. Where land was controlled by noblemen and/or the Church in other parts of Europe, in the province of Holland, circa 1500, only 5 percent of the land was owned by nobles, while peasants owned 45 percent of it.

It's hard to draw definitive cause-and-effect conclusions about such things, but it seems that this situation meant that ordinary Dutchmen were less inclined to adopt the posture of obedience that serfs and peasants elsewhere were forced into. Instead of owing fealty to lords, people paid rent to one another or bought and sold property. Such language itself speaks clearly to the difference: theirs was a kind of protomodern society. Of course (to paraphrase Bob Dylan), everybody has to serve somebody, but to a remarkable extent the Dutch of the sixteenth century were their own bosses.

This independence perhaps played a role in the thinking of Erasmus as he developed his "liberal" humanistic approach to renovating Catholicism; surely it was a factor in how rapidly the Dutch took to it, and ultimately to the Protestant Reformation. A people largely independent of the main social organization through which Catholicism dominated became, not coincidentally, the most eager to bolt from Catholicism.

All of that held particularly for Amsterdam. Put this historic lack of fealty together with a theology of independent thinking in a vigorous trading city—a city where people make money on differentness, so to speak—and the result is a culture of tolerance.

The Dutch notion of tolerance—which would have such a broad influence on history, coloring the thinking of men like John Locke and Thomas Jefferson—would come into its fullest form a century later, but even here we can pinpoint a feature of it that is not generally understood. Amsterdam's sixteenth-century policy of looking the other way has a lot in common with the modern Dutch notion of *gedogen*, or toleration of illegal activity. A recent application of *gedogen* suggesting a deep history and multilayered understanding of "tolerance" pertains to marijuana "coffee shops," whose owners must apply for permits and pay taxes just like any other business owners even though the product they sell is technically illegal.

So tolerance in Amsterdam in the 1520s, as later, did not have the broad meaning the word would take on in the late twentieth century. It wasn't synonymous with "celebrating diversity." It was more like "putting up with," a concept born of necessity and practicality. Americans in particular tend to associate such concepts with idealism—to assume a philosophical grandeur at the root of their principles: "We hold these truths to be self-evident . . ." It's true that as this notion of tolerance developed, it would be subjected to moral scrutiny and be championed in church pulpits as an element of Christian belief. But the root of it in Amsterdam was something other.

In what would become a familiar pattern, Amsterdam's tolerance attracted people of what would later be termed alternative lifestyles. Just as, in the 1960s and 1970s, the city became a haven for hippies, freaks, squatters, feminists, gay rights activists, and countercultural environmental radicals, in the years immediately following Luther's manifesto—a time of free-form reimagining of Christianity throughout Europe, with sects coming into being that condemned holy images, that were opposed to war under any circumstances (and fought to the death to defend the idea), that defied any organized church, and that preached that the human heart had supremacy over holy scripture—Amsterdam served as a magnet. Many of these sects died out from sheer exoticism or were crushed out of existence by the Inquisition. But for a time they flourished, and Amsterdam emerged as a center of countercultural experimentation, sixteenth-century style.

The city's unofficial policy of tolerance did not extend infinitely. The court of the Holy Roman Empire, regionally based in Brussels, became increasingly impatient with it, for it allowed the city to become a hotbed of dissent from crown and church. In addition,

as breakaway sects multiplied, order within the city started to collapse. And that was the one thing the municipal leaders, who were
also businessmen in a city that thrived on trade with foreigners—by
allowing but properly managing foreign or unusual expressions—
could not tolerate.

The change in official attitude began on an afternoon in March
1534, when the residents of Amsterdam were stunned to see five
men marching down the street stark naked and proclaiming (following a logic all their own) God's blessing on the right side of the city
and his damnation on the left. Sheriff Huybertszoon dealt with the
problem in his typical fashion: knocking on a few doors, knocking a
few heads together, and then trusting that this latest bit of nonsense
would go away.

It did not go away—instead, Sheriff Huybertszoon did. The
Catholic overlords of the city—in The Hague, where the provincial court of Holland sat, and in Brussels, the regional center of
the empire's power—had a wider perspective than the city fathers
did. They saw that what had begun with Erasmus and Luther was
proliferating in bewildering fashion across the Continent. The
laissez-faire approach of Huybertszoon and the other city officials
was not sufficient. Huybertszoon was forced to resign. There was a
good deal of trouble trying to find a suitable replacement—someone
who could be relied on to pursue heretics aggressively—but when
they found him, Cornelis Wouter Dobbenszoon quickly indicated
a dramatic change in strategy by making it his first order of business to prosecute his lax predecessor for failure to perform his duties.
(Huybertszoon, however, had seen what was coming and fled the
country.)

The naked paraders turned out to be the advance guard of
another new sect, the Anabaptists, who went much further in their
zeal for reform than the Lutherans. The main tenet of their beliefs
was that infant baptism was wrong since the infant was not aware
of the meaning of the ceremony, so that adults had to be rebap-
tized (*ana-* being Greek for "again"). The Anabaptist enthusiasm for

stripping away layers of dogma and paraphernalia from Christianity also extended to literal, bodily stripping; perhaps related was a penchant for polygamy. Another naked display took place a few months later: in February 1535—that is, the dead of winter—an Anabaptist group, including women who had left their husbands home in bed, met at night to listen to the words of their prophet. After several hours, his sermon reached a sufficient pitch that it required him to strip off his clothes and hurl them into the fire, since all that was man-made was to be committed to the flames. The others followed him. Then they all went out into the cold night and ran through the streets shouting, "Woe, the wrath of God!"

The impact on the city was spectacular. Sheriff Dobbenszoon arrested the religious radicals and hauled them into jail, but they still refused to get dressed, declaring, "We are the naked truth." They were given food but would not eat from plates and bowls, which were an adornment. One man, a particularly hard-core adherent, demanded that someone chew his food for him because, he said, he was a child.

The Anabaptists disturbed the city in a way the Lutherans had not. Plus, the pressure was on from the court in Brussels. And Dobbenszoon had to prove himself. After a short trial, the city issued vibrant death sentences that followed the emperor's rules for dealing with heretics: the male troublemakers were publicly beheaded; the women were tied into sacks and drowned in the frigid water of the IJ.

The warning didn't take. Other cells of Anabaptists emerged in the city. The year before, a group had taken over the German city of Münster, declared rebaptism, polygamy, and common ownership of property mandatory, and otherwise set to making Münster the center of a new, pure Christian kingdom on earth. While the German Anabaptists still held sway (they would soon be captured, tortured, and put to death, and their bodies displayed in cages from the tower of the church—cages that hang there today, though without the bodies), Amsterdam's Anabaptists decided to make their city Mün-

The Water Problem 49

ster's twin: a second Zion. Forty of them chose a late afternoon in May—a holiday, when, as they knew, the crossbow militia held its annual feast, which meant everyone would be drunk. They had no problem storming Dam Square and taking over City Hall.

But Amsterdam—its political leaders, its merchants, its shippers and tradesmen—had no interest in becoming a new Zion. An angry crowd gathered in the square. A drunken man staggered to the door of the town hall and declared that for purposes of negotiation the rebels could consider him the representative of the city. There was a scuffle, and one of the Anabaptists stuck a knife in him. A vicious fight broke out, in which one of the mayors and twenty of his followers were killed. When the Anabaptists were finally subdued, they died in the most horrible way the authorities could dream up. Their chests were cut open, their still-beating hearts taken out and thrown in their faces. Then they were beheaded and quartered.

However horrific the punishments meted out, Protestant ire and acting out against the Catholic Church and allied civil authorities only grew, in Amsterdam and elsewhere. Yet another rebel churchman—the French theologian Jean Cauvin (John Calvin to the English-speaking world) would soon make a lasting impression on the Dutch. His clean-and-sober variety of reform, coupled with a clear structure for creating and operating a new church, appealed especially to poor and working-class Dutch and paved the way for an organized separation from the Catholic Church.

But the crisis that built up in the ensuing decades—a crisis that would give people in the various Dutch provinces a national identity and would transform Amsterdam into arguably the most powerful city in the world—was not just about religion. It was equally political and economic. The Catholic Church and feudalism had evolved together into a solid mass. The merchant-and-trader cities of the Dutch provinces, centered on a fundamentally different type of economy, did not fit with it. The forces involved in this crisis were at play across Europe, but they took on a particular resonance in the Low Countries, where ties to feudal authority were weak and where an entire generation had come of age under the influence of Erasmus's application of individual reason to faith issues. In the minds of Catholic leaders and officials of the Holy Roman Empire, a kind of mania seemed to be taking hold of the Dutch people. After the Anabaptist takeover of City Hall, and despite the satisfyingly harsh prosecution of the heretics, the imperial powers in Brussels decided not to trust the citizens of Amsterdam with their own governance. They removed the local regents from power and replaced them with a new crop of "sincere Catholics," most of them out-of-towners.

It was the first move in a contest that would soon erupt into open war. In an age before newspapers, pamphlets were the news medium, and those that passed from hand to hand in the Low Countries—and were read in Amsterdam taverns and on the public passenger barges that traveled between towns—began to repeat, over and over, an ancient word, with a new twist. The more highbrow pamphleteers put it in Latin: *liber*. Appeals by and for the upper classes sometimes cast it in French: *la liberté*. Most, of course, put it in plain Dutch: *vrijheid*. As happens so often in history at the dying of one age and the birth of another, an era of phenomenal ugliness, strife, and chaos was about to unfold. A printed appeal, a call to action that swept through the cities of the Low Countries in the midst of the chaos, written by a dashing young man who would become first national hero and then national martyr—a combination of George Washington and Abraham Lincoln—urged people to shake off the stupor of the centuries and see the new reality. "Awake," it called. "Do not be blinded. Open your eyes." And it breathed strange new magic into that old word *freedom*.

THE ALTERATION

The rise of Amsterdam from a minor port in a distant corner of Europe to global powerhouse and birthplace of liberalism was an element of a power struggle that occupied the whole continent and ranged across much of the sixteenth century. It's possible, however, to assign a single event as the launch point of that rise and to see it in terms of the interplay of three personalities.

The date was October 25, 1555. The place was Brussels: specifically, the grandly colonnaded palace of the ancestral rulers of the province of Brabant. The occasion was one of the most fastidiously ornate of the century—which is perhaps strange, considering that the reason that dozens of European nobles had gathered was to bear witness as the palace's current overlord, Charles V, perhaps the most powerful man in the world, whose titles included Holy Roman emperor and king of Spain, abdicated those thrones in order to live out his days in the warmth of the Spanish sun. Charles had modeled himself and his reign on ancient Rome (his court followers referred to him as Caesar), and he wanted to orchestrate his departure from the world stage as a kind of classical drama. He would not live long enough to appreciate how well he succeeded.

If the history of the city of Amsterdam can be described as one of the ascendance of liberalism, which is one of the defining features of the modern world, then the emperor who limped into the throne room in Brussels on that autumn day—ashen, beaten, epileptic, crippled by gout—symbolizes, as well as any individual could, the world of the past: Europe's past, the Western past, the tradition that underlies much of our modern culture and yet partly in opposition to which our modern selves came into being. Charles was the personification of European royalty and medieval heraldry. His grandparents were Ferdinand and Isabella of Spain, who had sent Columbus off on his historic voyage. He was heir to the Habsburg family dynasty, which began its rise in a Swiss valley ten centuries ago, reached the climax of its world-historic power with Charles himself, and finally collapsed in the trenches of World War I. He had fought and strived his whole life in the service of Catholicism: not so much the faith itself (he waged a conflict or two against popes, and once sacked Rome) as the force for controlling minds, wills, and peoples. When Martin Luther had stood before the Diet of Worms in 1521 and refused to recant what he had written against the Church, it was Charles, then only nineteen years old but assuming the full mantle of worldly authority, who heard him out, forcefully opposed him, and issued a ban against him, thus formally setting off the Protestant Reformation.

The chessboard assembly gathered in Brussels (there were knights, bishops, and queens) was aware of the accomplishments of the man who limped into the throne room, leaning on a strong young shoulder for support. Charles had fought off Ottoman encroachments, sailed the Mediterranean in swashbuckling campaigns to rid the sea of pirates, personally sent off Magellan, Cortés, and Pizarro on their voyages, managed Spain's South American colonization, extended his dominion to the Dutch provinces, through Germany, and across Italy, and in pretty much every way worked to hold up the pillars of the medieval world order: monarchic power, domination by the Catholic Church, feudal land management, divine right, mercantile colonization, and obedience to authority along the strict metaphysical lines of the great chain of being.

But he was done. Before him stood his replacement: his twenty-eight-year-old son, Philip. The transfer of power would be personally as well as historically striking. The father had been, in temperament, a warrior whose aggression was shot through with touches of refinement and diplomatic smarts. He had a command of most European languages and, though not native to Spain, won over his Spanish subjects by not only entering the bullring but acquitting himself well. Throughout his life he loved both music and fighting, a combination that was excellently illustrated when he was twenty-two and a friend playfully taunted him that music was for girly men. Charles erupted in anger and insisted they duel. He beat his friend in a bloody joust in which he himself sustained a permanent injury; then he made the friend viceroy of Naples. Later, he would attempt to end a war with France by challenging the French king, Francis I, to settle things mano a mano. (Francis said no.)

His son was neither a warrior nor a scholar—though he did like to pose for portraits in battle-ready attire. Despite the fact that the royal household commissioned whole volumes to be written expressly to teach him languages and rhetoric when he was a young prince, he was only ever comfortable in his native Spanish. (When he was king and foreign emissaries addressed him in Latin, he would brush them aside by saying their pronunciation was too poor to be understood.) He had been groomed from birth to become a king, and he came to like his comforts and deplored his father's tendency to roam across Europe and into Africa as perennial commander of the forces of Christendom. Once when they were traveling together he had complained about the discomfort of the road, whereupon his father had roared, "Kings do not need residences!" In this, Philip probably represented an epochal as well as a generational change: from peripatetic medieval warlord to tactical modern leader.

For centuries historians portrayed Philip II (as he was about to become known) more or less as a concentrated block of evil, but recent scholarship has moderated that view, giving us a more rounded portrait: of a loving father and husband as well as an able

tactician with a vision for his empire. A review of this recent scholarship is convincing in that what had come before was so clearly
written or influenced by Protestant enemies of Philip. Then again,
the central portion of any understanding of him has to be the extent
and zeal with which he wielded one of history's most vicious weapons, the Spanish Inquisition, and the systematic torture and violence he unleashed on many thousands of human beings. Perhaps
we can best say that he was no more malevolent than other absolute
rulers who had sway over half the known world. But the one thing
he possessed that his father did not—a fierce passion for the Catholic faith—would give his long reign a calamitous fire.

There was one other major player in this power transfer, whose
role was as yet unknown to the participants (including himself) but
who was not only present in the throne room that day but offered
the shoulder on whom the fading emperor put his weight as he
walked in. His presence was one of those incongruities that fate
inflicts on human affairs, particularly meticulously planned affairs:
in his refinement and grand good looks, and in the affection that he
showed the abdicating emperor as he helped him into his seat and
that was clearly reciprocated, he seemed more naturally a model son
and successor than Philip, who walked in behind them.

His name was Willem. He had been born twenty-two years earlier in a storybook castle overlooking the clustered dwellings of the
German village of Dillenburg. His father was the count of Nassau,
a minor nobleman, not a man of great wealth, and Willem grew
up, one of seventeen children, in a boisterous household of simple
comforts and old-fashioned learning. He would eventually have
inherited the estate and lived out his life tending to it as his father
had, but for one thing. His uncle, his father's elder brother, who had
greater wealth, land, and titles, had married a woman whose family had considerably more wealth, land, and titles. This couple had
a son who, when he came of age, went off to war and was killed.
Whereupon it was revealed that all of the wealth and inheritance
that had come to the son from both his parents had been willed to

his cousin, Willem of Nassau. With that twist of fate, eleven-year-old Willem became one of the richest noblemen in Europe.

It so happened that Willem's uncle and Charles, the prematurely aged emperor who was now about to give up his throne, had been childhood friends. When the emperor learned of events, he insisted on taking the now fantastically wealthy and titled youth into his protection and had him brought to his court at Brussels. Willem's life changed in an instant: from romping with dogs, visiting tenant farmers with his father, and sitting in the evening with his siblings before the massive hearth, it was now banquets, masked balls, jousting tournaments, and sitting for portraits. He pushed his native German into the background and learned to speak French and Dutch, the languages of the court at Brussels, and Spanish, the language of the kingdom. When his family next saw him, he was nearly a man and in his bearing as aristocratic as the title by which he would henceforth be known: the Prince of Orange.

Willem's background says a good deal about the complexities of identity in the sixteenth century. In his teens, he seems to have accomplished the difficult trick of becoming fully a member of the ruling aristocracy yet never letting go of his rural, central European roots. Then there was the most historically decisive layer, for he came in time to identify himself with the Low Countries. From Brussels, he eventually moved north to the city of Breda. He got to know Dutch society, the most striking and unusual feature of which, for him, was how it was clustered into towns and cities. In these cities, he learned, power was not something that flowed from the castle down to the peasants. It was in the hands of herring merchants and cloth traders, men who owned soap works and timber yards and shipyards, the regents who sat on town boards, who were nominated to their governmental position by those same wealthy men of business, the members of the water boards of each community, and the *dijkgraaf*, literally "dike count," who had overall responsibility for the never-ending task of managing the damming and rechanneling of water, and which is still an important position in the Netherlands.

Charles took to the boy and kept him close to his royal person. They were much alike: not bookish but smart, and full of adventure. The boy enjoyed people and society and became a popular figure at court, yet he was delighted to leave it behind and go on hunts, and he took up military training with zest. He became an excellent soldier and leader; at the age of twenty he was named lieutenant general of the emperor's army in the Low Countries.

The most interesting feature in the interpersonal dynamic between the emperor and the boy lay just below the surface. Charles's motive in bringing Willem to him when he was young was not merely to please an old friend; rather it had everything to do with geopolitics. Willem's German parents had converted to Lutheranism, the dreaded heresy that the emperor was doing his best to quash. Charles pulled to his court the suddenly wealthy youth— whose newly inherited lands covered large swaths of France, Germany, Luxembourg, and the Low Countries—not out of kindness to the family but as a strategic move on the chessboard of Europe. His plan was to raise the boy himself and so personally take him, and his holdings, out of play for the Protestants and make them part of his empire.

And indeed, Willem dutifully grew up Catholic, regal, and "Spanish." Charles—the brilliant old schemer whose handcrafted plots had included colonizing Mexico and Peru (along with decimating the natives and their godless cultures) and squeezing money out of German Protestants to finance his defense of Vienna against the Ottoman sultan Suleyman the Magnificent—must have been pleased with this small success as he sat back in his velvet chair and surveyed the distinguished audience who had come to bear witness to his taking leave of the world of power politics. There were troubles on nearly every front of the empire, but in this at least—the plan to take a boy from the wilds of Germany, turn him into the excellent specimen of manhood who now stood at his right, and so bring him and his lands into the empire—things had gone as planned.

In fact, life had substantially improved on his original idea, for he had taken to the boy as to a son, saw greatness in him, and had groomed him to be proxy ruler of the Dutch provinces. Charles's plan for the Low Countries included making them, as it were, more medieval: building up the historically weak Dutch nobility, creating a line of Dutch noblemen who would get power and prestige from the court, and who would in turn do the king's bidding. With the transfer of power complete, Charles left it to his son, Philip, and the young Prince of Orange to make this happen.

As Philip began his reign, he quickly discovered that his adventurous, war-loving father had left vast problems behind. Foremost among these was money. Income from taxes totaled 1 million ducats, and the government's debt stood at 7 million ducats. Interest payments were crippling. Philip had to raise money. The Dutch cities—money-producing engines without parallel in Europe—were the only option.

The Dutch, though, were brewing a resentment against their Spanish rulers, who had pressed them for extra taxes time and again. The leaders of the States General—the governing body that represented all the provinces—knew that Philip needed them, and so they made a proposal. They would agree to tax their citizens again and raise 3.6 million ducats for the king over nine years—more than enough to bail him out of his financial crisis—but on the condition that they dispense it when and as they saw fit. The king was outraged, but he accepted the terms. Unwittingly, he was taking the first step toward losing the Dutch provinces.

Philip does not seem to have had a master plan for his rule, but his father had written a sort of "how to run an empire" guidebook for him, which the son did his best to follow. It had general advice ("maintain friends and informants in all areas") and region-specific wisdom ("Remember that the French are always discouraged if they do not succeed immediately in anything which they undertake").

When it came to the Low Countries, Charles wrote, "As we have seen and discovered, the people there cannot tolerate being governed by foreigners." Philip seems to have disregarded this caution. Whenever he deviated from his father's plan, it was in pursuit of his own ideals. Philip had what might be termed reactionary tendencies. He loved to watch knights joust and periodically ordered tournaments—replete with chivalrous decorum, thudding hooves, and roisterous bonhomie—that would last for weeks, never mind that these were, by the 1550s, largely a thing of the past. Philip's Catholicism was of a piece with this. It grew more passionate as he aged, but from the first it differed from his father's. Where Charles had ordered the execution of more than two thousand Protestants for heresy, it was for political reasons; Charles was also known to express sympathy with points of Protestant doctrine.

Philip was deeply devout, both in the sense of piety—he went on regular retreats to monasteries—and also in ways that get at the definition of fanaticism. After his marriage to Elizabeth of Valois, for example, he took her, in March 1561, as a kind of date, to an auto-da-fé—the ritual sentencing, parading, and execution of heretics (in this case twenty-four of them) by the Inquisition. He was an obsessive collector of holy relics, whose powers he swore by. At the end of his life he had more than seven thousand sacred bones and other relics in his possession, including 144 heads of saints, thousands of arms, legs, and other pieces, in addition to hairs supposedly of Jesus and Mary and bits of the True Cross.

In Philip we see the true merging of secular and religious powers, resulting in what is tempting to look at in modern terms as psychosis (one of his standard justifications was to say an act he wanted to be performed was in "God's service and mine, which is the same"). Yet psychosis also involves an inability to function, and Philip did indeed function, through a nearly forty-year reign. He was a man of his time, preoccupied with the trappings of the past yet dealing with forces of the future, waves of change that were altering the framework on which his world was built. Protestantism was a threat from below—masses of people were defecting from the faith—but also from above. Princes and bishops across Germany, Switzerland, Sweden, and Denmark had renounced the Catholic faith and thus presented a dangerous challenge to Philip. In England, Henry VIII had reformatted Christian worship in wholesale fashion; the result would be the creation of the Anglican Church.

The Dutch provinces were part of this upheaval, but as far as Philip was concerned the difference was that these provinces were his territory, which he had sworn to maintain. They were a financial engine that powered his government. And they were slipping away from the faith.

His conclusion was clear ("God's service and mine, which is the same"): he would exert every force to stop Protestantism in the Low Countries. As he later opined to his fellow Catholic warlord Holy Roman Emperor Maximilian II, "To think that a passion so great as this about choice in religion can be resolved by soft means [is] a complete illusion." He made two decisions. The first was to maintain a standing army of three thousand Spanish soldiers in the Dutch provinces. These had been brought in as a defensive tactic in a war that he was in the process of fighting against France; he now proposed to station them permanently. Second, with the support of the pope, he would reorganize the Catholic Church in the provinces. This would keep the flow of church revenues out of the hands of abbots in the country, many of whom were showing signs of rebellion. It would also let Philip appoint his own man as the cardinal who would lead the Dutch church. And, most ominously, it would bring the Inquisition into Dutch life as an instrument with not only ecclesiastic but also secular authority.

Much of his plan was kept secret at first. Philip relied heavily on the Prince of Orange for its implementation. Willem was, by all accounts, a willing vassal, at least as far as he understood the plan. He was now one of the most important figures in the Low Countries, who managed the trick of being a popular figure both at court and among ordinary Dutchmen. In fact, he could come off as a bit of a harmless fop whose good looks and fortune shielded him from serious matters. As he later wrote of this period, "I had nothing so much in my head as the play of arms, the chase, and other exercises suitable to young lords." Very shortly after the unexpected death of his wife, Anna, he was eagerly in the hunt for a new one. He thought he had found her in the young Princess of Lorraine, but when he approached the girl's widowed mother, who at thirty-five was nine years older than him, she offered herself instead. He politely declined.

But he also had serious business to do. At the king's bidding, Willem talked the English into providing a loan. And he did his best to keep the most prominent Dutch leaders in line, arguing that the future of the provinces lay in working with, not against, the Spanish government.

Then the scales fell from Willem's eyes. The war with France had ended, and the king sent the Prince of Orange as part of a delegation of three "royal hostages" to negotiate a peace treaty with Henry, the King of France. Willem rode into Paris in June of 1559 to find the city fully decked out for an elaborate armistice celebration. There were contests and balls, and Willem was briefly distracted by a seventeen-year-old duchess. Then came the royal hunt in the Chantilly forest. Hunting was a serious business for King Henry, and he chose this as the moment to speak of the future. Like everyone else, he had taken a liking to Willem; of all those in King Philip's delegation, he preferred to discuss the matter with him.

What had brought the French and Spanish kings to the negotiating table was the foolishness of the situation, in which two Catholic kingdoms were at war with each other while the faith itself was being undermined across Europe. As the king talked, Willem realized he was speaking of ideas that Philip and his closest advisers were in the process of hatching, which had been kept from him but about which Henry assumed he knew. The plan was for a full-scale suppression of Protestantism in the Low Countries—in particular Calvinism, which had overtaken Lutheranism in just a few years to become the main threat to the Catholic faith. Unlike other, more radical Protestant offshoots, Calvinism didn't abjure wealth; you were allowed to make money and still be a good Christian. And

Calvinism had a strong vein of political righteousness in it: it honored obedience but also held that there was a point at which it was appropriate to rebel against unjust rulers, which made it both especially attractive to ordinary Dutchmen and particularly threatening to Philip.

Under the oak canopy of the forest, the French king prattled on—systematic torture, mass beheadings, an impressive preview of coming attractions—and Willem kept his alarm hidden, pretending he was already aware of the plan, playacting that would result in the nickname history has given him: William the Silent.

Overnight, Willem changed from satrap to rebel. A revolution was in the offing, a war of independence against an arrogant foreign monarch, and Willem would be its leader.

At least, that is the standard historical view, which lasted for more than four centuries. In fact, a close reading of the historical record (the scholarly research project www.historici.nl has identified and cataloged more than twelve thousand extant pieces of correspondence associated with Willem) shows that, far from having leapt to the head of the Dutch revolutionaries, Willem was caught more or less right in the middle of two extremes: those who pushed for an all-out war of independence and those who vowed to remain loyal to the Spanish king. As someone who had been raised at the Spanish court he was unable to abandon it with the snap of a finger; for the next few years he would try to appease both sides, try to hold together the world as he knew it. And yet the event in the French forest does seem to have marked a turning point for him: he became convinced that Philip was ready to take measures against the Dutch provinces that could not be tolerated, and he determined to take action.

He was not alone. As news of Philip's intentions spread, so did outrage. Going back to the 1400s, as merchants and tradesmen in Amsterdam, Utrecht, Rotterdam, and other Dutch cities flourished in their nonfeudal system, they had built up a series of "privileges and liberties" that local governments granted to them in exchange for their avowal of obligations that they had to the community. These privileges and liberties included a principle of free trade, as well as regulations that favored local merchants or tradesmen over outsiders (i.e., protectionism). They also covered quasi-democratic principles, such as a right to have a say in their taxation. The privileges and liberties—which are forerunners of modern political rights and freedoms—extended eventually to the provincial level, so that the governing bodies of the provinces were bound by them as well. Philip's father had promised, under his signature, that his rule would never violate these principles, which by this time the Dutch considered hallowed. Philip's new decrees trampled all over the privileges and liberties.

In late July of 1559, King Philip appeared in Ghent at a meeting of the representatives of all the Dutch provinces to announce that he was leaving the Low Countries, moving his court to Spain, and stationing his soldiers in the provinces for their protection. During an adjournment, the Dutch representatives prepared a response. The king read the response with fury, for in it the Dutch leaders informed him they would suspend payment of the nine years' tax unless the king withdrew the Spanish soldiers.

Philip was now in an impossible position. He had recently experienced the greatest military disaster in Spanish history to date—his expedition to retake Tripoli from the Ottomans was ambushed by a Turkish fleet, resulting in the sinking of dozens of Spanish ships and the surrender of ten thousand soldiers—and he was desperately short of funds. He raged at the impertinence of the Dutch, scoffingly asking whether their remonstrance also covered him, considering that he was also, technically at least, a Spanish soldier. But in the end he had to relent. He needed the money and he needed it at once. Shortly after, the Spanish soldiers left Dutch soil—most of them to replace those that were lost off the coast of Africa.

Among the surprises to Philip in this affair was a signature that stood out prominently in the formal complaint: Willem, Prince of Orange. Some days later, Willem was among the dignitaries who were assembled at the port of Vlissingen to see the king and his entourage off. According to a third-party account, as the king was about to step onboard his ship, he had an encounter with Willem. The king told him in effect that he knew full well the Dutch estates would never have had the gall to treat him this way were they not being led by someone higher, meaning the Prince of Orange. Willem, who was still trying to maintain a middle ground, deflected, saying that the Dutch provincial councils had made their own decisions. Whereupon the king let loose with an angry tirade, which the witness who recounted the story felt reflected the king's sense of having been personally crossed. It was "not the estates" that had betrayed him, he cried to the younger man, whom he had known since they were children and whom his own father had seemingly favored, "but you, you, you!" Philip boarded the ship and never returned to the Dutch provinces.

———

New laws went into effect in Dutch cities shortly thereafter. Protestant worship would be not only a religious offense but a crime against the state. The heresy laws to be enforced by the Spanish Inquisition on the Dutch populace were lampoonably brutal. For example, death was the penalty even if one repented and came back to the Catholic fold. The only difference was the manner: repentent men were beheaded and women buried alive or drowned, whereas those who refused to acknowledge the evil of their ways were burned at the stake. Considering that perhaps half of the three million inhabitants of the Dutch provinces had left the Catholic Church by this point, most of them to join Calvinist congregations, the implications were rather vast.

These decrees had an explosive and broad impact on the Dutch. Essentially, the Dutch population broke down into three groups: ordinary people, merchants, and the nobility. Calvinism had taken hold especially among farmers, shoemakers, shipwrights, and other workers; their new congregations were forums for both spiritual cleansing and political protest. For many merchants, who had to pay the largest share of the taxes that Spain levied, the heresy laws were added insult to financial injury. The nobility was tiny compared with that of other European countries (it comprised less than one-tenth of 1 percent of the population, and many of these people had no land but rather were businessmen who happened to have titles), but the noblemen played a role in the government and the king's decision to place his trusted courtier Antoine Perrenot, aka Cardinal Granvelle, in the position of senior minister of state usurped their time-honored right to be led by one of their own. Dutchmen of every class were outraged by portions of the new heresy laws that gave the Inquisition the power to strip someone suspected of anti-Catholicism of his or her property—another violation of their ancient liberties. Philip thus succeeded in bringing, for the first time, a large number of people from each of these three groups of Dutch society into alignment.

War is always messy, not just in the way it's fought but in who is fighting and why. Ardent Calvinists used the outrage that the heresy laws stirred up to promote their faith. But many who remained Catholic also joined in the rebellion. One of the first noblemen to openly object to Philip's plan was Lamoral, the Count of Egmont, who was not only a proud and eminently correct Catholic but a member of Philip's council of state, which administered the Dutch provinces, and a military hero who had recently won battles against the French in Philip's service. In 1564, before the council of state, he gave the first airing of what would become a familiar theme of Dutch tolerance—based not on ideals but on practicality. The king should abandon his campaign to crush Protestantism as a heresy, Egmont told the assembly, because the Dutch provinces were geographically different from other parts of Europe. We are not "bounded by oceans and mountains," his logic went. That is, since the Netherlands was an open landscape, rulers had to expect a free flow of information and ideas and to put up with it, even if some of those ideas were repellent.

With his this-behavior-is-going-to-happen-anyway-so-we-might-as-well-tolerate-it reasoning, Egmont sounded a refrain that would be repeated in the twentieth century in, for example, the decisions to decriminalize soft drugs and prostitution. No doubt he did not have it in mind to establish a tradition of loosening constraints on personal behavior, but in trying to maintain a balance between duty and liberty, he adopted what would become a uniquely Dutch approach.

Meanwhile, Philip had his inquisitors working in the provinces. The most infamously efficient was Pieter Titelmans, who operated in Flanders and was particularly skilled in his ability to sniff out information—from booksellers, in markets—then move through the phases of arrest, interrogation, and execution. Over the course of several years, he averaged about two cases per week, each one of which, as was intended, sent out ripples of fear and, as was not intended, built anger and solidarity.

People got creative with their forms of resistance. Since it wasn't safe to hold non-Catholic services in towns, "hedge sermons" sprang up, held at locations in the countryside that could be announced at short notice. At first they were small affairs, a dozen or so people listening to a Calvinist preacher, but very quickly they became immensely popular, with thousands at a time crowded together in a field outside the city walls, safely beyond the jurisdiction of the king's men. (The Flemish artist Pieter Breughel painted his pastoral *Sermon of St. John the Baptist* at this time as a sly blessing on this activity, a reminder that the first sermons were all in the out of doors.) Pore through some of the original documents of the period, in which local clerks were forced to write out decrees from the inquisitors to city residents, and you find snide little graffiti in the margins, as in one case in Ghent in which the clerk scribbled, beside Titelmans's name, "Alias Tyranny."

In what sounds like a Monty Python strategy, one weapon used by the Dutch rebels was . . . satire. It was an age in which the divine right of kings was so ingrained that it was nearly impossible for people to imagine directly challenging a monarch, and also a time when ceremony and ritual were so refined that slight changes could be used to make political points. Thus on April 5, 1566, a scene played out at the palace in Brussels that needs some interpreting if it's to make sense to modern eyes. More than two hundred Dutchmen of the so-called lesser nobility, which is to say merchants who happened to have inherited titles, processed through the archway of the palace and politely demanded an audience with Margaret, the Duchess of Parma, whom Philip had appointed regent of the Dutch provinces. The date they chose for the event—the Friday before Palm Sunday—would have said something in itself, suggesting Jesus's entry into Jerusalem and thus peace. Then again, Jesus was the righteous Son of God—what did that imply about how these Dutchmen saw themselves?

They presented themselves as "good and loyal servants and faithful vassals" of King Philip. They were so obsequious in their manner that one of Margaret's advisers dismissively referred to them as a bunch of beggars. And they were indeed begging—for the relaxation of the onerous heresy laws. But there was also a strong warning—that "a general uprising could break out"—and after their leader read their petition they all executed a graceful little half-turn movement—the "caracole"—which was a battle maneuver that mounted soldiers did in order to fire pistols at an enemy.

Margaret was bewildered by this mismatch of courtly signals—which was the idea. As the historian Peter Arnade says, the ambiguity allowed the Dutchmen "to imagine—even scheme—revolt while professing allegiance." The confused duchess acquiesced: she gave the order to suspend the burnings at the stake and the work of the inquisitors. The minor nobles were overjoyed. That night they held a drinking party, at which they decided that they liked being called beggars. Again mimicking courtly refinements, in particular the chivalric orders (the Order of the Fleece, of the Garter, of the Dragon), they—and by extension all the Dutch rebels—would henceforth become the Order of the Beggars. News of the satiric order caught on and spread throughout the provinces. The rebels adopted a mock chivalric fashion: gray cloak (gray was the color associated with the poor), a begging bowl attached to the belt, and, as a topper, a flourishing "Turkish" moustache. Paintings, prints, and medals of handsomely dressed-down Beggars circulated. The look became a fad among young people.

Until this point the rebellion was largely confined to the southern provinces. Then, two months after the Beggars' banquet, their leader, Hendrik van Brederode, who had read out the petition to Margaret of Parma, came clattering into Amsterdam at the head of a contingent of mounted rebels, bringing news of events in the south. Van Brederode had been among the earliest and most eager rebels. He was a vigorous, hard-drinking, death-defying sort who was seemingly afraid of no one—"a madman if ever there was one," a mate of his called him—and after attending several mock banquets, dressed variously as a beggar or a cardinal, he took charge of the effort to spread the rebellion northward.

As they did wherever he went, crowds turned out in Amsterdam. The city had followed its own trajectory through these turbulent times. Its Catholic leaders, installed by Philip, with their close ties to Rome and to Philip's court, obeyed the dictates of king and church—sort of. In fact, there were more and more Calvinists in Amsterdam, and Willem Bardes, the man who had taken over the job of *schout*, or sheriff, in 1542 and kept it until 1566, adopted the look-the-other-way policy in handling religious differences. He chose not to disturb Calvinist services, and, when pressured to make arrests, he gave residents warnings so that they could flee.

Bardes was smart and well liked—he knew his town and how it worked and how to keep things going in tough times. But he had been forced from office earlier in the year and replaced with a hardliner named Pieter Pieterszoon. After a visiting Calvinist minister held the first hedge sermon just outside the city's Haarlem Gate—which drew a huge but orderly crowd—Pieterszoon decided to go on the offensive. When it came time for the next "secret" sermon, he led one hundred armed men on horseback on a flanking maneuver, apparently intending to attack the gathering. But the Calvinists had protection: the sheriff's men were met by a large group armed with bows and arrows, who faced them down.

This was the atmosphere in Amsterdam when Van Brederode appeared. There were lots of restive Calvinists in the city, eager to take some kind of action. But what could people do?

As it turned out, the suspension of the Inquisition was like the sudden unlocking of doors that had long been barred: all over the provinces, decades of pent-up feeling burst forth in violence—directed not at the king but at the structures of Catholicism. It began in Flanders in the south, when, in the summer heat, a hedge sermon got out of hand and the crowd started attacking a nearby Catholic church. Within three days, more than four hundred churches across the south were ravaged, the "graven imagery" that John Calvin preached against hacked with clubs, angels' wings and saints' heads clattering to the marble floors. People tore down holy paintings, ransacked monasteries, raided monks' cells, put rocks through stained glass windows. The "iconoclastic fury" of 1566 was under way.

The first attack in the south took place on August 11. Twelve days later, a group of merchants were gathered in the morning along the Warmoesstraat in Amsterdam, exchanging news. The street ran perpendicular to the harbor, along the river. The houses on its western side had their backs to the water. Many of these were the property of merchants, who could have goods delivered right to the back by boat and then hoisted up into their upper floors for storage. The street along the front thus served as the city's financial center, where men haggled and gossiped. A group appeared, newly returned from Antwerp, and they breathily told of the goings-on in the south. For proof, they had with them some crumbled marble: bits of church altars and holy statues.

The news spread. At lunchtime, the Catholic officials of Amsterdam hurried through the streets hauling all of the valuables from their various orders to be stashed away for safekeeping. The sight of berobed clergy up to their necks in delicate items of wrought silver and gold inflamed things further. At two o'clock, a children's baptism in the Old Church—at which it was normal practice to ward off the devil—was interrupted by somebody shouting, "You priests, stop summoning the devil from these children! You've deceived the world long enough with your lies!" A woman in a pew took off her slipper and aimed it at the head of a wooden statue of Mary. Some young toughs started hurling stones at the stained glass windows.

One of the city's mayors happened to be in the church at the time. He flew out the door, headed straight for City Hall, and burst in to a meeting of his colleagues crying, "In the Old Church they're beating all the saints to pieces!" Whereupon one of the others, of Calvinist inclinations, responded, with dry Protestant pique, that they were in fact statues and not actual saints.

These were unprecedented times, but a familiar sequence of events ensued. After the initial rampage, the city fathers opted not to punish anyone but, instead, to allow Calvinists something they had been pushing for: permission to hold church services. It was *gedogen* all over again: *Yes, this is illegal behavior, but we will allow it.* They stipulated that Calvinist worship had to take place outside the city, but they also let Calvinist ministers make home visits to parishioners who were sick.

But this time, *gedogen* didn't work. In less than two weeks, the court in Brussels fired off a letter with an order: "Stand up against the church desecrators." The subsequent crackdown resulted in another, more furious bout of Catholic bashing.

The woman called Margaret of Parma, who was technically governing the Dutch people, had come into the world, forty-four years earlier, as the result of a liaison between Philip's father, Charles V, and the daughter of a Dutch carpet maker. The Holy Roman Emperor did the manly thing and acknowledged her as his offspring, and she was raised as royalty. At the age of eighteen she was married to another regal personage of nonstandard pedigree: the Duke of Parma, who was the son of Pope Paul III's illegitimate son—that is to say, the pope's grandson. When Philip left the Low Countries, he had appointed her his proxy ruler. She had been well educated, but probably no amount of education could have prepared someone to govern in such a tempest. She appeased the Beggars, infuriating her court as well as the Dutch loyalists, then she cracked down on the iconoclasts, leading them further along their path of revolt.

But just when it looked like her rule was dissolving into chaos, the situation changed. She knew there was serious disagreement among the Dutch leaders who wanted change. Van Brederode and his followers pushed for rebellion. Egmont, who had made the geographic argument for why Philip should allow the Dutch their tolerance, was among those of what might be termed a moderate-medieval sensibility: they saw that Protestantism was a fact, but they could not and would not openly oppose their king. Willem of Orange was in between these positions, advocating religious tolerance in a world of hardening intolerance; his letters show him constantly angling, trying to puzzle out a solution.

What shifted the balance was the iconoclasm. Its fury and violence had shocked many of the Dutch themselves, so much that some of the Dutch leaders who had been leaning toward rebellion began to waver. Sensing this, Margaret did some skillful politicking and turned some Beggars into loyalists. At the same time, her soldiers attacked, and easily won back, cities that had gone fully in support of the rebels.

The rebellion began to fragment. Willem traveled ceaselessly during this period, crisscrossing the countryside on two very different missions. He was trying to broker a deal in which the Dutch rebels would desist if the king allowed Protestant worship in the country. But he was also trying to get Dutch cities to contribute to a fund for the general defense, in the event that Philip mounted an all-out attack. Here he was faced with a classic problem that comes from a lack of national identity. Cities were willing to shore up their own defenses, but they did not have the sense of a larger purpose that would enable them to commit funds or arms to be shipped elsewhere.

As the situation grew more dire, Willem got bolder. One reason may have been exposure: as he traveled from town to town, arriving on horseback, erect and serene, with a chiseled visage that seemed made for reproduction in busts and engravings, ordinary people turned out to greet him. The cheers, the expectations evident in the faces: it was a kind of energy. He was becoming the de facto Dutch leader. He spoke out more directly, not for attacking the king but for "religious peace"—tolerance of religious differences. The moment would eventually be seen as a watershed in European history, and the principle would become the foundation of a set of concepts we take for granted today: tolerance, diversity, pluralism, civil rights, the idea that any single person is of equal value to another. Espousing it in the 1560s would turn out to be a little premature. It is all the more remarkable, then, especially given his background, that Willem came to this view and pursued it in the midst of such upheaval.

In September 1566, while in Antwerp, he took the step—which Margaret had not authorized—of allowing Calvinist worship. Soon other cities in the south followed suit. In December, Willem arrived in Amsterdam. Still trying to push for tolerance and hold off war, he wrote to Margaret, warning her that in Amsterdam "distrust, bias, and hostility of the citizens against the magistrate are so great and have been so prolonged, that is to be feared that one day there will arise great difficulties." Working with the city leaders, he hammered out an agreement that allowed Calvinist worship in the city, with restrictions.

Then came the blackest possible news—precisely what Willem most feared. Philip had finally understood the situation: the iconoclasm had brought him clarity. He had ordered an army into the Low Countries, ten thousand strong. Tolerance was weakness; he would show strength.

Soon two dreaded syllables—"Alba"—were echoing through the provinces, as word spread that the king had called on Fernando Álvarez de Toledo, more commonly known as the Duke of Alba and popularly referred to as the Iron Duke, to take charge.

Alba—a tall, thin, angularly handsome man approaching sixty years of age—had been at war since he was sixteen and was probably the greatest military tactician of the age. He was a rigidly puritanical Castilian nobleman, exacting in his Catholicism and in his indefatigable prosecution of a military campaign. He had developed a reputation for what others considered unnecessary brutality but which he saw as precisely necessary force. In a battle against French troops, for example, he offered them their lives in exchange for surrender. They fought on, only to surrender later. Alba hanged every one of them, reasoning that to do otherwise would render meaningless his initial offer.

Alba was twenty years older than Philip and had known him since he was a small boy. As a child, Philip had studied the campaigns Alba had carried out under his father. They were alike in their religion and conservatism, but Alba was both smarter and narrower than his king. If modern parallels are of use, it might be appropriate to liken the relationship between the two men to that between President George W. Bush and his vice president, Dick Cheney.

Alba was profoundly devoted to both his king and the church and, as one of Philip's closest advisers, had pushed since Charles's abdication for a crushing military solution to the Dutch problem. Now he had his chance.

Alba's reputation was so forbidding that people began to flee the country before he had even gotten there. He understood spectacle as well as strategy: he knew how to create a theater of terror. He arranged the travel into the Netherlands of his ten thousand hardened regular soldiers, culled from the top ranks of Spanish, Italian, and German regiments, so as to gain maximum attention. His army moved like a snake, in three sections: its head reached an encampment first, purposely drawing attention, then moved on; the middle section appeared at the same spot the next day, increasing awe; the final contingent, resplendent with banners and instruments of war (including muskets, a military innovation that bewildered the Flemish who first encountered them), arrived the following day.

As Alba approached Brussels, the leaders of the rebellion were in disarray, deeply divided on what course to follow. Willem of Orange knew that any sort of revolt was impossible, at least for the time being, and beyond that he knew Alba well (they had both served Charles and had traveled together on the expedition to negotiate peace with the King of France) and was convinced that leaders of the Dutch insurrection needed to make a tactical retreat if they wanted to stay alive.

With danger mounting, he arranged a secret meeting with his friend Egmont, to tell him that he himself was leaving the country to regroup, to urge Egmont to do likewise, and to lay out a strategy for future military action. They chose a hunting lodge in the Flemish village of Dendermonde. Willem arrived first. Egmont called for him through the open door. "I'm here in the kitchen, sitting on the meat block!" Willem replied, with comic awareness of the contrast between how much was at stake and how humble the surroundings.

That was the extent of the comedy. Egmont made clear his belief that fleeing was wrong—under the code of chivalry, it would be a sign of dishonor to Philip, who was his king. From the first, Egmont had distinguished between principled disagreement with a policy, which was a just undertaking, and disloyalty to a monarch, which was for him an impossibility. Willem tried in effect to get his friend to lose his medieval shackles. "Cousin, if you take arms, I will join you," he said. "If not, I must leave you and quit the country. Have you forgotten how the Duke of Alba used to say to Charles V, 'Dead men make no war'? I won't wait for their justice or trust to their kindness." Egmont said that when Alba arrived he would show him respect, and he believed that Alba would do likewise.

When Alba rode into Brussels on an afternoon in August of 1567, he made straight for the palace. Margaret offered him her resignation, for while officially she was still regent it was clear that her stepbrother had put the Spanish soldier above her, and she knew what he planned to do. Alba then set up a commission that he called the Council of Troubles to deal with heretics. It would become known in Dutch history as the Council of Blood. With this official machinery in place, he arrested Egmont and several other Dutch noblemen, including the Count of Hoorn, who like Egmont had been a military hero in the service of Philip II, and imprisoned them in the castle of Ghent. People throughout the provinces were bewildered by the news. Throughout the crisis, both Egmont and Hoorn had made clear their unswerving loyalty to the king, so it was unthinkable that they should be executed.

The following June, in the Grand Place, the central square of Brussels, in an enormous public spectacle that quickly became the subject of story, song, and art, the Dutch nobles were beheaded. "I have satisfied myself over what they deserve," Alba wrote to Philip. "The example should be made almost immediately, and I consider it more effective if done in cold blood." Alba was now in charge, as he told the king: "No one dares to ask me if I have authority for what I am doing. I refuse to present my authority, saying only that I have to do what is in Your Majesty's service."

Heresy was Alba's central interest. His Council of Troubles—with a staff of 170 researchers, prosecutors, and soldier/executioners—got to work. According to Dutch sources, by its end the Council of Troubles put eighteen thousand Dutch men and women to death. Other tallies have it at closer to nine thousand. Alba's own head count was twelve thousand. But killings via the formal proceedings of the Council were only a fraction of the total. At the same time, Alba's army began its assault on treasonous Dutch cities. Around the country, as the acrid smoke from burning bodies blackened the air, people prayed to heaven. And if they knew where heaven was, they were as clear on the location of hell. An inversion of the Lord's Prayer that appeared in printed sheets in Dutch cities, twisted to refer to Alba, began:

Our Devil, who art in Brussels,
Cursed be thy name.

An eleven-year-old boy had left these hills and this green valley, with its half-timbered houses and its meandering river. He returned as a thirty-four-year-old man who stood at the center of a vast struggle over religion, power, and the changing meaning of freedom. Willem of Orange chose his German home as the base from which to plan a war against the empire that had raised him. Over the next four years the quiet medieval Castle Dillenburg was transformed into a military headquarters, with soldiers, spies, and diplomats coming and going.

Willem was the only major Dutch nobleman whom Alba had failed to subdue—which put him in the position of singlehandedly being able either to let the Dutch rebellion die a quiet death or to reignite it and turn it into a war of independence. After years in which he himself had struggled over the nature of the rebellion, he had finally embraced revolt and come to terms with the central role that religion played in it. He converted to Calvinism, and the conversion was a calculated political move. At least sixty thousand Calvinists had fled the Low Countries since Alba's arrival. They were living in exile in Germany, France, and southern England, and they were waiting for a leader. There were also Protestant communities and leaders elsewhere in Europe that could be called on to help. He organized soldiers, borrowed money, and sent spies to commune with merchants and regents in cities throughout the Dutch provinces. And he raised a navy, of sorts, by giving letters of marque to a ragged collection of semipiratical ships of various nationalities that were moored at English ports, whose captains had pledged him their loyalty.

And so battle commenced. Willem brought soldiers into the Dutch provinces from the north and the south. But French forces in Alba's service were waiting and devastated the Dutch and their French Huguenot allies. With German mercenaries, Willem entered Wallonia, in the south, only to find that the townspeople there had not been prepared and thought he was an enemy. Willem grew more desperate as time passed—his money was running out and mercenaries had to be paid. Knowing this, Alba played a slow, defensive game.

What changed in the meantime was the Dutch people. The human mind doesn't instantly adjust to embrace new concepts, and the idea of nationhood took some getting used to. One thing that helped the Frisians, Zeelanders, Hollanders, Gelderlanders, and other provincials to begin to think of themselves as one people was Alba's continued campaign to stamp out Protestantism—every town square was the site of burnings and beheadings as the Council of Blood moved across the landscape.

Another was the sophisticated propaganda campaign that Willem of Orange mounted. Like a modern politician, he gathered into his inner circle men who could spin his version of events. Dutch cities were flooded with pamphlets and posters that portrayed a righteous rebellion, in support of uniquely Dutch ideas about home, property, and individual liberties, against the tyrannical power of the Catholic Church and a foreign monarchy.

The Netherlands have always been ruled, Willem said in the first of these pamphlets, with the principles of respect for the "freedoms, rights, customs, traditions and privileges" that the Dutch developed over the centuries. And the Dutch people "owe obedience to the rulers only on condition that the freedoms are maintained." But King Philip had shown that his true goal was to "enslave the conscience, persons and possessions of the whole population—nay, to rob them of all their freedoms, rights and privileges." Willem went on to dissect the misuse of religion by the King of Spain: "Of course, this was all given the appearance of holy zeal and said to be done in the name of religion . . . but in reality it was greatly to the disservice of God, the king, and the country."

The language of subsequent pamphlets became progressively more heated. "*Awake*," he urged in the next one. "Do not allow yourselves to be further deceived."

Such a movement required a figurehead, and the propaganda carefully crafted Willem's image, raising him up to founding father status. Prints were run off by the thousands that showed Willem of Orange, the righteous defender of liberty, on one side, and Alba, the demonic enslaver, on the other. Songs were written that praised the heroism of Willem and the other leaders of the revolt. The most popular, the "Wilhelmus," is today the country's national anthem. Whenever a Dutch athlete wins at the Olympics, the lyrics accompanying the dirgelike melody harken to Willem's exile in the German castle where he was born and his exhortation to the Dutch to hold fast until he comes to free them.

All of this would not only serve its intended purpose of lighting the fires of patriotism in the Dutch but would later help the Dutch revolt to stand throughout Europe as a model of modern, principled revolt: the beginning of the age of individual liberty. Indeed, John Adams, while he was in the Dutch provinces trying to secure loans to fund the American Revolution, would write (with pushy flattery) that "the Originals of the two Republics are so much alike, that the History of one seems but a Transcript from that of the other; so that every Dutchman instructed in the subject, must pronounce the American revolution just and necessary, or pass a Censure upon the greatest Actions of his immortal Ancestors."

The parallels are indeed striking. In both the Dutch and the American causes, people had to struggle to expand their identities from the local (Virginians and Hollanders to Americans and Netherlanders). Both revolts had economic injustice at their heart. In each there was a foreign monarch whose behavior allowed for him to be easily demonized. And both had a founding father. The reasons for the similarities are fairly clear. Both countries came into being as a result of the unfolding of the concept of individual liberty. The differences between the two situations are partly explained by the two centuries separating them, in which, so to speak, society was able to integrate the longing for liberty.

The war progressed. Willem of Orange orchestrated a complicated rebellion, using religion or political leverage as needed and calling on sympathetic foreign rulers for aid. In particular, he groomed Queen Elizabeth—stoking her fears that Philip and Alba were plotting her assassination—in hopes that she would join in an attack. The fears were well grounded: Alba, at Philip's request, was working with English Catholics to try to dethrone Elizabeth and install Mary Stuart (an attempt that would fail). Elizabeth was harboring the loosely disciplined but growing fleet of piratical ships that had sworn allegiance to the Prince of Orange, which became known as the Sea Beggars. Willem hoped for an invasion of the Dutch provinces from across the Channel.

But events took a different turn when Elizabeth decided against getting involved in a war with Spain and, instead of assisting in a naval invasion, forced the Sea Beggars from English ports. Whereupon they crossed the Channel and, with surprising ease, took the Dutch port city of Den Briel, in the province of Holland.

The effect was electric. Up to this point the war had been fought almost exclusively in the southern Netherlands. The south was the obvious focus of attention: the cities of the south were the economic engines of the provinces, and the Spanish court was located there. The revolutionaries had for the first time struck at Philip and won. And more than that, they had brought the war to the north, just sixty miles from Amsterdam.

Alba had recently announced yet another tax on the Dutch— the so-called Tenth Penny tax—the purpose of which, everyone knew, was to maintain the army that was oppressing them. Coming in a year of harsh weather and poor crops, news of it pushed people to the brink and brought about widespread strikes. As word traveled that the Prince of Orange had captured Den Briel, it was cause for sudden hope, for something to believe in. Cities began to revolt on their own, even without the arrival of Orange's men.

Alba retaliated by sending his army to lay siege to one town after another. When a city capitulated, he let his soldiers pillage in order to punish the townspeople. In Zutphen, he wrote to Philip with satisfaction, his soldiers "cut the throats of everyone they found." The Spanish army rolled across the flat landscape, past windmills and carefully managed polders. They were heading toward the province of Holland, in which, by 1572, nearly every city had switched to the Calvinist party, the side of the Prince of Orange. Only Amsterdam— with its deep ties to institutional Catholicism extending back to the time of its miracle, and with its city council propped up by money and support from Philip—was still under Catholic control.

Before they reached Amsterdam, Alba's troops, under the command of his son Don Fadrique, came upon the small town of Naarden, fourteen miles to the southeast. It too had gone to the revolutionaries, and its gates were shut: the inhabitants refused to surrender. As the king's soldiers arrayed before the walls and began to unfurl their siege engines, the town's regents, shivering in a December snowfall, thought again and offered surrender if lives were spared. Don Fadrique's men entered the town and murdered the entire population: men, women, children. Alba informed Philip that his son's men "slit the throats of burghers and soldiers without a single man escaping, then they set fire to the town."

And so the Iron Duke himself processed in state into the city of Amsterdam. He set up a home there, on the Warmoesstraat, the busy center of merchant activity, and he rested. History books have portrayed Alba as evil personified, but he was apparently a human being, which some of his letters from this period seem to confirm.

He was in his early sixties and his health had been declining for
several years. Attacks of gout would get so bad that a whole army
would have to hold up until he could move again. As time went on
a blackness overtook him. "I do not know how it is possible that I
am alive, and so I believe that I am not," he wrote at one point to
his brother-in-law. The waves of killings, compounded by his being
forced to stay and administer martial law, were wearing him down,
and he wrote to a Spanish cardinal complaining about all that he
had to perform for Philip: "Making me come here to cut off heads,
as I have done, and then having the same punisher remain as judge
for so long, is something no one has had to do."

Yet he continued, and he used Amsterdam as his base as he
orchestrated an assault on the cities of Holland. The town of Haarlem was the next battleground. Alba committed thirty thousand
soldiers to taking it, and Willem sent everything he could to resist.
The siege went on through a savage winter. The inhabitants inside
the walls were hungry, but the Spanish soldiers were dying of cold.
When Don Fadrique wrote to his father telling him it might be best
for him to back down, Alba responded with what might be the ultimate father-from-hell letter: "If you strike camp without the town
surrendering, I shall disown you as a son. If you die in the siege
I shall go personally to take your place, though I am ill and bed-
ridden. And if both of us fail then your mother will come from Spain
to achieve in the war what her son has not the valor or patience to
achieve." When the town finally surrendered, the Spanish troops
systematically murdered every one of the two thousand Dutch soldiers who remained alive.

Alba was not the only terrorizer. The Sea Beggars had invaded
Holland under Willem's banner, but controlling them was another
matter. With Willem locked in fighting of his own to the south,
they made their way from one town to another, igniting Calvinist
passions, which combined with fury at Alba's depredations set off
a new wave of iconoclasm and anti-Catholic violence. Every kind
of official Catholic structure was attacked. Nuns and priests were

stripped and murdered. The pirates dressed themselves in the holy robes and marched drunken through the streets.

For ordinary citizens of Holland, these were months of double-sided terror, as both Catholic soldiers and Protestant patriots bullied and bludgeoned them into allying with their side. People didn't know if their neighbors were informing on them. Many fled their homes, only to discover the roads were crowded with armies, thieves, and ordinary townsfolk who were wandering aimlessly, looking for a way out.

Shortly after the Sea Beggars took Den Briel, the anti-Catholic violence they had touched off reached the town of Gouda. The prior of the Emmaus monastery there summarized the behavior of otherwise ordinary and decent Dutch men and women who "care not whether God's temples are despoiled, the holy statues broken, whether God's servants, the priests, religious and upright Catholics, are mocked, driven forth, plundered and miserably murdered." As such violence reached the doors of his monastery, he ran for his life.

Catholic professionals like him were heading for Amsterdam, the only refuge in what was otherwise hostile territory. Once there, he found that while the city council was still controlled by the Catholics in the king's service, outside City Hall a virtual civil war was raging. Streets were alive with chaos, fear, flash mobs of the worst sort. He found refuge in the Sint-Agnieten Convent, one of the walled orders that had dominant positions along the city's canals.

And so, panting and sick with fear, Brother Wouter Jacobszoon huddled at the window of his convent cell and observed the horrific transformation of his society—as medievalism convulsively gave way to modernity—from the same physical vantage point that, precisely four hundred and one years later, Kiki Amsberg would witness the flowering of hippie Amsterdam and from which I would look out on the city of the twenty-first century.

One night he saw fires in the distance, in the direction of Naarden, as the town that Alba had rendered extinct burned to the ground. Another day he reported that ten Beggars who had been convicted of setting fires in Amsterdam had been hanged. "They died," he reported, after they had confessed the error of their ways, "as Christians."

In early December of 1572, Alba's son Don Fadrique arrived in Amsterdam with his army. Brother Jacobszoon found it comforting to have the official Catholic protectors on hand but also unsettling, for his own space was invaded: "The whole of Amsterdam has been brought to indescribable difficulty now by the Spanish army, because the monasteries and monastic buildings are serving as shelter not only for soldiers but also for horses. No one can even turn around, and food has gotten expensive and scarce."

One day, the monk made the short walk to the Holy Place, the chapel built around the unburned host that launched the miracle of Amsterdam, to witness something that pleased him. "On December 4, with my own eyes, I saw Don Frederik and his entourage attend Mass at the Holy Place," he wrote of the Spanish soldier who was fresh from slaughtering untold numbers of Dutchmen. "He knelt there, very devout, during the entire Mass, on both knees on the stone steps of the sanctuary, and he had only one pillow under his knees."

"Don Frederik" may have had a starry-eyed fan in Wouter Jacobszoon, but his father had lost support. As Willem of Orange pressed his advantage in the north—scoring a naval victory in the Zuiderzee, forcing the Spanish to abandon their siege of the town of Alkmaar—advisers at Philip's court turned against Alba. They saw that his scorched-earth approach had had the opposite of the intended effect. Alba's own soldiers were close to mutiny. And the man was nearly out of his mind with pain and illness. Philip relieved him of his command; he died in Lisbon in 1582.

The Catholics still clung to power in Amsterdam, but Wouter Jacobszoon was increasingly miserable. At the mundane level, he had lived all his life in a monastery, among men, and found the nuns in the convent disagreeable. After a year, in order to tend to a sick prior, he moved to a convent across the canal but found the situation no better. He couldn't make the nuns listen to him. And their singing annoyed him to distraction.

But there were larger worries. His world was in the final stages of collapse. "Everywhere they go, the Beggars are setting everything on fire," he wrote. Things had turned topsy-turvy: "The most incompetent, the frauders, the exiles, the robbers, the murderers and heretics—these are the government of cities and countries." He didn't understand why God was letting this happen. At one point he decided the reason must be that Amsterdam had taken to the ways of sin, both to the Calvinists and to commerce. Another time, cowering in mortal panic, he blamed himself for the shrieks he heard outside: "O Lord, I have sinned against Thy Divine Majesty and therefore, I fear, brought all of these torments."

On May 26, 1578, Amsterdam's Catholic leadership finally caved in. The Beggars took control of the city government. Technically, it was the day that the city became Calvinist, but it might be more pertinent to say it was the day it became liberal. Ahead was staggering growth, a stock market, a harbor bristling with masts, streets filling with immigrants from all points of the compass. As the Dutch writer Geert Mak has it, "the 26th of May in the year 1578 is the exact moment when the real Amsterdam was born." It is with striking but perhaps typical Dutch understatement that Amsterdammers to this day refer to the event, into which so much calamitous history had gone, as the Alteration.

Calvinist worship was permitted. The annual procession associated with the holy host and the miracle of Amsterdam, which had launched the city on its rise, was banned. The dismantling of the Catholic orders began. The Sint-Agnieten Convent closed its doors. (A couple of decades later, its timbers would be used to build the frame of Kiki Amsberg's house.) As Catholic priests, monks, and nuns were being brutalized, Brother Jacobszoon, after some initial worries about where to locate street clothes, managed to escape from the city. He made his way south and eventually returned to his hometown of Gouda.

Before he left, he recorded a couple of parting images of the new city that Amsterdam was becoming. One was of the Damrak, the body of water that extended from the harbor into the city center, lined with ships: commerce was returning. Another was of drunken, delirious Calvinists, the city's incoming elite, behaving with inexplicable strangeness: a group of them had come upon a maypole, left over from May Day celebrations, and were pouring beer onto it—"as if the beer were water and the maypole needed watering," the monk wrote, in one of those odd and excellent little observations that ground the larger episodes of history.

If Amsterdam crossed the threshold into modernity on that day in May 1578, it celebrated the rite of passage, two years later, with a thoroughly medieval ceremony. The "princely entry" had of old been a staple by which monarchs knitted control and loyalty via pageantry. The last ruler to enter Amsterdam in state had been Charles V. In March of 1580, Willem of Orange resuscitated the tradition, standing on the foredeck of a galley draped with his noble colors (orange has been the Dutch national color, used for everything from the annual Queen's Day and King's Day celebration to the national soccer team's jerseys, ever since), at the head of a flotilla that entered the harbor and sailed majestically into the city center.

The entire population lined the streets and cheered. True, people had been warned by the Calvinist authorities that they would be fined if they did not, but no doubt there was a strong layer of enthusiasm. At strategic points the heroic prince could see tableaux vivants staged in his honor—live sculptural happenings in which costumed actors portrayed great events. The city's civic guard, its mayors, and its real nobility—the merchants and shipping magnates—greeted Willem in front of City Hall, on Dam Square, the spot where the dam had been built that gave Amsterdam its name. In the evening there was a performance of flaming arrows and, as a climax, a mock battle between two wooden citadels representing the fortresses of the Prince of Orange and the Duke of Alba, which culminated with Alba's burning to the ground.

It may have felt like an armistice celebration, but the fighting was far from over. Eventually history would come to know it as the Eighty Years' War. The Netherlands' struggle for independence would carry on through much of its golden age. Willem himself would die four years hence, at his headquarters in Delft, from an assassin's bullet (the supposed bullet holes are still lodged in the wall: a muted tourist attraction), after King Philip, with whom he had once cavorted as a boy, offered a financial reward for any good Catholic who could eliminate the man he called the "sole head, author, and abettor of the Revolt."

But if the period of the Alteration, culminating with the entry of Willem of Orange into Amsterdam, did not translate into victory for a new nation, it was a time of transformation. In this period, the northern Dutch provinces would sign the Union of Utrecht, a de facto constitution that, following on the decades of slaughter in the name of religion, would guarantee freedom of conscience. It would be a first draft of the concept of religious freedom and, beyond that, of the legal notion of equality. There is a connecting thread that runs from Willem of Orange's first articulation of "religious peace" (tolerance of religious differences) in the 1560s to the language of the Union of Utrecht ("each person shall remain free, especially in his religion") to the religious freedom clause in the First Amendment of the U.S. Constitution.

Of course, the horror that Brother Jacobszoon experienced shows the limitations of tolerance in its sixteenth-century form. Liberalism would become Amsterdam's new banner, but maintaining tolerance in practice would forever be a challenge.

Nonetheless, the policy was put in force almost at once as newcomers started to flood in. The great cities of the southern Netherlands—Ghent, Bruges, Brussels, and especially Antwerp—lost money and influence during the war. The Spanish sacked Antwerp in 1576 and laid siege to it in 1580. By the time the siege was over, the city that had once been the center of European finance was a shell. Its wealth, and more importantly its professions—the bankers and merchants and artisans—left by the tens of thousands, in one of history's great brain drains, and headed to the new power center in the north.

The results of this shift are visible, for the very way of seeing was in the process of changing. The art of the Flemish masters of the southern Netherlands, with its stiff human figures locked into metaphorical landscapes in which man submits to a greater will, would give way to the northern Dutch work of artists like Rembrandt and Vermeer. This new breed would be storytellers in the modern sense, alive to character, to the glories and writhings of the individual.

Part Two

(LEFT) An artist's rendering of Amsterdam circa 1300. The dam on the Amstel River, at bottom, gave the city its name.
Illustration: Paul Maas

(BELOW) A view of Dam Square today, looking in the same direction as the rendering: down the street that was built over the river, toward the harbor.
Photo: Gabriel Draghicescu

(LEFT) A depiction from 1560 of the procession celebrating the Miracle of Amsterdam that occurred in 1345.
Begijnhof Chapel, Amsterdam/Photo:Roeland Koning

(BELOW) A more recent procession.
Photo: Bart van Dijk

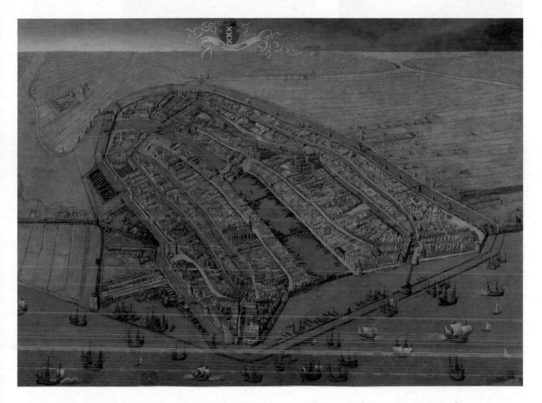

Cornelis Anthoniszoon's bird's-eye view of Amsterdam was presented to Emperor Charles V in 1538. It shows the medieval city set in the flat countryside, fronted by the IJ. The river Amstel cuts through the middle of the city. The dam that gives Amsterdam its name is directly in the center. Note also the intricate channels throughout the countryside by which water was managed. *Amsterdam Museum*

(ABOVE LEFT) Willem, Prince of Orange, aka William the Silent, the father of the Dutch Republic. *Rijksmuseum*

(ABOVE RIGHT) Dirck van Os opened his house to everyone wishing to sign on as a shareholder in the Dutch East India Company, making his Amsterdam home, in a sense, the birthplace of capitalism.
Courtesy Collectie Hoogheemraadschap Hollands Noorderkwartier, Heerhugowaard

(LEFT) The Duke of Alba, who brought the terror of the Inquisition to the Netherlands. Shown below are Alba's troops sacking of the city of Naarden, en route to Amsterdam. Alba informed King Philip that his men "slit the throats of burghers and soldiers without a single man escaping, then they set fire to the town."
Left: Liria Palace: The Alba Collection; below: Museum Boijmans Van Beuningen

The return of the second East Indies fleet, the event that ignited
Amsterdam's golden age. *Amsterdam Museum*

The world's first stock exchange, which, typically enough,
Amsterdammers built over water. *Stadsarchief Amsterdam*

Dam Square, with the new City Hall being built at left, in 1656, the height of the city's golden age. The painting shows a booming, mixed society—with people in European and Asian dress—and ships in the background. *Amsterdam Museum*

The VOC headquarters in Bengal, circa 1665. Amsterdam's golden age was built on wealth from outposts all over Asia. *Rijksmuseum*

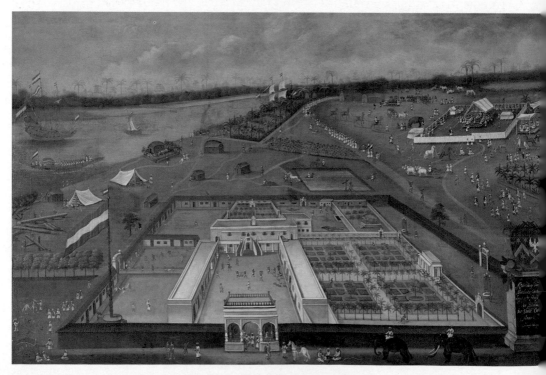

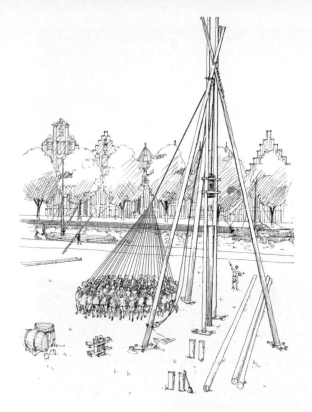

A modern illustration of a team of pile drivers at work in seventeenth-century Amsterdam. Each of the roughly 3,000 houses built on the city's insubstantial ground during the golden age required about forty piles driven in this backbreaking manner. *Illustration: Tim Killiam*

Jan van der Heyden's modernization of firefighting techniques in Amsterdam was copied around Europe. He showed off his wares in his art. In this cross section of a burning house, the man at lower left is using the old method; the team at right uses van der Heyden's engine and new long hoses. *Technische Universiteit, Delft*

Van der Heyden's painting of the new City Hall was intended as an advertisement for Amsterdam as the city of the future. *Louvre*

The interior of a seventeenth-century water coach, which traveled between Dutch towns on a regularly posted schedule. The convenience, comfort, and egalitarianism amazed foreigners. *Photo: Tim Killiam*

THE COMPANY

H e was thirty years old, at the peak of life and health, feet planted on the sound wooden deck of his flagship, the *Mauritius*, in command of 249 men spread over three ships and a pinnace. It was the twelfth of May 1595. They were nearly two months out of Amsterdam, had passed south of the Canary Islands, and were riding in fair weather off the coast of West Africa. Just today they had encountered five ships from the Caribbean bound for Europe, had a friendly exchange, and given over a sack of letters to be delivered to loved ones. Cornelis de Houtman, the young commander, a brewer's son from Gouda, was sailing purposefully, muscles braced against the pull and heave of the South Atlantic, on a mission that, for all its staggering scope, he had every reason to hope would bring not only riches to the city of Amsterdam but a historic transformation. Ship's logs don't record such things, but this was perhaps the last moment of happiness that he would ever know.

Shortly after, they crossed the equator, and it was like crossing from normal waking life into a nightmare. De Houtman and his crew seemed not to have prepared themselves for the tropical nature of the tropics. Men began to swoon from the heat. Prying open their casks of food, they were horrified at what they found. "Our flesh and fishe stunke, our Bisket molded, our Beere sowred, our water

stunke, and our Butter became as thinne as Oyle," wrote one of the
crewmen, according to an English account of the voyage that was
published three years later. "Whereby divers of our men fell sicke,
and many of them dyed."

Then things got bad. They swung far westward toward Brazil
before mounting a long, punishing eastward journey toward the
Cape of Good Hope. Scurvy swept through the decks. By August,
eleven men aboard the *Hollandia* had died and only three of the
ship's remaining fifty crewmen were not suffering from the agonies
of aching limbs and loosening teeth; the other ships fared only mar-
ginally better. They made their way round the Cape of Good Hope,
sailing through ravaging storms, and anchored at the tiny island of
Nosy Manitse, off the coast of Madagascar, to bury seventy men: in
six months at sea, more than a quarter of the expedition's crew had
died.

Resting on this primordial scallop of land, they searched in vain
for the fresh fruit or vegetables that they knew they needed to dis-
sipate the effects of the disease (though, in the absence of an understanding of the need for vitamin C, they attributed scurvy to "too
much salty food," which they thought fruit and vegetables would
counterbalance). During this landfall, organization collapsed. One
of those who had died had been the captain of the *Hollandia*. Cornelis de Houtman's second in command was a man named Gerrit van
Beuningen. From the beginning, the two had despised each other.
Now, Van Beuningen went over De Houtman's head and appointed,
as replacement for the dead captain, a man that De Houtman did
not want in that position. They weighed anchor to continue their
voyage, but the power struggle devolved into dissension among the
crew; the chaos, plus the need for fresh fruit, forced them to put in at
St. Augustine's Bay on the west coast of Madagascar. They brought
their dozens of sick men ashore and made an encampment, and continued the dispute. The council of top officers backed De Houtman,
while the midshipmen signed a petition supporting Van Beuningen.
At some point, those who were not too ill went off to look for water

and food; they hadn't been gone long when they heard shots. Hurrying back, they discovered that, according to the journal, "the beach was full of black men, who had broken down the encampment" and were ransacking it, while the desperately ill sailors tried to fend them off. As the sailors came rushing back, guns blazing, the natives fled, but they had stolen nearly everything that had been brought ashore. Shortly after, De Houtman got wind of what was apparently an attempted mutiny and clapped Van Beuningen in irons.

Two months later the expedition had proceeded only to the southern tip of Madagascar. The ships lost their anchors in a storm and put in to port for repairs. Some of the men rowed ashore and went inland to scavenge. Returning to the beach, the English publication of the journal ran, "We went to seeke for our boats, but the wild men had smitten them in peeces, and taken out the nailes [and] stood upon the shore with their weapons in hand and threw stones at us."

Despite the exhaustion, death, loss of small boats, and tremendous division among the remaining crew, many of whom were demanding that they abandon the mission and return home, De Houtman managed to push his pathetic little fleet on what would now be the most difficult stretch of the voyage: across the Indian Ocean, toward the East Indies and the fabled Spice Islands. And somehow, after another four months of hell, without having so much as sighted land, they reached their destination, a pretty and vigorous little settlement of straw buildings on stilts surrounded by coconut palms: the town of Bantam, on the western end of the island of Java.

———

A year before, a man named Dirck van Os left his home in Amsterdam, walked a short distance northward, with the towering transepts of the Old Church rising behind the housefronts on his right, and entered a building on the other side of Dam Square. Here, in a ground floor "tasting room" in the home of a wine merchant with the rather fitting name of Marten Spil, he encountered eight men whom he knew well.

Van Os was thirty-eight years old, arrestingly handsome, clean-shaven save for a gingery, thinly curled moustache. If traditional history books used the deeds of businessmen as lynchpins rather than those of kings and generals, his name would probably resound still, for the activities he initiated or took part in would span the globe and encompass an enormous amount of history. He had come from Antwerp in the south, part of the mass exodus from Spanish troops, settling in Amsterdam only six years earlier. His intellect was voracious, and focused on business: he had expanded Dutch trade with Russia and was a shipper of grain, salt, leather, and whale oil. The others he met included Reynier Pauw, an Amsterdam-born dealer in wood and salt, Pieter Hasselaar, a brewer, and Jan Poppen, a German immigrant who owned a great deal of land in and around the city. They were big men, substantial in their physical presence (layers of doublets, cassocks, and thick robes; heavy lace collars and high hats) and in their work. The wine merchant's establishment sat on the Warmoesstraat, so close to the cacophonously busy harbor the men might have been distracted by the cries of gulls and calls of sailors readying vessels. But then, it was no distraction: via those ships they brought their heavy goods—copper, iron, tar, timber, hemp—into the city and sent them back out, from Russia to Italy, from the Baltic to the Mediterranean.

It was highly profitable business, but recently they had begun to ponder, and to plot for, something far grander. This generation had been weaned on a story of how global trade worked. The so-called rich trade—the highly prized luxury products of India, Ethiopia, the Spice Islands, and elsewhere—was controlled by the military-navigational complex of the mighty Portuguese empire. Portuguese ships, Portuguese navigators, Portuguese maps and mapmakers, Portuguese cannon, Portuguese factors (aka agents) who maintained, with the backing of papal bulls, a near monopoly over half the world's commerce: dating from Vasco da Gama's trip around the Cape of

Good Hope and into the Indian Ocean nearly a century before, this network had been a feature of European life. Everyone accepted it and believed in the indomitability of the Portuguese system.

But this view had begun to change. Partly as a result of the war with Spain (and thus with Portugal), a few Dutch travelers had insinuated themselves behind enemy lines, as it were, becoming firsthand observers of the Portuguese system. These travelers discovered signs that the great empire was tottering and was not nearly so indomitable as its propaganda machine had portrayed. Still, any city that dared to challenge Lisbon for control of the Indies trade would need to have a great deal in the way of infrastructure. It would need ships, a shipbuilding industry, sophisticated navigational know-how, and money. Rather suddenly, Amsterdam possessed all of these.

What's more, it had a great influx of new blood. After Antwerp fell to Spanish soldiers in 1585, that city's non-Catholic inhabitants left forever, and a large percentage of them settled in Amsterdam. These newcomers were mostly not poor, bedraggled refugees but successful merchants, artists, and bankers: people who had helped to make Antwerp the business and cultural capital of northern Europe. They brought with them money, contacts in other cities, knowledge . . . and one other thing.

Just as important for the economic revolution that was stewing in the city of Amsterdam was the very newness of the newcomers. In the early twentieth century, an Austrian economist named Joseph Schumpeter espoused a theory about economic innovation that has received a good deal of attention in recent years. Schumpeter said that the mechanism of capitalism was "creative destruction": that is, a capitalist economy functions provided it keeps innovating, with the new creatively destroying the old. And while innovation is a highly complex thing—involving social groups, fashions and tastes, wars and politics—there is a spark or kernel to it without which it would not come about. The spark of any kind of economic innovation, Schumpeter said, is always the same: a tiny group of people. What's more, this small group of innovators is almost never part of the current establishment, since the establishment has no need to change things. It is the small, daring group of newcomers who see an opportunity and push ahead. They confront risks and obstacles, including those put in their path by the establishment, and if they have luck and skill, they succeed. Then another group emulates what the first did; then others, until what was once risky and radical has become part of a new established order.

Schumpeter's theory fits all sorts of cases. It can be applied, for example, to the digital revolution. Companies like Apple and Microsoft were started by outsiders who had a vision and exploited an opening. But when the Dutch economic historian Clé Lesger applied Schumpeter's theory of innovation to the men who met in Marten Spil's Amsterdam wineshop in March of 1594, who were instrumental to one of history's great economic transformations— no less a thing than the first draft of capitalism itself—he found that the theory fit, but only partly. It turns out that while newcomers like Dirck van Os, who had fled war and persecution to root them- selves in Amsterdam, spearheaded this innovation, men of the city's old establishment also took part. Part of the explanation might be that the whole city was in such a state of bustle and transforma- tion that even its establishment was open to innovation and the risks that came with it. Then, too, another thing that helped drive innovation in Amsterdam—something that would work to the city's advantage time and again in the coming decades—was that Amster- dam was unusual in Europe in imposing virtually no restrictions on newcomers who would do business there. An immigrant didn't have to join a chartered company—in fact, he didn't even need to be a citizen. So the established businessmen were open to new ventures, and the immigrants faced no extra bureaucratic hurdles.

The nine men were joined by another, whom all were especially eager to see, for he, unlikely as he must have seemed with his dour demeanor, was in possession of the key to the success of their radical scheme. His accented Dutch gave him away as being another of the émigrés from the south. He had his own kind of heaviness, but his was the weight of gravitas: he was one of the most respected, and most rabidly conservative, Calvinist theologians of the Dutch provinces. The businessmen were not interested in receiving his spiritual blessing for their venture so much as his worldly knowledge, for Petrus Plancius happened also to be one of the great cartographers of the age. (His map of the world, published two years earlier, can still take your breath away with its vivid colors and lovely intricacy of detail.) He was also a savvy dealer in cartographic knowledge who made it his business to become friends with many of the greatest sailors of the age. A few years later, Henry Hudson would consult with him before venturing across the Atlantic in search of a northwest passage to Asia—a trip that would result in his accidentally encountering what would become New York and the Hudson River.

The nine businessmen and the theologian/cartographer had been working for some time on their secret venture. Two years earlier, Plancius had purchased maps from a Portuguese cartographer named Bartolomeo de Lasso that showed the route to the East Indies in thrilling detail. At that same time, the merchants sent a spy to Lisbon to get more information. Cornelis de Houtman was not, in fact, a professional spy, but he was apparently very keen for adventure. The merchants gave him a plausible cover: they loaded him down with merchandise samples and gave him credentials as a representative for Amsterdam businesses. He spent two years in Lisbon, gathering details, at regular intervals receiving more merchandise to keep his cover alive, and then came back to Amsterdam flush with the latest information on Portuguese trade agreements and activities in Asia.

It was presumably De Houtman's return from Lisbon that prompted the meeting at the wine seller's shop. He must have been impressive in the presentation he made to them, because in addition to formalizing their venture, committing 290,000 guilders to it and giving it a storybook-sounding name—the Compagnie van Verre, which might best translate as the Company for Faraway Lands—they chose De Houtman to lead the first Dutch expedition to the

East Indies. This despite the fact that he was no more a professional sailor than he had been a professional spy.

The four ships set sail with horns blowing and flags waving. It was a moment of patriotic awareness for the citizens of Amsterdam, awareness that their city was pushing itself into a new future, willing itself toward something grander than previous generations could have imagined.

The lack of experience behind it all—De Houtman's as a sailor and leader of men and the merchants' as managers of global convoys—showed in every facet of the sloppy tragicomic meander that ensued, from the moment the ships lost sight of Texel Island, and Dutch territory, to their finally, improbably, reaching their palm-fringed destination.

De Houtman's sources in Lisbon had told him that the town of Bantam, on Java Island, was both a center of pepper production and a spot that the Portuguese had not infiltrated. On arrival, he did his best to cast off the stench of failure and death with which the expedition had become clotted on its long, harrowing journey and introduced himself to the local officials as a would-be trader from a faraway land called Holland, fearsome in its power yet sublime in its fairness toward friends. He was welcomed by the governor and invited to meet with the sultan. Never mind the months of unspeakable hardship he had endured in the voyage to this point; never mind the purply skin and toothlessness left by the scurvy in its retreat or the miasmal rankness of having lived week upon endless week with cadavers and disease and rats and lice and human waste (it was common at the time for sailors to forgo the head and instead crouch in any out-of-the-way spot to relieve themselves): De Houtman dressed for the occasion in velvet, satin, and silk vestments that he had stored for the purpose, strapped on a rapier, and processed, together with as many men as could make themselves into an imitation of Western grandeur, through the tropical town. He had someone hold a sun shade over him as he walked, and a trumpeter went before, sounding blasts on De Houtman's orders. Europe had arrived.

At least, that was what he had hoped, to be the first Europeans, but the hope was soon quashed. The men took in everything they could as they walked the sultry streets of Bantam. They noted the dreamy array of foods on display in the thronged markets ("hennes, hartes, fish and Ryce . . . Oranges, Lemons, Pomegarnets, Cocombers, Melons, Onions, Garlicke"). They made wide-eyed observations of cultural differences ("the men sit all day upon a mat, and chaw Betele, having ten or twentie women about them, and when they make water, presently one of the women washeth their member, and so they sit playing all the day with their women"). And it wasn't long before they saw, interspersed between the faces of indigenous islanders and traders from Malacca, Bengal, Malabar, and China, the nervous, untrusting looks of Portuguese merchants, who saw the Dutch mission for what it was intended to be: an outright takeover of the monopoly that Portugal had enjoyed in the East Indies spice trade for more than eight decades.

But De Houtman's sources were largely correct: the Portuguese presence here was slight. De Houtman managed to hammer out a trade agreement with the sultan that gave the Dutch favored-nation status. But when it came time to begin bargaining for the prized product—pepper—De Houtman fumbled. The few Portuguese traders on the island didn't have much real power, but they knew how to make trouble. They began a whispering campaign, telling the sultan that the Dutch planned an attack. De Houtman erupted during the negotiations, fulminating about the presence of the Portuguese. The sultan took his behavior as proof of the warlike intentions of the Dutch and had De Houtman and the men he had brought with him imprisoned.

The Dutchmen on the ships reacted by blasting their guns at the town and at the Portuguese ships at anchor, "slaying divers of the people." De Houtman managed to win his release in exchange for a ransom payment. His small fleet sailed away from the port they had come to bargain with, having only caused trouble. For the next month they hugged the Javanese coast, picking up a few sacks of cloves and pepper but mostly bringing on more disaster. At a town on the northwest coast the locals offered them a feast and promised to sell them as much clove and nutmeg as they could carry; in the middle of the party they pulled out swords and killed twelve Dutchmen.

More dissension ensued. De Houtman was for pushing onward; others wanted to bring their nightmare to an end. Then suddenly one of the ship's captains died and it was widely believed that De Houtman had poisoned him. De Houtman was imprisoned. With both the commander and vice commander of the expedition under arrest, the expedition at last headed back toward home, stopping for four weeks of R & R on Bali, which one might be tempted to see as the only sensible decision of the entire journey. On August 14, 1597, three ships sailed back into a Dutch port, the fourth having been abandoned because there were too few sailors left to man it.

The hopeful leaders of the Company for Faraway Lands had had word of the imminent arrival of the ships and sent vessels out to greet their returning heroes. What they found was appalling. Of the 249 men who had left Amsterdam two years and four months earlier, only 89 skeletally emaciated sailors had returned. Both De Houtman and his second in command were under guard and charged with serious crimes. The decks were riddled with disease and tales of horror and mutiny. The word *disaster* seems eminently applicable to the voyage. It's not surprising, in that sense, that Dutch history gives it scant attention.

Yet when I scoured Amsterdam for remnants of De Houtman's voyage I did find a couple. High up among the rafters in the grand formal entry of the Royal Tropical Institute, seventy-four images sculpted into the tops of columns give an elaborate, though nearly impossible to see, visual depiction of the whole voyage. Near the city's waterfront sits a squat round tower called the Schreierstoren, which used to look out over the famous "forest of masts" that filled the harbor. Above its doorway is a memorial stone to the "first voyage to the East Indies 1595." It depicts four little ships teetering darkly on swirling waves and features the Latin epigram *navigare necesse est*, "to sail is necessary." The stone was placed on March 10, 1945, 350 years after De Houtman and his crew left that spot and while the city was still under Nazi occupation.

For excellent reasons, Cornelis de Houtman has not gone down in the ranks of history's legendary sailors. Nor was he destined to have a long career. The following year he found another backer and headed off once more to the East Indies, where, having once again raised the ire of the locals, he was killed in his cabin off Sumatra. But despite the black comedy and epic ineptitude of his first voyage, it was historic, because of two utterly unrelated outcomes. The lesser involved De Houtman's brother, Frederick, who had been aboard. While in the Indies, he and the expedition's navigator, Pieter Keyser, acting at the urging of Petrus Plancius, charted the stars visible from the Southern Hemisphere, becoming the first people to do so, and in the process identified the twelve southern constellations and gave them the names that apply to this day. (Frederick de Houtman would also take part in a later Dutch expedition, to Australia, where he would discover an island group that is still called the Houtman Abrolhos.)

The other historic result of the first Dutch voyage to the East Indies had to do with the reaction of the nine merchants who funded it—and, for that matter, of all Amsterdammers, who, as appalled as they may have been by the loss of life, were instantly aroused by the enchantment and allure and sheer possibility that the trip suggested. For although the ships returned with their hulls mostly empty, the modest quantity of pepper they contained was enough for the merchants to recoup their investment. Beyond that, the thing had been done: De Houtman had sailed halfway around the world, defied the Portuguese, and established business relations—albeit marred by the odd spear through the neck and cannonade reprisal—with the exotic and economically intriguing kingdoms of Java and the Spice Islands. Anything, it seemed, was now possible.

The inhabitants of Amsterdam—old guard and new arrivals, wealthy merchants and ready workers—reacted as one. Shipyards sang; the dark, twisting stench of pitch filled the air. Dirck van Os and his fellow backers doubled down their investments, dissolving their company, as was the practice on completion of a voyage, and launching a new one: outfitting new ships, raising new crews, this time with better leadership. As a Dutch historian of the nineteenth century put it in reference to this precise moment in the city's life, "Getting rich became the ambition of the day."

The nine merchants were not alone in reacting feverishly to the return of De Houtman's fleet—nor was Amsterdam. Businessmen in other seaport cities in Holland and Zeeland—Hoorn, Enkhuizen, Rotterdam, Middelburg, and Delft—cobbled together fleets of their own and flung them off southward, in the general direction of Asia. Seemingly no sooner had De Houtman's ships sailed away from the East Indies than the people of the coastal kingdoms of Java, Sumatra, the Bandas, and other of the lush islands in the present-day Indonesian archipelago saw more Dutch ships arrive. The mayhem quotient lessened; deals were struck: for nutmeg, clove, mace, and pepper. Two years after De Houtman's return, a second fleet sailed back into the IJ, Amsterdam's waterfront, after a relatively brisk and trouble-free fifteen-month jaunt to the East Indies. Its backers stepped aboard and were led belowdecks by their exultant skippers. We can only imagine the stunned, reverential silence as they took in the sight of more than one million pounds of pepper, cloves, and nutmeg, packed with exquisite care into the hulls. The silence was broken by bells pealing from church steeples. As someone on the scene intoned, "So long as Holland has been Holland, such richly laden ships have never been seen." Even after the staggering costs involved, the merchants turned a 400 percent profit.

More sails bent toward the East Indies—within four years of De Houtman's return, sixty-five Dutch ships had made the trek, essentially smothering the Portuguese presence—and more deals were struck, only the prices that Javanese merchants charged were now getting higher. And the sudden arrival of so much pepper in Europe sent prices on that end plummeting. It wasn't long before the merchants from the various Dutch ports realized they were competing against one another. When the price of pepper at Javanese ports had doubled, the merchants, who until that point had viewed one another with distrust, decided that they would have to work together.

They put the issue before the States General, the Dutch governing body in The Hague. It was an inevitable move, for this was now truly a political matter. The war against Spain and Portugal was ongoing, and the young Dutch government, based in The Hague, saw not only financial but military prospects in having the various merchant consortiums band together. In fact, as Johan van Oldenbarnevelt, the greatest Dutch statesman of the day, saw things, it was a matter less of prospects than of necessity. There was no certainty that the infant republic would survive; for it to do so, great, bold steps would have to be taken. What had begun with De Houtman's voyage was now impelled by the Dutch shipping network in Europe. The very fact that men like Dirck van Os had taken over a large amount of European shipping traffic meant that that network had to be used in the service of the country. "Expand or die" might well have been the motto. And expansion of trade into Asia would further impel an expansion of the war. Which was to say, the new venture would need guns.

As he tried to put together a consortium of companies that would trade in the East Indies, Oldenbarnevelt found resistance among the non-Amsterdam merchants, who feared that the city would dominate any joint venture. They had cause for concern. Copies of a new engraved plan of Amsterdam, commissioned by the city as a form of promotional literature, hit the streets in 1599 with the modest title "Amstelodamum, Urbs Hollandiae Primaria, Emporium Totius Europae Celeberrimum": Amsterdam, First City of Holland, Cele-

brated Emporium to All Europe. Only two years after De Houtman's
return, the city was marketing itself with very un-Dutch braggado-
cio. Nearly half of the plan was taken up by the harbor, with hundreds of two- and three-masted ships at anchor or under sail, being
serviced by fleets of lighters while others were being assembled in
the vast shipyards. One area was helpfully labeled "ships to the West
Indies" and another "ships from the East Indies or Java," giving clear
indication of the city's global reach.

Oldenbarnevelt employed all his political skills to bring the
competing interests together. He got Amsterdam's merchants to
make a concession: instead of occupying half of the seats on the
new company's board of directors, Amsterdam would get eight out
of seventeen. As a final push to win an agreement, Oldenbarnevelt
brought in Maurice of Nassau, who as son of Willem of Orange, the
assassinated father of the nation, had great prestige throughout the
country, to give the venture his blessing.

The result of months of negotiations was an entity that was
unique in world history in several ways. It would be a private, for-
profit venture, yet with governmental oversight and with not only
the power but an obligation to wage war on behalf of the Dutch
Republic. It would have the authority to build and maintain military
forts and, from these, to impel foreign leaders and populations to
trade with it. It would negotiate treaties with foreign governments.
It would get support from the national government, especially military support, so that the leaders of its expeditions would be not only
sailors and trade representatives but naval officers. It would also
be a complex business operation, divided into six city chambers,
each with its own fleet, largely under control of its city's wealthy
merchant investors. As historian Jonathan Israel observes, it was
"a unique politico-commercial institution, and one that could be
imitated nowhere else in the world, because the United Provinces
were the world's only federal republic in which a collectivity of town
governments, committed to the advancement of trade, industry, and
navigation, also wielded great military naval power." In other words,

the unique features that had developed in the Low Countries in the sixteenth century—leading to a society that was based not on the feudal system but on individuals who bought and sold property and banded together to promote their mutual interests—had given rise to the world's first multinational corporation, the Verenigde Oost-Indische Compagnie, the United East India Company, which soon became universally known by the logo of its interlocked initials that would appear on ships in harbors around the world: VOC.

This is a book about Amsterdam, not the Dutch East India Company, but the two are so intensely woven together that it is worth laying out a few broad VOC facts. It's by no means a stretch to say that the VOC remade the world. And to a large extent Amsterdam made the VOC. And in refashioning the world, the VOC in turn completely transformed Amsterdam.

Like the oceans it mastered, the VOC had a scope that is hard to fathom. One could craft a defensible argument that no company in history has had such an impact on the world. Its surviving archives—in Cape Town, Colombo, Chennai, Jakarta, and The Hague—have been measured (by a consortium applying for a UNESCO grant to preserve them) in *kilometers*. In innumerable ways the VOC both expanded the world and brought its far-flung regions together. It introduced Europe to Asia and Africa, and vice versa (while its sister multinational, the West India Company, set New York City in motion and colonized Brazil and the Caribbean islands). It pioneered globalization and invented what might be the first modern bureaucracy. It advanced cartography and shipbuilding. It fostered disease, slavery, and exploitation on a scale never before imagined. It shuffled the global ecosystem—by design and by accident, with consequences we face still—by ferrying plants, animals, and insects across the planet. Over the course of its history the VOC sent more than a million Europeans to Asia, and hauled 2.5 million tons of Asian products back to Europe, four times more than its nearest competitor, the English East India Company. It took over kingdoms that did not bend to its wishes, making its officers island potentates; it slaughtered entire populations. The business of the VOC in Asia is typically described as buying spices for resale in Europe. In fact, it was vastly more complicated—and the company's success came in large part from comprehending and exploiting that complication. For example, De Houtman was probably unaware that much of the pepper he was trying to purchase "from the source" was grown on other islands and that some of the Javanese he was attempting to bargain with were themselves middlemen. In addition to the Indonesians, Chinese and Indian transshippers had been working the tropical waters for centuries, helping to fuel two of the world's great cuisines as well as providing ingredients for local medicine. The genius of the VOC was in threading itself through this highly evolved network. By the end of the golden age a century later, the Dutch were selling spices not only to Europe but to China, India, and even to the Spice Islanders.

Along the way, the company developed many of the modern principles of business administration and management, as it figured out the intricacies of shipping copper and silver from Japan to China, selling those products there in exchange for silk and porcelain, then trading those in the East Indies for the spices that it then shipped to Europe. It made porcelain, coffee, tea, and dozens of other things literally household words in the West. It sold Indonesian sugar in Persia and Indian fabrics in Yemen. For two centuries it was the only outside entity permitted trade (or any other) access to the closed empire of Japan.

By these means, the officers, merchants, and soldiers of the VOC engineered not just their own rise but the advent of modern economies in Europe and beyond. Whole populations of the world became for the first time dependent on the foreign sale of their goods thanks to the VOC's muscular expansion of global trade. The company tutored goat herders in western Anatolia in upgrading their production of mohair yarn; as the yarn was transformed from a local to an export product, the region edged from peasant agriculture to become part of a global economy, and its people became proficient in new management techniques and mathematical concepts. People in India, China, West Africa, present-day Vietnam, Cambodia, Laos, Thailand, and Indonesia likewise shifted from being local cultivators to participants in global trade networks, in pepper, cinnamon, ivory, copper, silk, and many other products. The expansion of Dutch shipping affected Europe as well, as it brought Polish grain growers, Scandinavian processors of iron and tar, French grape producers, and Spanish salt refiners into a global network. All of this involved not just creating a transportation system but augmenting it by refining systems of insurance, storage, and processing. On the heels of the VOC's success, Amsterdammers developed ancillary trades. They cultivated European markets for new products— coffee, tea, tobacco—with great care. All three of these were sold as wondrous medicinal cure-alls and marketed and advertised in often strikingly modern (if sometimes a bit coarse) fashion:

Tea rejuvenates the very old
Tea warms the piss of those who are cold

went one catchy jingle.

The common thread through this activity was that it was all geared to the individual. It was the beginning of consumerism, which, for better or worse, is surely a component of liberalism.

The VOC was successful on a scale that few companies have achieved. It paid its investors healthy annual dividends over a period of nearly two centuries. Indeed, for all its achievements in shipping cargo and negotiating deals, in hauling crates of silks and spices and bending tropical kingdoms to its will, its greatest impact on the world—its most far-reaching impact on the development of liberalism—was in this, the realm of finance.

Say you are a tourist in Amsterdam. You arrive the way most do: by train, at Central Station. Stepping out into the city, worn and dazed from your journey, you confront an unholy mess of trams and buses in the foreground and a smeary polychromatic chaos beyond. Walking forward, you cross a trafficky thoroughfare and come to a stop at one end of a fusty-looking rectangle of water, a canal of sorts, carrying toward the city center. The massive tourist barges that call this spot home sit quietly in their bays; a few are making seemingly impossible maneuvers as they get themselves into or out of their narrow slots. To your left, the gabled back ends of buildings along one side of the Damrak (as the canal is called) come right down to the water. Across the noisy stretch of traffic that runs along the water's other edge is a matching lineup of brick buildings, the graciousness of whose gabled tops clashes forcefully with the kebab stands, marijuana dispensaries, beer palaces, casinos, sex arcades, Automat sausage vendors, and displays of dusty postcards and wooden-shoe key chain fobs that occupy their streetfront space. It is such a wearyingly ugly wreck of neon and litter and urban detritus that you turn away at once, in search of some other, less blasted and violated part of the city: in search of some history.

But wait. What you have before you is a chance to engage in one of the most rewarding aspects of travel, which is also one of the most enjoyable things about reading (and writing) narrative history: the possibility of lifting the veil of the present and systematically willing a particular iteration of the past to reconstitute itself. With a little help, this powerfully unlovely view can be reenvisioned as the urban landscape that spawned one of the basic features of economic liberalism and one of the building blocks of the world we live in: the stock exchange.

This little area was the beating heart of Amsterdam at the start of its golden age. Behind where you stand, in place of the crenellated Victorian-era towers of the train station, was the harbor itself, a thicket of wooden spikes and sailcloth, constantly alive with pumping, hauling, swabbing, jibing, trimming, augering, sawing, climbing, crawling, and cursing. (In the nineteenth century the city fought vigorously against the national government in The Hague, which, in the way of bureaucracies, had decreed that Amsterdam's train station would be built here, cutting the city off from the waterfront to which it had always been wedded; the bureaucrats won, and Amsterdammers still sneer at Central Station as if its construction had personally offended them, never mind that it was built in 1889.) Thus, with the ships of the harbor coming right up to where they would have nudged your backside, the bridge you are standing on—the New Bridge—marked the gateway between the city's two realms: water and land.

One of the buildings along the left side of the canal had served as home to the Duke of Alba while he lorded over Amsterdam. Another, a generation later, was the wineshop of Marten Spil, where the nine Amsterdam merchants gathered to found the Company for Faraway Lands. Then, on April 1, 1602, following the negotiations in The Hague at which those same nine men, plus eleven others, signed on as directors of the Amsterdam chamber of the East India Company, a curious assembly of people from all walks of life began streaming into another private home closer to Dam Square. Whether because he was felt by others to be elementally important to the success of the new venture or because he himself believed it would stand a chance only if he took personal charge of it, Dirck van Os turned his house, in the street called the Nes, into what you might care to think of as the birthplace of capitalism. Here, over the next five months, anyone wishing to purchase shares of stock in a new type of corporation would have to come. His street-level rooms must have been as bustling as a busy shop, for during that period 1,143 individuals signed up to buy shares in the Amsterdam chamber of the VOC, for a total of 3,679,915 guilders, which constituted 57 percent of the company's stock.

What made the Dutch East India Company different from all previous companies was its permanence. Where companies before had always formed around a particular venture and dissolved when the venture was complete, the VOC continued. (Technically, it was granted an initial charter for twenty-one years, but the charter was perennially renewed.) This was more than just a novelty: it meant that investors were buying not into a voyage but into the company itself. And it allowed for a far-reaching innovation, for Amsterdammers who signed the subscription book could read, on the first page, that they were entitled to sell their shares to someone else. They were further assured that if they did so the transfer would be rigorously monitored, and the subscription book stipulated the process for selling shares.

Almost immediately after all shares were bought, so-called aftermarket trading began. The truly revolutionary innovation of Amsterdam's stock market lay in the fact that it became the world's first market in the sale of company shares: a secondary securities market. If a company's shares of stock are frozen, its ownership is frozen and the business is a private affair. But if those shares, or derivatives based on them, can be resold, then you have a financial marketplace, which is a kind of living thing, constantly churning. It can then become a means of individual expression and power, allowing for anyone with a few extra coins to play a part in the great economic drama of society. It becomes a vehicle for economic liberalism. This was the collective insight of the society that launched capitalism in its modern guise.

It was a remarkable feature of Amsterdam's society that all sorts of people—not just professional merchants and traders but coopers, blacksmiths, weavers, glaziers, basketmakers, bronze founders, cutlers, rope makers, and others, including no fewer than seven housekeepers—tramped into Dirck van Os's home to buy the original shares in the VOC. Indeed, one of the oldest and most celebrated shares of stock in the world tells a modest little story of its owner. In August of 1602, an elderly and very wealthy woman named Agneta Cock entered Van Os's home and agreed to pay 4,800 guilders for shares in the VOC. We know she must have done so because two and a half years later her grandson was born, and a year and a half after that, in 1606, Agneta Cock's estate, including the VOC certificate, was registered over to him. (We know she was wealthy because 4,800 guilders was an enormous sum: one could rent a fine house in Amsterdam for 100 guilders a year.) The papers detailing Hendrick Janzsoon Cock's inheritance were eventually housed in the archives of the Amsterdam Orphans' Chamber, and there they remained. The reregistered VOC certificate, bearing the name of Agneta Cock, was until recently considered the oldest existing share of stock (which, for the record, is not technically true since the VOC issued receipts rather than shares). This piece of paper, which gained a flurry of fame when it was used as the plot vehicle in the 2004 movie *Ocean's Twelve*, bears, in accordance with VOC rules, the signatures of two directors of the Amsterdam chamber. One of those—bold slashes of ink that turn the curtness of the last name into a flourish—is Dirck van Os. In 2010, Agneta Cock's certificate lost its claim as the oldest share when a Dutch history student found, in the West Frisian Archive in Hoorn, a VOC receipt that predates hers by a few months. In any case, the point holds that the Amsterdam chamber of the VOC expressed the outward expansive impulse of the entire city, an impulse that ordinary Amsterdammers felt as strongly as did major businessmen.

Now, once again: you are standing on the New Bridge, with Central Station behind and the canal called the Damrak stretched before you. But you are looking not at Amsterdam today but at the city of 1602; in fact, let's be very precise and say it is August 31, 1602, the day that subscriptions for VOC shares ends and thus the date when trading in those shares could legally begin. The harbor bristles behind you, and (as today, minus the tacky neon and the candy wrappers blowing down the sidewalk) the rickety stretches of gabled brick buildings line the canal in front of you.

So the connecting point between the harbor behind you and the city in front of you—that is, the logical nerve center of this city that is with incredible rapidity becoming the entrepôt of the world—is the bridge on which you stand. This very bridge, for all the inconsequential drab humbleness of its twenty-first-century self, became, as of late August 1602, the financial district: the de facto stock exchange. Here investors encountered one another, agreed to buy or sell VOC shares, then, following the rules, marched together along the Warmoesstraat to your left toward the East India Company headquarters (the red-and-white-brick building still stands and today houses part of the University of Amsterdam), where they formalized the stock transfer with the company bookkeeper. Buyer and seller got signatures from two of the VOC directors, paid 2.20 guilders tax plus 0.60 to the bookkeeper, and the transfer was complete.

This secondary trade was vigorous from the start, for the good reason that the fortunes of the VOC fleets were public knowledge. Within days of Dirck van Os's closing his doors to initial subscribers in the company, news arrived of a successful convoy and the price of VOC shares went up 15 percent; at other news shortly thereafter they went up by 40 percent; and not long after that their value doubled. There was money to be made—not only in the backbreaking and seriously hazardous work of sailing around the world and haggling for spices but in the far more gentlemanly pursuit of speculating on that work.

As any casual investor knows, straight transfers—simple buying and selling—account for only a portion of possible financial transactions. Derivatives—financial securities derived from stock—are not an invention of the Wall Street bubble of the late twentieth century. Nearly all variations on financial transfers in use today—call options, repos, futures contracts, short selling, naked short selling—were invented or pioneered in Amsterdam in the seventeenth century, as traders sought innovative ways to speculate on the underlying price of VOC shares. We know from the existing books of Amsterdam notaries, for example, that futures trading on shares of stock—an agreement to buy at a set price on a future date—began with open-air meetings on the New Bridge in 1607.

Derivative devices such as short selling—selling shares one

doesn't actually own in order to profit from an expected downturn in price—open the door to financial scamming, and two years later the first scandal erupted in Amsterdam's open-air securities market when a powerful trader named Isaac le Maire, at the head of a consortium of traders, engaged in short selling of VOC shares. This in itself was not problematic, but the details made it so. Le Maire—one of the more flamboyant figures of Amsterdam's heyday—had been part of the brain drain from Antwerp to Amsterdam in 1585. It was perhaps natural that he and Dirck van Os would join forces; they had both taken part in that migration, and both were ambitious businessmen at a time and place that favored big ambition. The two had collaborated to open the city's trade into Russia. Le Maire had then watched from the sidelines as Van Os and others founded the Company for Faraway Lands; he was inspired by Cornelis de Houtman's ragged voyage to launch an East Indies venture of his own. He had then joined his colleague Van Os in becoming one of the founding members of the VOC. But in 1605 the two men split: Le Maire was forced out of the company in a dispute over financial irregularities. As a result of this public humiliation, he seems to have turned his energy to getting revenge. He secretly undertook a mission to the French king, Henry IV, and set in motion plans for a French East India company. Acting on this privileged information, Le Maire gathered his consortium of short sellers in order to take advantage of what he expected would be a dramatic drop in VOC shares due to competition from the new company. But he miscalculated: plans for the French company died. When VOC shares did not drop in value, Le Maire led his fellow short sellers on a rumor campaign—company vessels lost at sea, and a sizable fortune with them—which did indeed send share prices plummeting. The rogue traders, having sold at a higher price shares they did not own, then bought the same amount of shares at a far lower value and delivered them to their buyers, pocketing the difference. (Technically, in modern parlance, what Le Maire and his confrères engaged in was naked short selling, a riskier activity than short selling today, since there was no broker involved.)

Van Os and the other directors of the VOC intuited what was happening—that the value of the company was dropping less for real-world reasons than through manipulation—and further, they believed they knew who was behind it. They issued an appeal to the States of Holland, the provincial governing body, to make such practice illegal. What is interesting about the matter is that within a few years of the launch of the first modern capitalist venture came the sort of unscrupulosity that has ever since been a feature of capitalism, followed by the first concerted effort at financial regulation. The directors, in their appeal for reform, cited biblical principles of fairness and decency. They pointed out that widows and orphans had their savings in the company, which meant that willingly depressing its value was a strike against society's most vulnerable.

The governing body sided with the directors and banned the practice. The ban didn't hold for long, since it was in the traders' interest to allow short selling, but then again both the ban and the failure to enforce it indicated the government's willingness to play an active role in this new game. And that willingness—the enthusiastic support of government for trade—would continue to serve the city of Amsterdam.

Meanwhile, as the VOC prospered, it paid dividends to its stakeholders. This was at first a creaky process, since the directors had decided that these should be paid in kind. So, for example, in April 1610, Agneta Cock's little grandson would have been inundated by a dividend on the order of 5,000 pounds of mace, the spice derived from the outer covering of the nutmeg seed: that is, 3,600 guilders' worth, or 75 percent of the value of the shares in the company that his grandmother had bought. Later dividends were paid in sacks of pepper and nutmeg. While some Amsterdammers were happy to jump into the spice market as resellers, it was quickly found to be a cumbersome means of recompense, and by 1618 dividends were paid in cash. Whether or not stakeholders received fragrant sacks as part of their profit taking, the association of spices with high value became embedded in the culture. To this day, if in Dutch you want to express your feelings about the forbidding price of the new watch or car your spouse has an eye on, you say the item is *peperduur*— "pepper-expensive."

Short selling, futures trading, stock jobbing: all of this ornate activity had been taking place outside, on the New Bridge, amid the rain and wind and the jostling and cursing of sailors. Sometimes in foul weather traders were allowed to gather in the St. Olof Chapel on the Zeedijk (which still exists, a hundred or so paces to your left), but clearly an institution was in the making—within a decade or so of the founding of the VOC, Amsterdam had three hundred licensed brokers and trade negotiators—and it needed a home. Construction on one was finished in 1611; it was built by the city's leading architect, Hendrick de Keyser, who also designed the East India House. The new Amsterdam Merchants' Exchange, when complete, had a grandeur that suggested the role the city saw it playing. It stood like a Renaissance castle, a rectangle of elegant colonnades around a central courtyard. It was conceived as an actual marketplace: trading was still conducted in the open air, but under sweeping vaulted roofs. Each commodity being traded (for the exchange was meant not only for VOC shares but shares in beer, salt, wood, copper, wine, cotton, and other goods) had assigned areas among the pillars.

The Amsterdam exchange straddled the water on the other side of Dam Square. What you see at the far end of the Damrak is a later iteration of the stock exchange, built in 1903 by Hendrik Berlage, who was the city's chief architect of his era. Berlage's building has since been repurposed. The current home of Amsterdam's stock exchange—which these days trades around $3 trillion in shares in a given year—is now just beyond Berlage's structure, out of sight from where you stand, housed in a modest palazzo of a building tucked between Berlage's modernist take on a medieval bourse and the Bijenkorf department store. NYSE Euronext, as the Amsterdam Stock Exchange is now officially called (after mergers with the New York Stock Exchange, the Brussels Stock Exchange, and the Paris Bourse), is the oldest stock exchange in the world, according to both its Web site and the guard who chatted with me as I poked around its lobby one day. Antwerp and London both claim the oldest stock exchange, which is true in a sense (Antwerp's building predates Amsterdam's by eighty years) but theirs were commodities markets. Taken in the modern sense, of a market where shares of company stock are traded, which is the essence of capitalism, Amsterdam was the originator.

Of course, the Amsterdam Stock Market was not an end in itself. Those pieces of paper that changed hands were valuable because they represented other things. Indeed, over the course of the next few decades they came to represent, not to put too fine a point on it, *everything*. Europe was in the early stages of its infamous period of exploitation of the wider world. The image we have of Europeans of the seventeenth century—semimedieval peasants rooted to their villages, their entire lives, including all they consumed, comprised of what was available within a few miles of their homes—is in need of updating. Europe was exploring the world with vigor, and Europe was ready to exploit—to consume. And the Dutch were on their way to becoming the greatest shipping nation the world had ever seen. The genius of Amsterdam in particular—the economic foundation to the political and social liberalisms it was soon to spawn— lay in its identifying and solving the problem that Europe's would-be consumer culture faced: life was staggeringly unpredictable. Fate was swift and could blindside anyone. Plagues swept in on a sudden wind. A returning fleet would be swallowed by a storm. Life was carried on perilously close to its natural state, which Thomas Hobbes would famously describe a few decades later as "nasty, brutish, and short." Nobody could count on anything, and therefore business suffered. Price and availability were wildly variable.

Security was what was needed, and Amsterdam's stupendous rise can be seen as a result of the awareness that, if you provided this, virtually everyone would thank you for it. Your enemies, your competitors, would be grateful to you for giving them a small foothold of safety and would repay you over and over, even if they hated you at the same time.

The first step in achieving this security was providing a central stock exchange. Another was having insurance offices and other services, as well as hotels and facilities for traveling merchants. All of these services came into being and were clustered in the buildings laid out around the exchange. But also part of the plan was the concept of a central storehouse. Shortly after the founding of the stock exchange, Amsterdam went about making itself into the Amazon.com of the seventeenth century, the place where everything was available to everybody. But of course it was an analog emporium: nothing was virtual; everything was real, in all its bulky, aromatic, or reeking glory. That meant an unfathomable amount of hard work. And it meant that the city—a city with barely a foundation, which had been tenuously built on marsh and swamp and for which inundation was a constant threat—would have to transform itself to hold all the goods of the earth.

Amsterdam's physical self as it developed in the seventeenth century—and as is largely still evident in the city center today (one notion that repeatedly strikes you if you live in the city center, with its teetering brick facades and undulating parade of gables, is that it's always the seventeenth century here)—was a product of this awareness and this decision. The city morphed itself, carved itself, flooded itself, dammed itself, built itself up brick by brick around this idea, which is part of the foundation of liberalism. For individual freedom can come about only, can be conceived only, if there is some sense of security to life. In fact, the city's rise—its coming role not only as the world's economic entrepôt but as a center of scientific learning, art, shipping, and much else—can be seen as the antidote to the frightful vagaries that Hobbes had in mind, as expressed in the full quote from his *Leviathan*:

> In such condition there is no place for industry, because the fruit thereof is uncertain: and consequently no culture of the earth; no navigation, nor use of the commodities that may be imported by sea; no commodious building; no instruments of moving and removing such things as require much force; no knowledge of the face of the earth; no account of time; no arts; no letters; no society; and which is worst of all, continual fear, and danger of violent death; and the life of man, solitary, poor, nasty, brutish, and short.

If you wander around Amsterdam's fabled canals, especially the Prinsengracht, the outermost central canal, which was specifically designated for commerce, you'll note that a lot of the gabled brick buildings that line them have shuttered windows right in the middle of each story. These were warehouses. Indeed, in a sense the whole city became a warehouse. A trader kept his office on the ground floor of his house, the room that connected to the street. His family lived behind. And the upper floors were packed with whatever goods he dealt in. If you turn your gaze upward, you will see a beam jutting right out from the top of each canal house, with a metal hook hanging down from it. Hoist beams are still used, though mostly for moving furniture. In the seventeenth century, you worked a rope and pulley to haul your crates of goods to the upper floors. Particularly in the case of spices, being able to store quantities kept prices from fluctuating wildly, which was good for everybody.

How vast an enterprise was this? As a snapshot: in 1625, VOC warehouses in the Netherlands contained almost four million pounds of pepper. The year after, thanks to especially successful voyages, there were nearly six million pounds of pepper packed into the quaint little canal-side buildings of the city's middlemen, not to mention warehouse upon warehouse filled with cinnamon, stockfish, tea, whale oil, sugar, salt, soap, sail cloth, silk, beer, tobacco, and other goods, waiting to ship out again. A generation later, when Cosimo III de' Medici traveled to Amsterdam, his gushing observations suggested an awareness that Italy's own grandeur, that of the high Renaissance over which his grandfather and namesake held sway, was a thing of the past and that what he saw in this city of business was the future: "Greater trade is done in Amsterdam than in any other city in the world. Foreigners are astounded when they first see it, and it appears that the four quarters of the world have despoiled themselves to enrich her and to bring their rarest and most curious treasures into her port. Anyone who considers the present state of Amsterdam . . . will be amazed that the city with such small beginnings and in such a short time has become enriched to such a degree of greatness, beauty, and magnificence."

Before this could happen, before the city could become the world's emporium, it had to grow. The Amsterdam in which Dirck van Os opened his house to subscribers to the VOC, the Amsterdam of Agneta Cock, was still a small medieval city hunkered inside its walls, surrounded by a moat: far too small for its ambitions. Its size had been restricted by legal decree. There was still a war on, and it was feared that any outlying buildings could be taken over by the Spanish and used as bases for attack. Thus it was against the law to build outside the city walls.

But as the city grew, people wantonly ignored the law. Look at any of the many maps and paintings that exist from, say, 1600 to 1610, and you find dozens if not hundreds of buildings of various types beyond the walls, along with neatly laid-out gardens and fences. Despite potentially putting themselves in harm's way, people were defying the city ordinance, for the oldest of reasons: it was cheaper. Land was cheaper, and, crucially, beyond the city walls you didn't have to pay city taxes.

By 1610, the old way of doing things had completely fallen apart. The city needed to expand and to raise the money for its expanded urban infrastructure by selling off parcels. There lurches onto the panel of history at this point the curious figure of Frans Hendricksz Oetgens. He is the man most responsible for the great expansion of the city in its golden age: for the physical manifestation of Amsterdam's commitment to liberalism. At the same time, he demonstrated a ruthlessness, cunning, and utter lack of civic responsibility that could have served as a model for people like Bernard Madoff, Charles Ponzi, and other individuals synonymous with the scheming and rapacity that would accompany financial liberalism through the centuries.

As far as we know, Oetgens lived his whole life within the city of Amsterdam. He was born in 1558, near the start of Philip II's long and bloody reign as Spanish monarch. He had come of age amid the first period of the Dutch war of independence from Spain, when Willem of Orange led Dutch patriots against the Duke of Alba. He started humbly, training as a mason, and in the years after Amsterdam threw off its Catholic overlords he helped to build it anew. The first building project that we know he worked on was the Zuiderkerk, or Southern Church, the third of the city's three great churches. He also had a role in constructing the exchange building. As he prospered, he bought one of those houses on the right side of the Damrak that today make up a row of urban detritus; there he lived with his wife and their six children. Later he joined Van Os and others in becoming one of the directors of the Amsterdam chamber of the VOC. Oetgens ultimately worked himself into the position of *fabrieksmeester*: city builder. It was, at this unique moment, perhaps the most important job in the city. It was an ideal place, and the perfect time, for a man of ambition.

Oetgens can perhaps be said to have had some ambition for the city, but it is beyond doubt that his greatest ambition was reserved for himself and his fortune. He urged the city's panel of four mayors to give up the long-standing policy of barring building outside the defensive walls. They acquiesced, putting him in charge of the expansion project, an action that could have been the inspiration for the fox-guarding-the-henhouse saying. Oetgens worked with the city carpenter, Hendrick Jacobszoon Staets, to map out precisely where the city would expand. Meanwhile, he won an appointment as one of the four mayors and from there got several friends appointed to positions in the city government. Most notable of these was his brother-in-law, Barthold Cromhout. Together, Oetgens and Cromhout oversaw the expansion of Amsterdam. One of their first achievements was to have committee meetings held in secret. Next, they proceeded to buy much of the land that they had targeted for inclusion in the city. This was mostly swamp, which Oetgens and Cromhout got for next to nothing since of course the owners of the land were ignorant of the secret expansion agreement. Their plan, then, was to wait for the value to rise. One example, cited by Clé Lesger: a stretch of land just beyond the western walls of the city that Oetgens, Cromhout, and two of their cohorts purchased for 16,179 guilders in 1611 was valued in 1615 at 122,247 guilders.

Oetgens and other speculators orchestrated dozens of such deals. Eventually the land was divided into lots and sold to individuals in a curious process that became known as an Amsterdam auction. I attended an Amsterdam auction conducted by the city's association of realtors—for repossessed real estate in the city continues to be sold by the same process. An Amsterdam auction consists of two parts. The first is like an ordinary auction: bidding starts low and rises. But the highest bidder does not necessarily get the property. In one case I observed, bidding on a house and garage began at €200,000. With the usual waves and gestures, people in the crowded, boisterous rotunda of a room pushed the price up, until the gavel came down at €430,000. A man rushed to the table set up in front of the room, where a panel of two realtors and the auctioneer held court, signed a paper, and shook hands. Then the auctioneer started round two by naming another figure: €300,000. Silence in the room. Rapidly, then, he descended: "€250,000 . . . 200 . . . 150 . . ." When he reached €60,000, someone in the room burst out with a single sharp syllable: "*Mijn!*" Saying "mine" in the second round is the unequivocal signal that you will take the property at that price. That is to say, the small bald man in the gray suit who now darted to the front table had agreed to buy the property for €60,000 more than the round one price of €430,000—or for a total of €490,000. If the round two figure had dropped to zero, the highest bidder of round one would have gotten the property.

The Amsterdam auction seems to have developed in the era of the city's expansion as a way to spice up the bidding process, for it adds some extra layers of complexity. For one, the top bidder in round one received (and still does receive) a cash prize for nudging up the value, whether or not he was topped in round two. This practice led to its own form of speculation. Some people took to bidding on properties even when they had no money to pay for them, in hopes that they would win the reward money and then get beaten out in the second round. Someone who was caught—stuck with buying a property he didn't have the money for—was called a sheep. A sheep spent two months in prison as punishment. But the air was so thick with the scent of money to be made that many people risked it.

Meanwhile, the larger illegality in the expansion that made Amsterdam the jewel of the golden age, the flagrantly corrupt speculation of Oetgens, Cromhout, and others, which was an appropriate coda to what might be Europe's first great expression of economic liberalism in the arena of real estate, was met by one of the first systematic attempts at regulation. In this case, Oetgens, the villain, had a counterpart. Also on the city government was a man named Cornelis Hooft. In Dutch history he is best known as the father of one of the great poets in the language, Pieter Corneliszoon Hooft (who isn't read much these days and is probably familiar to most

Amsterdammers only by virtue of the fact that the city's toniest shopping street is named for him). But more importantly he acted as whistle-blower as well as moral, legal, and political block against the unscrupulosity of Oetgens and Cromhout. Hooft was a stern-looking, deeply religious man who became so famous for his sense of fairness that the greatest of Dutch dramatists, Joost van den Vondel (also little read today but namesake of a large park in Amsterdam), characterized his role in the city's history in verse:

Hoe heeft hem Amsteldam ervaeren wiis en simpel:
Een hoofd vol kreucken, een geweten sonder rimpel.

Or: "How did Amsterdam know him but wise and simple: / A brow of folds, [but] a conscience without a wrinkle."

Once Hooft saw what was going on, he launched a sustained attack on Oetgens—or rather, two attacks. One was based on the liberal concept of free trade: Oetgens and his cronies were using their inside knowledge to confound the free market. The other was moral. Quoting from the Bible and classical authorities, Hooft played the part of prosecuting attorney, telling his fellow municipal leaders that each of them had a duty toward the city that he likened to the role of a foster parent toward an orphan. Amsterdam, he said, was a child, a perennial child, who had to be protected and nourished and helped to grow. For base personal gain, the speculators were violating their sacred moral responsibility.

Hooft won his case. Oetgens and Cromhout fell from power. They soon got themselves reinstated, though, and restacked the council with men sympathetic to their views (that is, other speculators). The fight went on for years, with twists and turns, but in the end it can be said that the speculators won. They enriched themselves fantastically, at the city's expense, and were allowed to get away with it because so many of the city's other supposed foster parents decided to join them at their game. On one of the lots of land that Cromhout had schemed to buy he built a home, and later his son rebuilt it. Today, you can see a ghost of the family association on its facade in the form of a bas-relief image of a twisted log: the name Cromhout means (appropriately) bent wood. Ironically enough for a structure that might be said to stand as a testament to immorality, the building has served, since the 1970s, as the home of the Bible Museum. Recently the street-level rooms were configured into a museum showcasing the Cromhout family's wealthy lifestyle in the eighteenth century.

While the speculation battle raged, work was going on to develop the new districts. And for all the corruption on one side, the care and foresight that went into the overall development was probably unprecedented in human history. In one swoop, the surface size of the city was increased fivefold. The development took the form of three new canals that would wrap in a semicircle around the medieval center. The sensibility behind it all was strikingly modern. Each of the new canals was given a fancy name to attract the nouveau riche merchant class to build gracious homes: Prinsengracht (Prince's Canal), Keizersgracht (Emperor's Canal), Herengracht (Gentlemen's Canal).

Before building could happen, the swampy terrain needed to be pumped. First, the perimeter fortifications had to be built. Then mills had to be erected. Then the new canals had to be dug and a system of locks constructed so that the canals would be flushed daily. Try as one might, it is impossible to imagine the effort all of this took. For of course it was done without machinery. You get the gist from the occasional print or painting that shows wheelbarrows and shovels, men's legs planted in thick mud, boards laid down for the barrows to traverse the glop. But still, in the span of a single lifetime:

Six miles of canal were dredged by hand and foot (using water wheels powered like stationary bicycles).

Twelve miles of canal-side land were built up, with mud from where the canals were dug out and with sand hauled in via barges, to raise the ground level enough above water to build on.

Somewhere around one hundred bridges were constructed.

A dozen miles of canal-side road were laid brick by brick.

And then came the houses: upwards of three thousand of them, every single one built, with outrageous improbability, on shifting marshland, requiring the backbreaking work of pile driving by manual labor. This in itself was such a supreme effort that the Dutch word for pile driving—*heien*—is the root of a number of sayings, songs, and folktales. A single house required maybe forty pairs of piles, each a stout, straight log of Scandinavian pine, to be jammed forty or sixty feet into the peat, sand, and clay. The grandiose City Hall, built on Dam Square in 1653 (today known as the Royal Palace), required 13,659 piles. Were you to travel to Amsterdam in its glory days, probably the sight you would have been most struck by would have been that of the triangular "trees" of support posts dotting the landscape, each with a block of iron weighing maybe half a ton poised above the pile. Teams of thirty or forty men, keeping time by chanting songs and fueled by ready barrels of beer, simultaneously pulled ropes to heave the *heiblok* into the air; then, on the call from the *heibaas*, they would let loose and the weight would slam down, hammering the log a little deeper into the ground. The Scandinavian logs are still there: the canal houses you see in Amsterdam's central ring today (except for those that have had their foundations replaced) rest on piles that were rammed into the earth in the 1600s. That they are still holding up so much of the city is the result of a bit of seventeenth-century genius. The engineers knew that the logs would not rot once they were below the waterline. The problem was the tops had to rest in the air, where masonry fixed them to the bricks, in order for the mortar to harden. The solution was to dig ditches where the piles would be driven to a point below the waterline and then temporarily pump water out of them. Once the mortar had dried, the water could be let back in the ditch, and the pile, safely under water, remained preserved from the ravaging effects of oxygen.

This went on throughout much of the century. As you read the next two chapters, keep it in the back of your mind: while Rembrandt painted and directed his business empire, while Spinoza stood before a synagogue tribunal on the charge of heresy, while the merry companies patrolled and caroused and scientists tinkered with lenses and sliced into corpses, the entire city, throughout its golden age, was a construction site, a work in progress.

Amsterdam's canal ring, when completed, was the greatest urban feat of the age, a model for cities from England to Sweden. Peter the Great set himself up in the city for a time, studying its engineering and urban planning techniques, and then put them to practice in constructing St. Petersburg, which was likewise built on marshland. For four centuries Amsterdam's canal ring has been a wonder, worthy of tourism and imitation, for reasons that UNESCO identified when in 2010 it named the district a World Heritage site: "It is a masterpiece of hydraulic engineering, town planning, and a rational programme of construction and bourgeois architecture." In other words, the reason early modern Europeans marveled at Amsterdam's golden age urban core was that it *served* people, extraordinarily well. And the people it served were not princes or popes but merchants and tradesmen. As Europe lurched toward secularism, democracy, modernity, a society based on the individual, it became intrigued by this city that had remade itself to serve the ordinary individual and his or her upwardly mobile aspirations. The new city Amsterdam became brought the world to one's doorstep. Ships anchored in the harbor, where goods were then transferred to small vessels and ferried right into the canal zone, to be unloaded directly into homes that were also warehouses. A man could sail from China or Japan to Amsterdam and enter his front parlor and the bosom of his family almost without touching solid ground. The canals were like arms that the city sent out to reach around the globe and gather its plenty back to it.

The rings of concentric canals, with radial canals and streets serving as spokes, was likewise set up for bourgeois living. Everything was within reach of the ordinary man or woman. And while there was of course a division of rich and poor, the classes were not divided by neighborhood. Rather, the rich lived on the canals and the poor lived on the streets interspersed behind each canal. This division had long been obvious to me, but I had never stopped to consider the cultural meaning behind the fact that the poor were not ghettoized. It was brought home to me by Paul Spies, the director of the Amsterdam Museum and custodian of the city's historical artifacts, one day as we sat in his office in central Amsterdam, in what was built (in 1580) as one of the world's first orphanages, looking down onto the museum's collection of "merry company" portraits of the men who had conceived and built all of this. "When they constructed their ideal city in the seventeenth century, Amsterdammers kept rich and poor together," he said. "They all lived in the same neighborhoods—everyone met at church. This came out of the Dutch mentality of modesty. In other countries in Europe, where the rich had their own neighborhoods, the separation said, 'I'm the master, and you are totally dependent on me.' But we had the Calvinist mindset, which said, 'We are all small people. None of us are gods.'"

This mentality of modesty also had its origins in the communal sensibility that is so elemental to the country's water-bound culture, and Spies pushed me to see it as part of the explanation for why the world's first stock exchange was founded in Amsterdam. Here, once again, we find the irony that a collective sensibility is somehow tied to what we think of as extreme individualism. For if on the one hand the stock market can be seen as an instrument of individual empowerment, you can also look at it as a collectivist enterprise. As Spies said, "With stocks the impulse was, 'Let's share the risk and maybe we'll all get ahead.'"

One of the defining features of our time is the push in the political arena for greater individual freedom of movement, especially economically. In the United States, this is typically a conservative position, associated with the Republican Party. In Europe, it is a Liberal position (with "Liberal" here relating to individual economic freedom). In both places, the position defends the rights of individuals to make money and sees the threat as coming from either the government or society—from "socialism" of one kind or another. The left-wing position, meanwhile, tends to put society ahead of the individual. But the example of Amsterdam as it took a lead role in developing liberalism—the broad principle of individual freedom, which underlies both sides of this argument—shows that there was a constant dance between society and the individual. The communal desire to share risk brought about the first multinational corporation and the first stock exchange. For the residents of Amsterdam, a communal urge to work together led to scintillating and unprecedented individual success and advancement. And as that individual success fueled their society, the society crafted a new kind of urban space, one that further promoted cooperation as a strategy for advancing individual power.

THE LIBERAL CITY

Opinions differ on the question of whether a golden age is something you can experience while it's happening or whether it only comes into focus on reflection. When the poet Randall Jarrell half joked that "the people who live in a Golden Age usually go around complaining how yellow everything looks," he was voicing a suspicion that no matter how grand and prosperous and momentous the time in which you are living may be, its grandeur is inevitably stained by the incessant drabness of the present.

Then again, in various eras and contexts you find people who proclaim outright that, in effect, these are the good old days. And there are indications that Amsterdammers who were alive during the city's golden age had an inkling that something very special was going on. For one thing, the city commissioned a history of itself as early as 1614—after successive waves of VOC ships had returned from the East Indies but before much of the city's spectacular new canal belt could be built, and certainly before its great artistic and scientific flowerings—which was a pretty clear indication that the residents already felt the throb of history in their achievements. And in that history book, the author, Johannes Pontanus, actually applied the term in question to his city. After summoning the mythological ages of man that the ancient Greeks wrote of—gold, silver, bronze—he decided that the period of astonishing transformation that he was trying to describe on the fly deserved the golden epithet.

Of course, the rich and the poor experienced the age differently. But even the poor—some of them, anyway—felt the jolt of possibility. Let's follow, as an almost random example, a poor newcomer who arrived in the city just about at its height. Her name was Geertje Dircx. She was born in Edam, to the north. She had been married to a sailor, and he died. We know that she had worked at an inn in Hoorn and had some family in a village called Ransdorp and that her brother was also a sailor; but the fact that she headed for Amsterdam tells us that in her widowhood she could depend on no one and so had to find a future for herself.

She might have traveled by water coach, a transit system that had become commonplace in the province of Holland by the 1630s and that foreigners marveled at. These were passenger boats that glided along the canals and rivers, towed by horses, and they signaled, even before one entered the city, a newly developing society, one that stressed order, comfort, and egalitarianism. The boats were covered, were lined with benches, could hold up to fifty people, and followed a regular schedule between towns, of which one could find printed copies. Passengers paid fares based on the length of the journey; various currencies were accepted. Everyone, rich and poor, used them, and foreigners often found this free mixing of castes to be one of their first experiences of the novel Dutch egalitarianism. Food and drink were sold onboard. People got drunk. In the evening, songs broke out, sometimes fights. If there was a dark corner, a prostitute might try to make a quick florin from a traveling salesman.

The passenger boats wound their way close enough to the landscape as to be in it, and slowly enough for travelers to exchange words with farmers in their fields. The countryside of Holland unfolded for a traveler, as it still does, in its endlessly massing flatness. There was the green of the polder, cut by the straight lines of water channels. The horizon was a line studded by cows and an occasional tree. Then there was the sky and its cloudscapes: tunnels and chasms and cathedrals and phantasmagoria of clouds, mounting the heights and marching in vaults and columns, ennobled by sunlight or furiously crosshatched by the force of an impending storm. (The Dutch sky is seemingly unchanged; my favorite word used by Dutch meteorologists is *wolkenvelden*: cloudfields.)

Then walls and church tops would rise up for interested passengers to observe: a city. And one hubbub, of insects and birds, would be replaced by another, of people and commerce. Then would come the bells. Foreign travelers to the Low Countries always remarked on the ceaseless donging of church bells in Dutch towns. A resident could tell with his eyes closed where he was in Amsterdam from the distinct timber and carillon of the Zuiderkerk, the Westerkerk, the Oudekerk, the Nieuwe Kerk, the Noorderkerk.

Once ashore, a newcomer like Geertje Dircx would want to wander and begin exploring sites that had become legendary in just a few years. The main site was the city itself, its alleys and quays. The sleek new canal rings were already talked of as the physical manifestation of this golden age that had descended on the city. Some of the new houses, which doubled as warehouses, were five stories high: skyscrapers to someone coming from a village. At the time Geertje Dircx arrived, the first portion of this ongoing urban development project was finished, with new brick homes lining both sides of each canal; further along in the direction of the river the work of the pile drivers and bricklayers was still going on. The ring canals were then (as now) both a tourist site and a trap, for newcomers would be confused by the semicircular construction: you would start out walking south along a street and, without making any turns, end up heading north. You also had to watch out for the coaches, which had only recently come into normal use among the wealthy and which would go barreling crazily through the narrow streets and over the hump-backed bridges.

The Amsterdammers themselves were as well a source of confusion for newcomers. When Willem of Orange rode into the city in triumph Amsterdam had had 30,000 inhabitants; now there were close to 140,000, plus swarms of undocumented aliens, which a scholar recently estimated would have numbered in the hundreds of thousands, flooding into the city to work on the expansion or looking for places on VOC ships. And the inhabitants were a bewildering mix. At least a third were foreign born. Most immigrants were from Germany and Scandinavia, but Geertje would have also seen and heard Africans, Turks, Inuits, Laplanders, and others. The city was a cacophony of languages.

It was also, however, very well organized, and that too would have taken some getting used to. Amsterdam comprised a maze of bureaucracies and societies that had to be negotiated. There were taxes to be paid on everything from beer to rent. Nearly every profession had a guild, and each guild had rules to follow. It must have seemed that the city had invented every possible job for a human to do, and some that humans had no business doing. There were people who only made balances for scales, people who only made glue, and people who only bored pearls to be strung. The textile industry employed not just weavers but wool washers, nap shearers, bleachers, dyers, and fullers. Wire drawers worked gold, silver, and copper into wire, for use in jewelry, which more and more ordinary people were wearing, and scientific equipment. *Vuilnisvaarders* hauled dung. *Piskijkers* (literally: piss lookers) could cure whatever was ailing you (or said they could) by studying your urine.

A small-town girl would have been rendered dizzy by the activity and, in this city that had set itself to be the entrepôt to the world, the display. Among the canals you could find live elephants and armadillos, pickled snakes and frogs, microscopes and telescopes, old Chinese porcelain and new delftware. And of course spices and herbs not only for cooking but for aiding digestion, loosening stools, dilating cervixes, and warding off disease: stores went far beyond garden-variety pepper and cinnamon to include exotica like scammony, zedoary, galangal, spikenard, euphorbia, tragacanth, coloquintida, and what was billed as dragon's blood.

There was food everywhere to goad poor and yearning immigrants. There was a poultry market and a butter market, vegetable markets and butchers' stalls. Street hawkers sold cinnamon cakes and roasted nuts. At noon our traveler might see and smell, through house windows, families sitting down to bowls of pea soup or the national dish of *hutspot*—a stew of vegetables, chopped meat, ginger, and lemon juice—along with knobs of hard dark rye bread and beer for young and old. Peering through the stained glass windows of finer houses our woman from the provinces would have noted that the wealthy were now eating on porcelain, drinking from porcelain mugs, employing finely wrought silver cutlery. Nowadays, after a meal, people were fanatics for tobacco; men, young and old alike, would pull out their long-stemmed pipes and start puffing.

Geertje would likely have found temporary residence in the Jordaan, the area of the new part of the city that sat astride the canal belt, which mostly housed the poor and working classes. Life was rougher and shaggier here, the houses were smaller and more cheaply constructed, and there was more unpleasantness, since zoning laws prohibited smelly industries like tanneries from setting up in the main part of the city (two windmills nearby were known as the Big Stink Mill and the Little Stink Mill).

We don't know when she first arrived in Amsterdam, but in 1642 Geertje Dircx began her own upwardly mobile trajectory when she made her way to the Breestraat, or Broad Street. It ran through what had until recently been one of the fashionable neighborhoods of the old city, until its wealthier residents began to decamp for the new canal zone and their places were taken by members of Amsterdam's large Jewish population, as well as by artists and artisans. Geertje needed work, and she had gotten a tip. There was a couple who lived here, in a grand, double-sized house. They had recently had a baby; the wife was doing poorly. They needed help. Geertje stood on the stoop, perhaps still heavily swaddled in her North Holland dress, with the bonnet drawn tight around the sides of her face. A bonnet might have obscured some of her features, but it could not have masked the fact that she had eyes that danced, eyes that, whatever

she had been through, showed a keen will to survive, someone still
vibrant to life's possibilities.

If the golden age meant that there were ways for a peasant girl
from the country to advance herself, for a smart, ambitious boy from
a moderate background the future was positively fat with promise.
Claes Pieterszoon was born two years before Cornelis de Houtman
set off on the disastrous voyage to the East Indies that would, despite
its immediate failure, launch the VOC, which in turn would fuel
the city's rise. Claes's father was a linen merchant. The family house
stood virtually within the shadow of the New Church, and the boy
spent his childhood playing in the streets behind Dam Square, in
the very center of old Amsterdam. He would have marched with
friends down to the harbor to see fleets of VOC ships returning from
impossibly faraway lands and wandered eastward toward the river to
inspect the progress of the new canals and houses. In time, his older
brother went to Leiden University to study for the ministry. Claes
followed but chose medicine.

In 1617, he was back in Amsterdam, ready to start a career as a
doctor medicinae, what we would call a general practitioner. He knew
right where he wanted to be: on one of the new canals, convenient
to the upwardly mobile gentry who were moving in there. He bought
a house on the Herengracht and shortly afterward married a young
woman named Eva van der Vroech. One account says Pieterszoon's
mother wasn't pleased with the match, which seems strange because
his family was part of the conservative wing of the Dutch Reformed
Church, and so was the young woman's family. Eva had an uncle
who had snapped his sword while hacking at a Catholic statue during the iconoclastic frenzies, an incident that her family recalled
with pride.

Claes Pieterszoon, who at this time had a bit of baby fat to his
features and wore his beard and moustache long, was possessed of

a sober and wide-ranging intellect, which soon attracted the attention of others. As a physician, he was conscientious and became known for his warm bedside manner. Science was beginning to develop basic principles to be applied to the natural world, but the new fascination with observation was still in its early stages. Most medical men preferred to rely on the teachings of the ancients. Claes Pieterszoon went both ways. On the one hand he was the main force behind a significant modernization: the city's codification of its sixty-odd apothecaries, which involved listing which of the hundreds of compounds were to be prescribed for what ailments and even provided for government inspectors. But as a physician he was old school. The Englishman William Harvey published his revolutionary theory of the circulation of the blood in 1628; Claes Pieterszoon didn't buy into it. The prevailing thinking, which went back to the Roman physician Galen, was that the body produced two kinds of blood, one made by the heart and the other by the liver, and that the lungs pumped the blood. The two-bloods theory was the basis for the method of bleeding patients in order to cure disease, and indeed for much of medicine. Harvey thus had good reason to expect the medical establishment to frown on his theory ("I tremble lest I have mankind at large for my enemies . . . respect for antiquity influences all men"), and many physicians did. Pieterszoon was a deeply conservative man, and he preferred to scour the texts of ancient writers for answers, just as he relied on the Bible as his moral guide. He even made a joke about his refusal to go with the new theory, saying that he would rather be wrong with Galen than "circulate" with Harvey.

As a representative of Amsterdam's golden age, Pieterszoon was in this way typical: it was a time of constant clashes between ancient and modern, and nearly everyone had in his or her makeup a mix of the two. This dividedness is one of the biggest obstacles to our comprehending the early modern personality. The inability of Claes Pieterszoon to see the truth of Harvey's theory seems especially bewildering in view of the fact that his greatest passion as a medical man was for anatomical dissection. He was among the first to study the functioning of several parts of the human body, and he described them in minute detail. Like a good Dutchman, for whom an understanding of the channeling of water was second nature, he described an intestinal valve as functioning "like our locks, the gates of which go up and down, and are so sound that they can open for ebb tide but are able to withstand the force of the flood."

By the early 1620s he was one of Amsterdam's most distinguished citizens. Politics in the city were divided into two Protestant-aligned factions: the ultraorthodox, who believed that the city's sudden rise, along with that of the young Dutch Republic, was due to the will of God and that every act, public and private, should not only expressly follow God's commandments but be based on the conviction that mankind was fundamentally depraved and only divine grace could bring salvation, and the liberals, who pushed for a bit of lightening of this unyieldingly dark view of things and who advocated tolerance in a wide range of matters. Pieterszoon was temperamentally orthodox, and that faction on the city council sought him out to join their number. Doctors were now newly respected—people believed that they were not all necessarily quacks (a word, incidentally, of Dutch origin) but that some of them could actually alleviate suffering on occasion—and it made sense to bring an up-and-coming medical man into the city's affairs. It was the beginning of a lifelong career in city politics—four times he would serve on the four-person panel of mayors—which Pieterszoon would pursue alongside his medical practice.

Accompanying his sobriety, piety and civic-mindedness, Pieterszoon had a good deal of vanity. He collected fine things and worked with very modern energy to cultivate his public image. Indeed, he rebranded himself. To his dismay, his name was a common one in the Dutch provinces. There were Claes Pieterszoons digging ditches and baking bread. He, however, was anything but common, and he was in the market for an appropriate association by which to recast himself. Since their introduction into the country in the late 1500s, tulips had steadily become a Dutch passion. People loved their color and stateliness. Tulips adorned the homes of Pieterszoon's wealthy clients. They were dignified, upscale, exotic, increasingly expensive, and emblematic of the times. The physician appreciated all the associations the flower possessed. In 1621 he took the bold step of changing his name. The flower had originated in central Asia and reached Europe by way of Turkey. *Dulband*, the Persian word for turban, which the flower looked like, became, in Dutch, *tulp*. When Pieterszoon and his wife, Eva, moved from their Herengracht home to another on the next fashionable canal, the Keizersgracht, and then shortly after to yet another home on the third new canal, the Prinsengracht, he hung a sign above the door to announce his practice. It was a painting of a tulip. From that moment, Claes Pieterszoon became Dr. Nicolaes Tulp. He had expanded his first name to its formal size, quietly jettisoned the tie to his father's name, and added the floral crown. And thus was born a new dynasty. When a daughter was born the following year, he named her Catharina Tulp, and his son, two years after that, was christened Diedcrick Tulp. As a member of the city government, he was expected to choose a coat of arms and an insignia, with which he would stamp documents. He chose the tulip. He ordered one of the first full-sized coaches to ferry him around town on his rounds and had it emblazoned with a tulip, so that people clogging the roads knew to stand aside for Dr. Tulip to get to his patients.

Again, the paradoxical, not to say schizophrenic, nature of the age shows itself in riddle form. Granted that the convention of given name plus family name was not firmly fixed, it seems strange to us that a man so conservative that he would not change his medical perspective in the face of the evidence of his own eyes would take the seemingly radical step of changing his identity as if it were a suit of clothes. And for such a sober, serious, prudish man, a man of weight and bearing—to choose a flower?

He seems to have eventually had reason to regret the step. A few years later, in the mid-1630s, the unprecedentedly vigorous city, and the Dutch provinces as a whole, would become swept up in the first of the many speculative frenzies that would afflict the capitalist world in the subsequent centuries. Recent economic bubbles have been centered on the dot-com industry and on real estate. In Dr. Tulp's Amsterdam, the focal point was, uncomfortably for him, the tulip. When prices for the rarest varieties reached their height, single bulbs were going for thousands of florins, the equivalent of the price of Dr. Tulp's grand canal house. In retrospect, the lunacy of tulipo-mania makes perfect sense, or at least fits a pattern of human nature. As John Kenneth Galbraith puts it in his *Short History of Financial Euphoria*, "Speculation . . . comes when popular imagination settles on something seemingly new in the field of commerce or finance. The tulip, beautiful and varied in its colors, was one of the first things so to serve. To this day it remains one of the more unusual of such instruments. Nothing more improbable ever contributed so wonderfully to the mass delusion here examined." Recent scholar-ship has questioned how widespread tulip speculation was, and thus how devastating the crash was, but there is no doubt that after the bubble burst the tulip suffered a serious image problem, going from a symbol of refinement to a symbol of folly. Dr. Tulp had the shingle over his door removed. But he could hardly change his name, which was by then known far and wide.

Two big things happened to Dr. Nicolaes Tulp in the year 1628. His wife, Eva, died, and he was named professor of anatomy. His wife's death was a blow, but the tradition was that one didn't mourn long; he remarried less than two years later, to a woman he had known since they were children living in the same street. The anatomy appointment meant that henceforth he would conduct the city's annual public dissection of a human corpse in a building on the New Market square that had originally been one of the medieval gateways into the city but that now served as both a weigh station for goods transported by ship into the city and, in its upper reaches, as the anatomical theater of the surgeons' guild. The dissections were for the benefit of medical men, of course, but they were also open to the general public. And, again in that way the golden age had of confounding things we keep in separate compartments, the dissections were scientific but also religious and even theatrical events. Prayers were said at the beginning for the soul of the person whose body was about to be sliced into. At the end, there was a feast, and everyone got drunk. More than a few people, in their cups, must have tried to make off with body parts, for the city saw the need to issue a decree that anyone stealing bits of corpses from the public dissections would be fined six guilders.

The anatomy appointment cast Dr. Tulp as genuinely a public figure and cemented his position as the premier man of medical science in Amsterdam, perhaps in the whole Dutch Republic. It also fed into his weakness for self-promotion. During the course of his lifetime Tulp commissioned, by my count, eight full-scale portraits of himself, one life-size marble bust, and a gold and silver medallion featuring his image. An officially important subgenre of the portrait was the group portrait. It seems obvious that, on accepting the role of professor of anatomy, Tulp would back the idea of commissioning a group portrait showing him as the head of the city's men of medicine, sagely instructing them in the miraculous inner workings of the human body. And Tulp being Tulp, it should be no common group portrait, for a number of important vectors came into alignment in it. It had to showcase the lead role the city saw itself taking in advancing science. It should also identify clearly, and flatteringly, the other scientists of the guild. And Tulp had ideas about how he himself should be portrayed. Somehow the painting had to be both deeply traditional and clearly modern. It should be a serious piece of propaganda for Amsterdam, for science, and of course for Dr. Tulp. But where could the surgeons' guild find an artist capable of capturing all of this?

They found him in Leiden. That is to say, he had been born there, the son of a miller and a baker's daughter: working-class parents who wanted to lift their son up a rung, even though (or perhaps because) he was the ninth of their ten children. They sent him to a prestigious school where he would study Latin and get onto the track of a civil servant. But all he wanted to do was paint and draw, and finally they gave in and apprenticed him to a local master. They had given him a name that was unusual even then (a search of Amsterdam's burial register up to 1811, for instance, turns up only eight individuals with the name or variations thereof, and none before him). So some people may have snickered at being introduced: who calls their son Rembrandt? The last name that he began attaching to his paintings in 1632—van Rijn—reflected, of course, the river that shaped much of the country, but more particularly it referred to the name of the mill where his father made his living.

He had a hint of extra fleshiness as a young man, as well as frizzled gingery hair and, needless to say, explosive talent. He was passionate: religiously devout and hungry to understand what seemed beyond understanding, the swirling tub of human emotion. His goal, he wrote (the only time he committed himself in writing to a singular purpose), was to express "the greatest and most natural emotion."

He developed a dexterity with what were called historical paintings. We would call them religious paintings (though some were of mythological rather than biblical subjects), but they were fundamentally different from those of Michelangelo, Raphael, and other earlier artists. Those artists were commissioned by churches and their work was installed behind altars: the artists were workers in the business, the industry, of religion. But these were different times, and this was a different place. The Dutch provinces had broken free of Catholicism and were on a new trajectory, in the service of individuals, which encouraged them in turn to be interested in individuality: their own and that of their subjects. The clients of Dutch artists were not priests and popes but herring wholesalers and flax merchants.

And yet, those merchants were pious men. They and their wives wanted paintings that helped to instruct them in the history behind the Bible: they wanted the stories in living color, to be displayed in their own homes, for themselves and their children. So they commissioned vivid, twisting depictions of the angel stopping Abraham from sacrificing Isaac, the blinding of Samson, Jacob being shown Joseph's bloody coat, and Christ driving the money changers from the temple.

Rembrandt became very good at producing such scenes, and at pouring fresh drama into the traditional molds. Along the way, he began to do something else. He started putting himself in the compositions. This in itself was not new: artists had been inserting their likenesses into canvases for centuries. Usually, though, the figure was in the back, set off from the action, gazing at the viewer, as a kind of extra signature and a way to deepen the engagement, to say: Yes, you and I both know this is a painting; I hope you like my work. Rembrandt was doing something more: retrofitting himself into the psychological action. In his *Stoning of Saint Stephen*, his earliest signed painting, done before he had turned twenty, at least three figures seem to be portraits of the artist as a young man: the saint himself, his principal tormenter (who holds a rock the size of a bread loaf over the martyr's head), and a figure who, in the traditional style, looks out at the viewer.

What was going on here? From our psychological perspective, we might say the artist was making a statement or inquiry about himself, the sort of thing that most people at the threshold of adulthood do. He was wondering who he was. Am I a saint or a guilty sinner? Am I someone who violently refutes the manifestation of God's grandeur? The third painted self, in the traditional stance of staring out at the viewer, which is tucked precisely in between the other two, seems to be posing this quandary, asking the viewer to help him figure himself out. If this is true, then the artist was doing something that is commonplace now but had rarely been done before: using his art for his own emotional needs.

This idea comes a bit further into focus when you put the triple self-portrait against the backdrop of other work Rembrandt was then doing. Between the ages of twenty-one and twenty-five he made at least twenty self-portraits, in an intensity of guises and techniques. In some of the etchings his face is so engulfed in shadow it all but demands you to read it as a reflection of inner darkness. The art historian H. Perry Chapman says of this series, "In their extraordinary psychological presence we can recognize the initiation of one of the most concerted efforts at self-representation in the history of art."

Rembrandt was not the only one staring at himself. As Dutch society moved in its own direction, away from church and monarchy, portrait painting became an industry. Painters created portraits of beggars with as much care as, a generation earlier, someone like Rubens devoted to kings. Gabriel Metsu, who likewise trained in Leiden before moving to Amsterdam, specialized, as did his Delft contemporary Johannes Vermeer, in genre paintings that were less portraits than posed individuals: a woman holding a sick child on her lap, an old man selling poultry on a street corner. People loved these manicured real-world scenes, dickered for them, hung them in their homes and their workshops, as if to say: Look at us! Still lifes were part of the same trend. They were frankly not devotional art but decorative art. Maria van Oosterwijk was that rare thing: a highly successful woman artist. She specialized in richly rendered still lifes, usually of flowers, and her customers included European heads of state. A portrait of her done by Wallerant Vaillant, a French-born portraitist who also worked in Amsterdam, shows an attractive, elegantly dressed woman; she is posed with paintbrushes and palette in one hand and an open book on her lap, indicating her passions. The frustration is that so little is known about her life, other than that she started her career in Delft and ended it in Amsterdam. The lack of information may have to do with her sex: as a woman, she was not allowed to join the painters' guild.

But what made Rembrandt stand out from the rest of these highly skilled and successful artists? Why did the illustrious Dr.

Tulp look to Leiden in search of the man for the job of portraying him and his fellow surgeons? Rembrandt's fame as an artist had to do with technical brilliance and an inventive, theatrical approach. He was a master realist. But it's fair to say that what truly struck, even stunned, his contemporaries was his seeming to have turned his subjects inside out. He didn't just paint what they looked like; he painted who they were. This was something new, as was the desire for it. You can hear that shock of the new expressed in the slightly dazed-sounding amazement with which his friend Constantijn Huygens—poet and secretary to the current Prince of Orange, who became his early patron and booster—tried to explain Rembrandt. The artist, Huygens wrote, "gives himself wholly over to dealing with what he wants to express from within himself." Three and a half centuries later, the art critic Robert Hughes said much the same thing: Rembrandt is "the supreme depictor of inwardness, of human thought." This still strikes a viewer today, though we may have to excavate some layers of psychological sophistication that have built up over the centuries in order to appreciate what a revelation his painted faces would have been to the Dutch of the seventeenth century. And, once again, it's curious to ponder the medieval/modern split of the golden age Dutch: why the staid burghers would have experienced such naked interiority not as shockingly inappropriate or indecent but as a wonder to grasp at and savor.

The man who seems to have brought Rembrandt to Amsterdam was Hendrick van Uylenburgh, an art dealer who had apparently bought paintings from the artist in Leiden. Rembrandt moved into Van Uylenburgh's studio late in 1631 or just into the year 1632, at age twenty-five, and not long after walked three or four minutes down the wintry street to the Waag, the old gatehouse and current weigh station, whose upper floor housed the surgeon's anatomy theater. (The city's annual dissection was always held in winter so as to slow decay and stench.) There he observed Dr. Tulp demonstrating to his fellow surgeons upon the body of Adriaen Adriaenszoon (aka Aris the Kid), an executed thief who, coincidentally, had also emigrated from Leiden to Amsterdam. The resulting painting is one of the most admired and written-about of all time. *The Anatomy Lesson of Dr. Tulp* has been restaged, cast into fiction, anatomized by surgeons, dissected for hidden meanings. The postures of the men depicted, the features of the corpse (its curiously elegant fingers), the hank of tendon that Tulp stretches upward with the forceps, the position of the fingers of his other hand (with which, it has been suggested, he is showing the others the finger movement that the tendons in question effect), the swaths of darkness around the perimeter of the canvas and the glow emanating from the men's straining faces and, most of all, from the dead body, even the book that stands opened at one end of the painting: every element has been analyzed. As a whole the painting gives a frank statement of a time and place and conviction. We here in Amsterdam, it says, are committed to science.

For all the attention that has been paid to the painting over the centuries, we have no direct sources on how it was originally received. It seems safe to infer that it caused a sensation. We can guess that because immediately after the painting's unveiling Rembrandt became famous in Amsterdam. Everyone wanted to commission him; never mind that he raised his fee to a hundred guilders a portrait, about half the annual salary of a skilled laborer. Amsterdammers were entranced by the way he had with individuals, the way he seemed to know and be able to communicate to posterity just who they were. And thanks to the fact that he could work with astonishing speed he became a masterpiece factory; in one two-year period alone he painted forty-two exquisite, fully realized portraits, not to mention creating dozens of etchings and drawings. A shipbuilder named Jan Rijksen and his wife, Griet Jans, were among those who stood in line following the unveiling of *The Anatomy Lesson of Dr. Tulp* to pose for Rembrandt. Dirck Janszoon Pesser, a brewer, and his wife, Haesje, commissioned a pair of portraits. So did a furniture maker named Herman Doomer and his wife, Baertjen, and cloth dealer Nicolaes van Bambeek and his wife, Agatha. All of these people, and many others, are centuries dead and gone, and none made what you would call a lasting contribution. Yet they exist. They have Wikipedia entries. They live on canvases hanging in Amsterdam's Rijksmuseum, the Metropolitan Museum in New York, Buckingham Palace in London, and the Hermitage in St. Petersburg. Each of these human beings facing you as you stand in those museums has a past and present. They have interior lives. The subtitle of this book declares it to be about the subject of liberalism. I haven't used the word in a number of pages, but this is the essence of it: the emergence of the individual, with a self-consciousness, with the freedom to do, to expand, to make money, to become, to forge a career, to win fame, to change his or her identity even. When you try to describe it in words it comes across as an abstraction: the origin of liberalism in seventeenth-century Amsterdam. But it's actually a simple thing, which is on display in the great museums of the world.

The art historian Ann Jensen Adams relates the rise of portraits in this period of Dutch history to people's seeing themselves in new, individual identities in a society that had thrown off the old rules, that was no longer bound by church and monarchy. There was a new social mobility. Not coincidentally there appeared in Amsterdam a new kind of literature: self-help books, telling you how to behave as a wealthy merchant, what was the appropriate form of civic-mindedness, how to be a burgher's wife. This was a new society in the making, and its members were inventing the rules. And, sober and pious though they remained, they were fascinated by who they were becoming.

It may not be coincidental that René Descartes, the so-called father of modern philosophy and founder, in terms of philosophical underpinnings, of the modern self—whose *Cogito ergo sum* ("I think therefore I am") formulation reoriented all knowledge on the individual self—arrived in Amsterdam at almost the same time as Rembrandt and lived in the city for much of the next five years. I say it may not be a coincidence because Amsterdam had become a magnet for people of a modernizing bent: for liberals. Its burghers may have gone around in sober black coats with somehow even more sober white lace collars, but (again, the whiplash contrast) it was simultaneously a hotbed of reform and experimentation. While elsewhere in Europe the Catholic Church and various monarchs were inhibiting scientific tinkering, here people were grinding lenses for telescopes and perfecting the microscope. There were forty publishers in the city, and dozens more in other Dutch cities, and they were the most liberal—and the freest from constraint—in Europe. Descartes had come to the Dutch provinces to have published what would become arguably the touchstone of modernity, *A Discourse on the Method of Rightly Conducting One's Reason and of Seeking Truth in the Sciences*. The manuscript of Galileo's *Discourses and Mathematical Demonstrations Relating to Two New Sciences*, which was too incendiary for other European countries, found a Dutch publisher in Leiden. The Blaeu family of cartographers, who served as mapmakers to the VOC, ran Europe's biggest printing press on the Bloemgracht in Amsterdam, employing eighty men and cranking out ever-more-refined perspectives on the globe. Dutch presses published tracts written by opponents of both the English monarchy and the French king Louis XIV, literature that would have brought a death sentence to a publisher in England or France.

Descartes tramped around the city as awestruck as any tourist and provided a kind of advertisement for Amsterdam's golden age when he wrote to a friend of the wonder of watching "ships arriving, laden with all the produce of the Indies and all the rarities of Europe." He went so far as to relate the various kinds of openness that the city fostered to the personal freedom he required: "Where else on earth could you find, as easily as you do here, all the conveniences of life and all the curiosities you could hope to see? In what other country could you find such complete freedom, or sleep with less anxiety, or find armies at the ready to protect you, or find fewer poisonings or acts of treason or slander?"

All of this boundary-breaking activity can be related to *gedogen*, the look-the-other-way form of tolerance that had guided Amsterdam in dealing with Anabaptists and other radicals back in the sixteenth century (and that still governs its approach to sex and drugs). And ultimately it relates back to water: to people who banded together to make their home out of what was once sea and in whom an ethic of cooperation became hardwired, so that tolerance of otherness trumped ideologies. At least much of the time.

———

Rembrandt may have been ambitious, but he was also a home-body. As far as we know, once he made the move from Leiden to Amsterdam he almost never left the city for the rest of his life. Not only that, but many of his dealings were confined within a very small area of the city center, really just a handful of blocks. He lived first in the Academy of Van Uylenburgh on the Breestraat. His first great commission was executed in the anatomy theater a few min-utes away. After he married Saskia van Uylenburgh, a cousin of his boss and landlord, he and his wife moved a few blocks away, to a house on the Nieuwe Doelenstraat, on the site of what is today a big, modern café called De Jaren (where, coincidentally, I have written a good portion of this book). A minute's stroll from there, across a little iron bridge, brings you to a handsome Renaissance-style build-ing that was headquarters of the men who were appointed by the city to check the quality of cloth that was manufactured. A drab enough sounding occupation, but it says something about Amster-dam at the time that its commitment to quality control of products it shipped was such that these men warranted a group portrait. The result—*The Staalmeesters* (*staal* means "sample")—has long been considered among Rembrandt's greatest works, due in part to his having managed to bring energy and mystery to a subject that by rights should be crashingly dull. (The image was also translated into pop consciousness as the logo of the Dutch Masters cigar brand a century ago.)

Even closer to Rembrandt's first home outside the Uylenburgh academy, just a few steps from his front door, was the Kloveniers-doelen, the meeting hall of one of the city's civic guard companies. The group portraits of these companies are likewise stock images in all our minds: long-nosed, florid-faced men in floppy black hats and long white collars, hoisting either pikes and muskets or, when they are seated around a banquet table, heavy goblets. For the purposes of this book, what is worth pointing out about the civic guard companies is that they spoke to what had come into being in Dutch cities in the seventeenth century. It was individual townsmen who controlled their city, fostered its trade, and protected its citizens. It is their pride in that fact—and its uniqueness in Europe—that is reflected both in the canvases and in the genre itself.

But how to make such a staid genre come to life? That was the question before Rembrandt when the *kloveniers*' guild (a *klover* was a kind of musket) asked him to paint them. The circumstances of the commission say a bit more about Amsterdam's liberal culture. The banquet hall of the *kloveniers* was a public space, right in the center of town (the building has since been reworked into a hotel). The idea was to cover the walls with group portraits of the various companies, so that anyone who came in could admire not only the individuals whose likenesses were there preserved but the bond they represented between individuals and the community. The paintings were public statements that said in effect: Here we don't depend on kings or armies or hired guns; this is our town and we take care of it ourselves.

There were seven paintings commissioned for the hall, by six different artists. Why Rembrandt's massive effort—which we know as *The Night Watch* (a name that was first used a century and a half after the work was made)—became one of the world's most famous paintings, up there with the likes of the *Mona Lisa, The Scream*, and

Whistler's Mother, has seemingly little to do with the circumstances in which it was made. True, it was (contrary to some accounts) a hit right from the start. But its fame dimmed subsequently, as did that of its creator. For a few years, from his midtwenties to his midthirties, Rembrandt's intensity fit that of the moment, when Amsterdammers' self-consciousness as innovators and liberals came to a head, but otherwise the drama and emotional depth he incessantly searched for was a bit unseemly to the staid Dutch: he was, ultimately, too emotional a painter for them. He came back into vogue only in the nineteenth century, when the Netherlands was trying to forge a new national patriotism and identity. *The Night Watch*, so grand and opulent and stately, was chosen as the centerpiece of the new Rijksmuseum and given a hall all its own. What Rembrandt had painted to represent the civic-mindedness of Amsterdammers, which afterward the Dutch pushed away as rather un-Dutch in its grandeur, was now repurposed as the embodiment of Dutchness. And so, late in the day, Rembrandt became a national hero. In 1852 he was memorialized with a statue. Today, larger than life, he presides over the café patios and outdoor marketeers of Rembrandt Square, a few minutes' walk from his old stomping grounds.

The house where Rembrandt and Saskia lived on the Nieuwe Doelenstraat was a flashy rental. But it wasn't good enough. He had to buy a house—a grand and expensive one, two doors from Van Ulyenburgh's studio. He spent money freely in these days: on the house, on jewels for Saskia. He was a young man on the move, taking on commissions as fast as humanly possible, and there was no reason to think the flow of work and money would ever end. He worked with demonic energy, not only painting but running an academy, teaching students, and dealing in other people's artwork.

The house he bought (which is today an expertly tended museum devoted to his life and art) became his nemesis. He paid too much for it—with the flight of wealth to the new canals, prices in the neighborhood had dropped, but the owners of this house had held out for a high price and he was willing to pay—and around the time they moved in his career began to falter. Why? The American Rembrandt scholar Gary Schwartz—sitting in the living room of his own luxe villa, a 1725-era house in the village of Maarssen on the outskirts of Amsterdam, which he and his Dutch wife, Loekie, bought as students in 1968 for, he told me, a pittance—gave me his theory of Rembrandt's decline. Alongside the emotional intensity of his work, Schwartz stressed "a problem with authority. The norm was to form a relationship with a wealthy patron. Rembrandt did that. But, time and again, he started fights. He burned bridges."

Amsterdam was an oligarchy, run by a handful of wealthy merchant families. When he was fresh from Leiden and had completed the Tulp painting, Rembrandt was the hot young artist everyone wanted to have "do" them. But he didn't tend the relationships. One of his fellow artists actually complained that Rembrandt, as the city's leading painter, was dragging down the whole guild by not kowtowing to the great families. He was a workaholic, who would rather paint than attend obligatory social functions. And he got into fights with rich patrons about money and commissions.

Rembrandt's opposite on the Amsterdam scene was a former pupil, Govert Flinck. Flinck was happy to perform the social obligations Rembrandt despised and was also willing to change his style to suit changing tastes, making his paintings lighter and softer. By the time of the commission for the *kloveniers*, Flinck, the new golden boy, was given not one grand panel but two to paint.

Meanwhile, life at home had also clouded over. Saskia had delivered three children, all of whom had died in infancy. In 1641, she was pregnant again, and this time she was ailing. Rembrandt must have been in a panic. He needed help.

Thus Geertje Dircx from Edam, who had lost her husband and come to Amsterdam in search of work, showed up on the doorstep of his fine house. It isn't clear whether Saskia was still alive when Geertje began working in the household or if she had already died, leaving Rembrandt with a newborn son to care for. In any case,

Geertje took over the household and, after Saskia's death in June 1642, two recently widowed people who had each been drawn to the magnet of Amsterdam were living together under the same roof: one a peasant woman from the north, the other one of the world's great artists. So began a love affair. It's said that his *Danae*, a masterwork charged with golden light in which a voluptuous nude woman languishes in bed, one arm raised to welcome her lover Zeus, was first modeled on Saskia but that Rembrandt then painted her with Geertje's face. He also gave Geertje some of his dead wife's jewels.

The golden glow in their relationship seems to have lasted for quite a while, but when it left it didn't just fade but went black. Seven years after Saskia's death Rembrandt took on a new housemaid, a twenty-three-year-old beauty named Hendrickje Stoffels, and fell for her at once. At this point Geertje's forceful personality asserts itself onto the historical record. Reading between the lines of several legal documents, one concludes that there was a fight and that Geertje left the house and moved into rooms above an inn called the Black Bones. On June 15, 1649, in the presence of witnesses, Rembrandt made her a formal offer of separation, which included an annual "alimony" of 60 guilders. Geertje was furious and filed suit against him, claiming that he had promised her marriage and was in breach of his promise. Rembrandt didn't show up in court but instead tried another offer: this time 160 guilders per year. What he was most concerned about was the jewels that had belonged to Saskia and that he had given to Geertje: he wanted her to make clear in her will that on her death they would go to his son, Titus.

Another meeting took place, this time in the kitchen of Rembrandt's house. She found Rembrandt waiting with a notary, who would make the new agreement binding. Geertje arrived with a witness, a shoemaker named Octaef Octaefszoon who lived nearby. But things got ugly; Geertje exploded in anger and refused to sign.

Eventually, Rembrandt took a dramatic step—something that Rembrandt scholars for decades kept out of accounts of his life.

He had witnesses from the neighborhood testify that Geertje had descended into a life of loose morals, and asked a court to have her committed to a home for wayward women.

We don't know what truths lay beneath this sordid he-said, she-said affair, but Rembrandt's ultimate play—having a bothersome ex-lover committed to a workhouse—can't be seen as anything other than despicable. Gary Schwartz says he considers it evidence that the great miner of humanity's interior life was equally capable of great inhumanity. Geertje spent five years in the workhouse, was released in 1655 (despite Rembrandt's obections), and apparently died shortly thereafter.

What can we say about Geertje Dircx's experience in this new kind of society to which she had been drawn in the hope of benefiting from its lauded emphasis on individual freedoms? Maybe that the great promise was matched by great peril. Maybe that, as in any other society, fate was largely determined by power. Then or now, for someone like her, whether power is measured in money or titles or some other coin doesn't really matter; if you are among the least powerful, you'll probably lose.

Rembrandt's life after Geertje had some ups but mostly continued its downward trajectory. Hendrickje Stoffels remained his unwed partner; he painted several more images that would become iconic, including *The Jewish Bride* and more self-portraits, all of which, in contrast to the endless variation of emotions he captured in himself earlier, seemed to bear the same slightly dazed expression, puffed with age and splotched by sorrow. By 1660 he was bankrupt and, at the end of a long and tawdry process, lost his house and possessions. Two years later, still needing money, he sold Saskia's grave; her bones were removed to make way for someone else's. The next year Hendrickje died, and shortly after his son, Titus, died, at the age of twenty-six. Rembrandt himself died the following year, even as his work was being feted in foreign capitals. In one of those last self-portraits, as Simon Schama crisply notes, "Rembrandt's face is lit only by the illumination of his unsparing frankness." He was sixty-three but looked a decade older.

———

For all its superhuman scope, there is one remarkable gap in Rembrandt's career. The Dutch author Fred Feddes has marveled at how one of history's greatest visual artists could live in Amsterdam more or less exactly during the span of its golden age and almost completely fail to capture the explosive physical manifestation of its growth and glow. The city was not only transforming itself during his life but transforming what a city was and could be. It was refashioning itself around the individual, around human comforts and conveniences and profit making, focusing urban planning on what was good for business and pleasing to the eye. It was becoming a new kind of place. And Rembrandt ignored it all.

Or more: he willed it away. He didn't paint the new canals, the new buildings, the glorious churches, the forest of masts in the harbor, the spectacular new City Hall, which was a wonder of seventeenth-century Europe. Instead, he drew the pokey old City Hall—after it had been destroyed by a fire. And while the new one was being constructed, he put the building—which people were making pilgrimages to see go up—literally behind him in order to sketch a bucolic scene in the other direction, of the sleepy old Nieuwezijds Voorburgwal canal. He wandered in the city and the surrounding countryside with his sketchbook, and the results give a retro impression. A lazy windmill against a flat sky. A smudge of trees on a thin horizon. Thatch-roofed farmers' cottages. A cottage hemmed in by a rickety plank fence and towered over by trees. The city looks in his drawings like a medieval village.

Another artist of his time, one far less well known in our day but quite famous in his, was in this respect and others the opposite of Rembrandt. Jan van der Heyden was a teenager living on

Dam Square when the aforementioned fire broke out in the old City Hall, and the sight of it—the wonder and the horror—set him on his career path. He seems to have been struck by the fragility of the city: how quickly civilization can be swallowed up by chaos and destruction. He fashioned himself into the father of modern city services, beginning with firefighting. He invented the leather fire hose and perfected the water pump, making the first genuinely usable fire engine. He founded Amsterdam's fire department, became its fire chief, chronicled eighty city fires over the course of his career in order to perfect methods, and publicized his efforts for the benefit of others in Europe in a book he entitled *A Description of Fire Engines with Water Hoses and the Method of Fighting Fires Now Used in Amsterdam.*

Van der Heyden also invented the streetlamp and created perhaps the world's first assembly line so that unskilled workers could turn out the necessary parts. He and his brother founded a company to produce all of this equipment on a large scale and sold it to the city (to the same department of which he was the head). They outfitted Amsterdam's canals with 2,556 streetlamps and supplied its fire department with seventy fire engines. His designs spread around Europe: in France and Germany, the Van der Heyden fire engine remained the template until machine power began to take over in the late 1800s.

In addition to all of this, Van der Heyden was an artist. If you were to put his paintings of Amsterdam side by side with Rembrandt's, you would swear they depicted different cities in different eras. Van der Heyden—who has sometimes been called the Dutch Leonardo da Vinci—was interested in the practical functioning of a modern metropolis. As an inventor, he fussed over the optimal distance between lamp posts and worked out the ideal mix of oils to burn in the lamps. In his paintings, he gave precise renderings of what was new and grand: the canals and bridges of the new district and, seemingly most meaningful to him, the new City Hall, a temple to the people of Amsterdam that had arisen from the ashes of the fire that had dictated his life's course, its facade gleaming imperially in the sunlight. This painting was bought by Cosimo III de' Medici, the last Grand Duke of Tuscany, when he visited Amsterdam. Cosimo acquired Van der Heyden's regal image of City Hall as a souvenir of a futuristic city that impressed him as it did other golden age tourists.

There are almost never people in the cityscapes of Van der Heyden, a fact that precisely sets off the two sides of liberalism that he and Rembrandt evoke. The liberal passion that burned in Van der Heyden's breast was in the service of the kind of external structure that might provide a habitat in which personal freedoms could flourish. In a word: civilization. Ensuring that people could walk down a street in the evening without fear of getting clubbed in the darkness was the sort of thing that excited Jan van der Heyden. His artistic longing, if we can call it that, was to craft a city that would provide services and protections that would allow individuals to find a space opening within themselves, a space in which to explore who they were, to question their being and their place in the world. That internal space is of course where Rembrandt lived in his deepest self. Surely this is the reason he showed no interest in the outward growth of the new Amsterdam.

There is, however, a conjunction between the liberalisms of Rembrandt and Van der Heyden, a place where outer and inner personal spaces come together. Consider the archetypal monuments of certain cities, the buildings that seem to give clues to their souls. Think of the association of Paris with Notre Dame Cathedral or the Eiffel Tower, of London with Big Ben, of New York with the Empire State Building. Amsterdam, at first blush, has no such monument. The thirteen million people a year who visit the city are not in a rush to see the Royal Palace on Dam Square (which is what the seventeenth-century City Hall became when Napoleon Bonaparte took over and installed his brother Louis Napoleon as "King of Holland" in 1806). And the city's modest churches, most of which could fit inside Notre Dame, hardly have crowd-control issues.

People come to Amsterdam to see hundreds of far less extravagant buildings that line its canals: individual homes. These are also
works of art, but modest ones. Each is made of brick and traditionally topped by a decorative gable, which covers the roof line. The
changing fashions of passing decades of the seventeenth century
remain enshrined in the array of gables that confront you as you
walk down a street: step gable, spout gable, bell gable . . . Above the
door a gable stone might be set into the brickwork; this personalized
the house with a carving, say, of barrels, which said in effect, "Here
lives a cooper," or one of sheep that announced a wool merchant, or,
as a general statement of piety within, a picture of Adam and Eve or
the Flight from Egypt. Typically a canal house is reached via a small
platform between a porch and a step: a stoop (the word comes from
the Dutch *stoep*).

Each of these canal houses is an exquisite memorial to something so elemental to who we are that its significance might easily
escape notice. For each of Amsterdam's canal houses was built to
hold a family. Each represents what matters most to us. The idea
of family was not born in the seventeenth century, but the concept
of home as a personal, private, intimate space may have been. The
writer Witold Rybczynski, in his fine little book *Home: A Short History of an Idea*, traces the idea of the home as a vessel in which
our subjective selves can both rest and flourish to the kind of society that the seventeenth-century Dutch developed. That society
was not formed, as others in Europe were, by feudalism: by kings
and courts. Where elsewhere there were big cities and countryside,
the Dutch landscape was notable for being dotted with towns. The
Dutch were urban. They were also, going back into the Middle Ages
(and also having no doubt to do with the climate and conditions
in which they lived), modest, thrifty, careful, and rather obsessed
with household cleanliness: mopping floors and polishing silver and
scrubbing stoops.

The influx of wealth and the explosion of new ideas that came in the seventeenth century did not wipe out these traits but rather solidified them. The "modern" canal house of the seventeenth century was meant, first of all, for everybody. The egalitarian nature of Dutch society translated into a sense that, while a richer person's surroundings might be somewhat fancier than someone else's, out-and-out opulence was in bad taste. A Nicolaes Tulp or a Rembrandt at his height might opt for a double-sized canal house, but compared with their counterparts in Paris or London, wealthy Amsterdammers lived modestly. They had few servants, and relations between servants and their employers didn't follow the lines of the class system in place elsewhere. Rich people from other parts of Europe expressed amazement to see, for example, that in the canal house of a wealthy Amsterdammer the servant ate meals with the family.

Where in other European capitals through the Middle Ages buildings were large, often taking up a city block, with a common courtyard, and housed extended families along with servants and tenants, the Dutch kept things more intimate. Even wealthy households were small: the house contained the family and maybe one or two servants. This, as Rybczynski argues, led the Dutch to pioneer, in their canal-side dwellings, a new concept, that of the home as consisting of a man, a woman, and their children.

Another innovation followed from this. Elsewhere the border between public and private space was vague, partly because many people who were not related to one another often lived in the same house. Canal houses in Amsterdam would typically have a workshop just below street level and a room for receiving customers above this; the common courtesy was to remove your shoes not on entering these rooms but on going upstairs, into the area above the public space. Rybczynski argues that this taking off of shoes defined a border between public and private. The upstairs, where the bedrooms were, became, perhaps for the first time, *home*. Here was the intimacy of the hearth, the tiny bedroom with beds tucked snugly into closetlike corners, chairs that had some element of comfort to them. Here were fresh-cut flowers in vases and, of course, paintings on the walls. Here was *gezelligheid*, the untranslatable Dutch word that means something beyond coziness.

This, I think, is what attracts those thirteen million visitors to Amsterdam. A word you hear from tourists wandering the canal zone is *charm*. It's so charming. The last time I was in Paris I found myself subconsciously comparing it with my adopted city. There is no doubt that Paris wins the grandiosity contest; but at the same time that grandiosity—the high-walled temples of stone that populate nearly every part of the city, each lined with life-sized figures of French heroes, men of stone gesturing importantly to no one at all— feels a little silly. It certainly feels of another time, a time when the church or the state would mount these grand physical statements as emanations of its power. Paris's grandiosity is to Amsterdam's canal house cityscape what mythological figures are to ordinary people. Amsterdam relates to who we are today: it is, in a sense, where we began, we as modern people who consider individual human beings to be more important than institutions. These sleepy canal-side streets, with boats moored on one side and gabled brick houses on the other: this is the cradle of our focus on ourselves. It can't help but seem charming to us.

Maybe it's not surprising then that many of the city's museums are in canal houses and were once homes. There is Rembrandt's former house and that of the impressionist painter Willem Witsen. The Canal House Museum is in a building on the Herengracht that was in the eighteenth century the home of a banker named Jan Willink, before whom John Adams, emissary of his nascent government, appeared in an attempt to secure a loan to keep the American Revolution going. The Anne Frank House—where she and others were in hiding during the Nazi occupation—represents a different sort of living experience.

There was another Amsterdam house I had long wanted to see inside, but it involves some extra complication, since the family that has been associated with its interior since the seventeenth century still lives there. After a chance meeting and a bit of cajoling, I pulled my bicycle up one afternoon in front of a monumental structure along the Amstel River and found my new acquaintance—a man named Jan Pieter Six—waiting for me. He was in his early sixties, florid of face, with a tight mass of gray hair, round horn-rimmed glasses, and a *lintje*—a small ribbon signifying his having received a Dutch knighthood—pinned to the lapel of his immaculate suit. We stepped through the street-level doorway of the house and, as they say, into another world. This was traditionally the servants' entrance: delftware tiles—blue-and-white renderings of birds and cityscapes, dating to the seventeenth century—lined the walls of the hall and the kitchen, which lacked only an open hearth to signal its golden age heritage.

Here we met Jan Six's cousin, also in his sixties, an equally distinguished-looking man, though more casually dressed, as he was after all in the comfort of his home. His name, improbably enough, was also Jan Six. His father, the previous occupant of the house, was Jan Six. His eldest son, who was not home at present but whom I would meet later, is named Jan Six.

The arresting and arrestingly repeated name was the reason I had come to this fifty-six-room semipalace. Besides being a private abode, it is, and has been since 1915, the home of the Six Collection, arguably the world's grandest collection of art in a private house. The collection, which was begun in the 1600s, had, by the turn of the twentieth century, reached a staggering enough degree of grandeur that its caretaker, Jan Six, great-grandfather of the man in whose kitchen I shared a typical Dutch lunch of brown bread, cheese, and milk, sought out the Dutch government for help in managing it. The result, which has been squabbled over ever since, becoming at times a matter of debate in the national parliament, is an arrangement whereby the collection is in the hands of a private foundation that is owned by the family, which has a legal contract with the Dutch state whereby the government provides a subsidy to maintain the collection and the family promises not to sell anything and to open the house to the public on a limited basis (as of this writing on weekday mornings between ten and noon). Thus a tour group might find a family member in pajamas stealing around a corner. The fuss over the arrangement continues to the present. Over our lunch, Jan Six held forth with some vim for the benefit of his cousin Jan Six about a government minister's recent call that care of the house should be taken once and for all out of the hands of the family, on the grounds that they were not in a position to professionally oversee it. "Haven't we been doing a pretty good job of keeping things for four hundred years?" he said.

The Six Collection was once even grander: at one point it contained two of Vermeer's most famous paintings (*The Milkmaid* and *The Little Street*). The existing collection still overwhelms you. There is a Frans Hals. There is a Bruegel. There is a letter from George Washington to a Six. In one room you find a nineteenth-century diadem of pearls in a case and, above it, on the wall, a portrait of one of the Six wives—Lucretia Johanna van Winter, who sat in 1825 for the French artist Alexandre-Jean Dubois Drahonet—in which she is wearing the same diadem. A red ceremonial sash worn by the mayors of Amsterdam in the seventeenth century has been valued at more than $300,000; it sits nearly lost in the background of a display case chock full of silver, jewelry, seventeenth-century drinking glasses, and miniature paintings.

As wondrous as the collection itself is, I particularly wanted to see the drawing room of the house, which gives a glimpse of a moneyed existence in golden age Amsterdam: of what *home* would have felt like. It turns out to feel surprisingly comfortable. Wealth meant formality, but the vast chairs, covered in thick floral tapestries, are gracious and inviting. You can rest in them. The walls are cased in gold-colored wallpaper, which fairly strokes you with its emanations of opulence. The room speaks to you. The world is harsh and almost unremittingly cruel, it says, but here you may pause and be well and content.

The room spoke these things to one man in particular. He came from a family of cloth dyers but used a smart marriage and political connections to lift himself to the level of a society maven. The marriage was to the daughter of Nicolaes Tulp. And as a tastemaker of Amsterdam's golden age, he became the patron of the city's greatest painter, Rembrandt van Rijn. His name, of course, was Jan Six.

Before their falling out (following the pattern that dogged his career), Rembrandt drew his friend Six, and etched him, and, most famously, painted him. The portrait of the original Jan Six, the undisputed highlight of the collection, is actually slightly visible from the sidewalk outside the house, if you crane your neck and shield your eyes from the daylight glare. It hangs in the first-floor parlor. Under the latest agreement with the national government, the Rijksmuseum has the right to move it seasonally to its more public space. Otherwise, this picture that has been called the greatest portrait of the seventeenth century lives with the family.

The canvas shows a man in middle age, wealthy, dressing to go out. He is nearly ready. He wears an immaculate gray cloak with an orange coat draped over a shoulder; he has one glove on. The greatness, art critics say, is most clearly expressed in the hands. The gloved hand is almost a cartoon, patently a painted hand, a mock-up. The other also is composed of a few quick strokes, yet it is somehow living human flesh, pink-white, with blood beating in blue veins. It shocks with its daring to seem to be alive. Similarly, the gray cloak is perfect but the orange coat is roughly done, its buttonholes just dabs, slurs of paint; it has been said that one can see Rembrandt's fingerprint in one of these, an indication that he actually rubbed the paint onto the canvas. This image is not real, and of course you know perfectly well that it's not real, those slurs of paint say. But again with the face, you cannot but let yourself be tricked. It is an actual human's face: pale skin, mottled with age and cares and living, the eyes not meeting yours but staring into a middle distance, as if the evening's destination is not of interest to the man depicted—this man of prominence whose life is so much a part of Amsterdam's golden age—but something else on his mind is taking precedence. It's this interplay between realism and obvious plasticity that makes this, perhaps, the first modern painting. The artist both wants you to believe in the illusion and at the same time insists on breaking the illusion, on the grounds that maintaining the illusion throughout would be the ultimate falsehood: which you might say is the definition of the modern in art.

Later, I met Jan Six XI, son of the current master of the Six Collection, who is himself a dealer in Dutch seventeenth-century painting. He told me that he and his father are engaged in an ongoing battle about Rembrandt's portrait of their ancestor, as well as that of the original Jan Six's mother, on the opposite wall. The dispute is not about money or public access. It is about frames. The paintings are encased in gilt frames that were made for them in the nineteenth century and, Six the Tenth maintains, suit the period of the room. Six the Eleventh says that seventeenth-century taste would only have stood for black lacquer and that the family has a duty to return the paintings to the sort of stately, sober frames that Rembrandt intended for them.

The grandeur of the Six mansion is a far cry from the typical Amsterdam canal house. I had already long before gotten an excellent sense of that. The first year I spent in Amsterdam, I lived with my then wife and our two daughters in a solid example of one of these simple, ur-modern homes, on the Reguliersgracht, one of the canals that extend radially from the central canal ring. Many writers have remarked on the similarity between canal houses and ships and have related the development of the one to the other. The Dutch were a seagoing people, and these homes jut upward like seventeenth-century sailing vessels. They comprise a warren of tiny rooms, linked by corkscrew staircases and narrow passages. Such was the house we lived in. The staircase even had, in place of a handrail, a rope that you clung to.

The house was built around 1680, or at the very end of the period in which the great canal ring was constructed. Maps from a year or so earlier show three vacant lots, side by side, along the canal. The lots were bought by a little DIY real estate consortium consisting of a stonemason, a carpenter, and a diamond cutter. They built the three houses almost identically, and each man, with his family, took one. Mine was the home of the diamond cutter. The front room, looking out onto the canal, was probably his workshop and office. I took it in turn as my office and wrote a book there.

Thanks to the shifting of the wooden piles in the foundation over the centuries, the floor of the living room listed so severely that my daughter Eva, who was eight at the time, found it spectacular that she could not set a ball in the middle without its rolling sharply to one wall. When of an evening you looked out the tiny window in the attic, which was my daughter Anna's bedroom, you almost couldn't help but imagine yourself a citizen of late seventeenth-century Amsterdam: a person of no great importance, perhaps, but one who could feel lucky and content, able to make your own way in the world, with your belly full and your head singing softly with beer, and the light from Jan van der Heyden's streetlamps playing on the surface of a canal that brought the wide world to the doorstep of your own private home.

"THE RARE HAPPINESS
OF LIVING IN A REPUBLIC"

It may have been in the aftermath of the Roman destruction of Jerusalem's Second Temple in the second century AD that Jews first settled in what in Latin was called Hispania and Greek geographers referred to as Iberia: the peninsula that became Spain and Portugal. Then again, some traditions date it to half a millennium earlier. Whatever the origins, over many centuries the Iberian Jews developed a culture that was distinct from that of Jews elsewhere, inflected by Arabic, Spanish, and Portuguese flavors. Under successive rulers and ruling faiths—Visigoths and Moors, Muslims and Christians—they endured a panoply of persecutions, but somehow they flourished and produced their own golden age. One result of this period was a rich tradition of searching for meaning, which took religious, philosophical, and mystical directions. Life began to change for the worse in the 1300s, when the Catholic Church in Spain launched a policy of forced conversions. Many *conversos* truly did convert, and they and their descendants became Catholics. Others—called Marranos or Crypto-Jews—lived a lie, practicing one faith in secret and another for show. Then in 1492, with the defeat of the last Muslims on the peninsula, first Spain and then Portugal dealt with their remaining internal "enemy" by simply ejecting the Jews. A new diaspora began, with more than 100,000 people wandering the earth in search of homes. Sepharad is what Jews in late antiquity called the Iberian peninsula, and the roving descendants of those who had settled in Spain and Portugal became known as Sephardim.

The Dutch Republic, in the midst of its eight-decade war of independence against Spain, became a haven for Sephardic Jews. Amsterdam provided a welcome—of sorts. Just as it had done with various Protestant sects in the early 1500s, and as it would do with Catholics after Catholicism was booted out as the city's official faith, Amsterdam at first allowed Jewish families to settle provided they didn't worship openly. In 1615, however, the States General gave official Dutch sanction to the Jewish religion, and four years later Amsterdam's Jews were allowed to practice their faith in the open. Crypto-Jews threw away their crucifixes and rosaries and began to be themselves again. Meanwhile, more and more Sephardic Jews— many of whom were traders—poured into the city, attracted by its relative tolerance and free-trading spirit. The neighborhood where the Sephardim settled looked and felt like the former Jewish quarter in Lisbon. Cumin and turmeric scented the air. Children on the streets hollered to one another in Portuguese. There were syna-gogues, and the Jewish schools, where children studied Hebrew and the Torah, were considered the best in Europe. Businesses prospered; families grew.

Miguel d'Espinoza was the head of one of these families. Apply-ing his connections in Spain and Portugal to Amsterdam's shipping network, he built up a trading company that imported raisins, olive oil, and other Mediterranean products. With his second wife, Ana Deborah, he had three children. Their first was a daughter whom they named Miriam. Then came a son, Isaac, who died as a teenager. Their third child, who like his brother and sister was probably born at the family home in Amsterdam's Jewish quarter, became one of the world's greatest philosophers.

Over time his first name evolved from Portuguese (Bento) to Hebrew (Baruch) to Christian European (Benedict). History trimmed D'Espinoza to Spinoza. He was the first true philosopher of modernity, the first to argue systematically that religion and politics should be pulled apart (an idea that was pretty much viewed as insanity at the time), and an early advocate of democracy, though he later retreated from insisting that democracy was the only acceptable form of government in much the same way that some political thinkers in our day have. He anticipated the movement to separate superstition from faith in the Bible by looking at it as a historical document, and he argued that religion should keep its nose out of scientific inquiry. His take on one of philosophy's thorniest problems— that of the relationship between mind and brain—matches up with much of what scientists today have deduced from empirical study. Bertrand Russell called Spinoza "the noblest and most lovable of the great philosophers." In his time, and for a century after, he was one of the most hated. His has been called "a free man's philosophy." He was the first and maybe the greatest philosopher of liberalism, who made it his life's work to comprehend what "freedom" means and how individuals can be free.

Spinoza did all of this precisely because he was born in Amsterdam: because he was born into a transplanted Sephardic Jewish community trying to establish itself in a place where the forces of liberalism—individual freedom in its various guises—were rooting themselves. He took in the events of his time, the history and deeds of the city where he was born, and distilled that experience into a philosophy. Thus condensed and packaged, it became part of the genetic code of the modern centuries: it helped make them modern.

Spinoza was born in 1632, at the same time that Rembrandt was moving from Leiden to Amsterdam, into the academy of his patron Van Uylenburgh, right on the other side of the block of houses that comprised the main part of the Jewish quarter. It was the heart of the Dutch golden age, but Spinoza grew up in the protective cocoon of Portuguese Jewry. He went to a Jewish school a few doors from his house, next to the synagogue, where he studied Hebrew, the Talmud, and laws pertaining to Jewish observance. His first step outside

that world came after his older brother died when Spinoza was seventeen, followed soon after by his father. The boy was forced to leave
school to help run the family business alongside another brother.
The new name of the import firm—Bento y Gabriel D'Espinoza—
adds a dimension to his biography that is not often taken into con-
sideration. Among other factors influencing Spinoza's development,
he was also a businessman operating in the teeming, liberal, free-
trading city that had invented some of the basic elements of capitalism.

While trying to conduct business in and around Amsterdam's
harbor and between the columns of the stock exchange building,
Spinoza picked up currents of what was happening in the city. He
had a world-class mind and was used to soaking up information in
many languages (Portuguese at home, Spanish at school, Hebrew for
reading the Torah, and Dutch on the streets), and in his late teens
he began to reach beyond the boundaries of the Jewish community
in seeking to understand the world.

There was a lot to understand. In 1648, momentous news reached
Amsterdam. Marathon negotiations, conducted jointly in the cities
of Münster and Osnabrück, had resulted in twin peace treaties. The
warfare that had engulfed most of Europe for decades was over. The
Thirty Years' War, which had started out as a Catholic-Protestant
conflict but evolved in many directions, and the Eighty Years' War,
between the Spanish empire and the Dutch Republic, were at an
end. For the first time in living memory, Europe was at peace. Some
said it was the final peace: that the treaties were so momentous they
would make war itself a thing of the past. For the Dutch, it meant
the conclusion of the struggle that had begun in their grandparents'
or great-grandparents' time, when Philip II, the ardently Catholic
Spanish king, brought his armies and the Inquisition raining down
on the Dutch provinces. Although the Dutch nation was long since
a de facto truth, now it was proclaimed by official decree.

Amsterdam had played an instrumental role in the treaties, with
Adriaen Pauw, the son of one of the original founders of the VOC,

acting as a chief negotiator. The city reacted to the news by throwing parties. The mayors held a celebration on Dam Square featuring tableaux vivants: live human beings posing in scenes from the long struggle. The civic guards hosted sprawling banquets that everyone got staggeringly drunk at and that naturally had to be captured in group portraits. The city struck a commemorative coin declaiming in Latin that "one peace is worth more than countless victories." The wars to end all wars were over.

Less than two years later, the city was plunged headlong into a new crisis. The end of the war with Spain brought to the fore tensions between two Dutch parties that were vying for control. One thought the government should be centralized around the figure of Willem II, Prince of Orange, whose grandfather of the same name and title had led the Dutch charge against Spain. The other party supported a republican form of government in which power was held by the individual provinces. With the Spanish conflict at an end the republicans immediately called for troops to return to their homes. Holland—the biggest and most powerful of the provinces—led the way, largely out of self-interest: because it had the most money, it had to contribute the most to maintain an army. Amsterdam, the province's richest city, became the center of republicanism.

Willem, who was twenty-two years old and pumped up with monarchic ideas, took the call to disband the army as a direct attack on his power, since he was in effect the general of the Dutch troops. He had tried to block the peace treaty, which he believed (rightly) would embolden republican forces among the Dutch. He had also maneuvered with the English to try to preserve their monarchy (Charles I, who was Willem's father-in-law, had recently been deposed by Oliver Cromwell and was about to be beheaded), and with the French. Willem responded to the obstinance of the Hollanders with a rush of brute force that took the whole country by surprise: he had soldiers arrest six members of the provincial assembly and sent his cousin at the head of an army of ten thousand troops to invade Amsterdam. The House of Orange, which had once represented Dutch freedom and resistance to monarchy, now for many embodied something like the opposite.

In a flash, a civil war seemed imminent. At dawn, Amsterdammers swarmed onto the city fortifications to gaze at the sight of phalanxes of soldiers marching toward them. It had happened so suddenly that many people didn't even know who was threatening them. Rumors flew about marauding intentions. "The women mixed their laments with screeches," ran a news account. "The weakest of them feared for their bodies and their property and bewailed their misfortune that in the middle of the peace and in a city that was in the middle of the country they were unprotected from the will of soldiers."

As it happened, the prince's army had arrived late, due to bad weather, giving the city's leaders time to muster every able man. Instead of an assault came negotiations. The attack fizzled, and shortly thereafter Willem died from what was apparently smallpox.

Spinoza was eighteen; he may well have stood on the fortifications with his fellow townspeople to watch the business of choosing a form of government take this dramatic turn. Around this time he was doing a lot of reading and thinking about such matters: about politics, society, human nature. Was there such a thing as a right form of government? What was a government's responsibility to its people? What constituted moral behavior?

A seeming breakthrough in answering such questions had been achieved by René Descartes, the Frenchman who had spent most of his career in the Dutch Republic. Despite the revolutionary character of his philosophy, Descartes cowered in the face of authority and had tried to sidestep awkward issues such as the fact that his work seemed to undercut both biblical and monarchic authority. But the political implications of his philosophy were impossible to ignore for long. Spinoza never met Descartes, who had recently left the Dutch Republic for Sweden, where he was to die an untimely death, but Descartes had left behind a swirling controversy that had engulfed the country's intellectual circles. Descartes had absorbed all the new thinking and scientific study going on in Europe—from Harvey's discovery of the circulatory system to Galileo's astronomical observations—and provided what he and his followers heralded as a new framework for understanding these findings: a theory of knowledge based not on the received wisdom of the Bible and ancient authorities but on the human mind and its "good sense," as he put it. It was a system, in other words, based on reason. Not only that, but Descartes offered a "method for rightly conducting the reason." He proposed that Europeans scrap their whole educational system and start over, letting reason be the sole tool for determining truth in every human endeavor. Descartes's method opened the door to empirical scientific thinking, and it had implications for virtually every other field. If the human mind was the true basis for understanding, did it not follow that the central point of all endeavors should be the individual human being? Was not each person, no matter his or her status, of equal value and importance to every other? And did that not compel one to favor a form of government based not on theological power or hereditary ascendancy but on the say of every citizen?

Descartes's ideas—the first stirrings of what would be called the Enlightenment—would soon sweep across Europe. But the first place they made an impact was in the Dutch provinces, where the Frenchman had lived and published. Preachers and orthodox university professors accused him of being a radical, a revolutionary, and, most damning of all, an atheist. Meanwhile, the very things that incited such fury also attracted many intellectuals to his work.

In order to appreciate what the fuss was about, Spinoza needed to be able to read Latin. He signed up as a student in a Latin school on the Singel, the innermost of the city's concentric canals. The school's head, Franciscus van den Enden, turned out to be a Cartesian radical who promoted something called "democracy" and had as his dream to found a colony in North America that would be based on the principles that flowed from what Descartes had started.

In Van den Enden's utopia, every inhabitant would be equal to all others in every respect.

From Van den Enden Spinoza got more than language training. The older man was a true mentor in radical ideas, and Spinoza became a disciple. Van den Enden had emigrated from Antwerp, perhaps seeing Amsterdam as a freer place in which to peddle his beliefs. His school became a meeting place for young men—some of them, like Spinoza, the sons of merchants—who had been raised in a city that was the epicenter of trade and ideas. Many in this younger generation were not content simply to build on the fortunes their fathers had made. They had a bit of comfort in their lives; they were used to freedom, and they wanted to use it to push for answers. Van den Enden would later move on to Paris, where he would found a similar salon, mastermind a plot to overthrow Louis XIV, and be hanged for his efforts. His importance to history, however, would be via one of his Amsterdam students. His fame comes from the fact that he is the man who introduced Spinoza to the new world of philosophy that Descartes had launched.

Spinoza's time line is sketchy. We know he entered Van den Enden's academy in the mid-1650s. And we also know that around the same time he became interested in the ideas of one of the many sects that had sprung up in this newly dawning age of discontent. Put together the names of the more obscure sects and it sounds like a lineup at a folk festival: the Tremblers, the Enthusiasts, the Seekers, the Levellers. More well known today are the Quakers. What united all of these groups was a quest for truth and justice outside the established religious institutions and the existing economic system. A Dutch offshoot of the Mennonites was the Collegiants, and it was to this group in particular that Spinoza was drawn. The Collegiants were pacifists who believed in retreating from society; they formed communes and shared property. Many of their ideas would make their way into Spinoza's works.

Spinoza may have gotten his introduction to the Collegiants

through a man named Jan Rieuwertszoon, who ran a bookstore and publishing company out of his house in one of the narrow streets near the harbor. Rieuwertszoon was entranced by the new thinking that was pulsing through Europe, and he managed to make his little house into an important center for it. He published the works of Descartes in Dutch and sold them in his shop. He held salons where like-minded seekers and thinkers could gather and exchange ideas. In time he would publish all of Spinoza's works.

Somewhere in this period Spinoza made a conscious turn: he chose philosophy as his life's work. He formally relinquished his role in the family business and decided to take up Descartes's challenge to orient one's life around reason. Many young people make dramatic pronouncements about their life's path; few follow through. Spinoza did indeed spend the rest of his life working out a philosophy that tied together everything from God to politics to the nature of matter and thought, and he based it on a cold, scientific calculus. The irony is that while his philosophy appears so chilly on the page—broken down as it is into postulates, propositions, proofs, and corollaries— its ultimate concern is the warmest of things: the individual human being and his or her possibilities.

As he consorted at Van den Enden's academy amid the swirl of national politics, the young Amsterdam Jew found he had reasoned opinions about the circumstances that were in front of him. High-handed monarchs, he saw, were an abhorrence and an anachronism. He was proud of his city, both in its readiness to confront Willem of Orange and in its overall character, which he reduced to a single concept: its promotion of individual freedom. It was a city, he declared proudly and loudly, in which "religion and sect is considered of no importance."

The leaders of Spinoza's religion and sect, though, considered these things to be of great importance. There is certainty about one date in his life. On July 27, 1656, in the synagogue just steps from his family home, before a packed gathering of friends and neighbors, people among whom he had grown up, the rabbis of the Jewish community in Amsterdam took the drastic step of excommunicating him. Referring to the "evil opinions and acts" of the twenty-three-year-old, the rabbi who read aloud the proclamation declared that

> by decree of the angels and by the command of the holy men, we excommunicate, expel, curse and damn Baruch de Espinoza, with the consent of God, Blessed be He, and with the consent of the entire holy congregation, and in front of these holy scrolls with their 613 precepts which are written therein; cursing him with the excommunication with which Joshua banned Jericho and with the curse which Elisha cursed the boys and with all the castigations that are written in the Book of the Law. Cursed be he by day and cursed be he by night; cursed be he when he lies down and cursed be he when he rises up. Cursed be he when he goes out and cursed be he when he comes in.

Since we know none of the exact circumstances leading up to this event, it has long been a pastime among Spinoza scholars to try to figure out the "real" reason for his excommunication (or *herem*, the Hebrew term for banishment from the Jewish community). Maybe the point most worth noting is that there were so many reasons to choose from. In the small, tightly controlled world of Amsterdam Jewry, which had seen itself all but snuffed out in Sepharad and in which everyone was thus vividly aware of how precarious their existence was, obedience was expected, and stepping far over the line of accepted speech and behavior was unheard of. Spinoza trampled on the line, jumped across it, and mocked it.

In the main, Spinoza scholars have seen the excommunication as motivated by either theology or economics. Over the course of his life Spinoza provided plenty of material to support the theological argument. He skewered Jewish laws and practices as viciously as a stand-up comic might today—starting with the cherished notion that the Jews were "the chosen people." "In regard to intellect and true virtue," he wrote dismissively, "every nation is on a par with the rest, and God has not in these respects chosen one people rather than another." The idea that angels appeared to holy people in the Bible was, he said, "mere nonsense," and the elaborate elucidation of such superstitious beliefs in Jewish writing was "the acme of absurdity." Regarding Kabbalists—followers of Jewish mysticism, who included one of the rabbis who excommunicated him—Spinoza said that their "insanity provokes my unceasing astonishment." Organized religion overall received his most withering criticism. The paraphernalia of religion—holy books, incense, rules, circumcision, holy days, prescribed prayers—were just man-made trappings that existed only so that institutions could exercise control.

The brand of faith that Spinoza espoused would also have provided rich cause for excommunication. He believed it was wrong to think of God as the creator and the world as His creation. That sort of conception, Spinoza said, cheapened "God" by forcing the term into anthropomorphic garb. Rather, he held, God is the totality of all that is. Spinoza's use of the term "God or nature" has led some people to think he associated God with the life force—flowers and bees and such—but Spinoza's God is, so to speak, bigger than that. Spinoza's God is the infinity of substance, and substance included all matter and all thought.

Spinoza held that God exists—for Spinoza, God logically *must* exist—but Spinoza's God doesn't think or have pity or watch or feel compassion or answer prayers. Spinoza characterized the essence of spirituality as follows: "Whatever is, is in God, and nothing can either be or be conceived without God." Spinoza's God is without borders, beyond religion. Albert Einstein, on being asked by a rabbi if he believed in God, answered, "I believe in Spinoza's God who reveals himself in the orderly harmony of what exists, not in a God who concerns himself with fates and actions of human beings." That a lot of people might agree with that statement today points to one of the many ways in which Spinoza, at the dawn of the liberal era, set the template. But in the seventeenth century such assertions as

Spinoza made about God and religious practice would have meant excommunication from any congregation, Jewish or Christian.

At the same time, the *herem* against Spinoza could equally have had an underlying economic basis. While he believed in free trade, and was proud of his city for the economic miracle it had wrought, Spinoza had also witnessed some of the dark side of history's first experience with capitalism. As power had accumulated in the East India Company and its sister, the West India Company, those great concerns had strangled small businesses. Spinoza's family business—which fell on hard times—may have been one of the small businesses that were hurt by their practices. The vast trading companies, with their monopolies, routinely manipulated markets to their advantage, forcing ordinary citizens to pay inflated prices for goods. And while society flourished in innumerable ways during the period, the ranks of the poor kept growing: proof that capitalism in and of itself was a pitiless machine that needed to be controlled. The republicans whom Spinoza admired called for an end to the great trading companies, which, they said, had become a danger to society and, to boot, violated the principle of free trade.

The leaders of Amsterdam's Jewish community were conservative and deeply cautious men. They were aware that their people had only recently arrived in the country and that they lived there at the discretion of the Dutch. Yes, there was a policy of religious toleration, but laws could be changed at a moment's notice. From their first days in the provinces, the Jewish elders allied themselves with the conservative faction in Dutch politics, which in turn was closely connected to the big trading companies. Prominent Jews were investors in the VOC. The fact that the orthodox Calvinist faction had pushed through a law requiring VOC board members to be loyal subscribers to the Calvinist faith did not bother the Jewish elders; nor did the staunch Calvinists in the VOC mind that Jews were significant shareholders. In this turbulent era, the orthodox had to stick together. So a young Jew who attacked the VOC was a threat to the well-being of the Jewish community.

While there was ample reason for Jewish leaders to expel Spinoza from their community, it's possible to see also some level of irony in their action. Sephardic tradition, forged under the hot Iberian sun, was unusually open to philosophical inquiry. After Spain and Portugal had ejected the Jews, Amsterdam had opened itself to them and offered a place for that tradition to live again. Spinoza, one might say, simply took up the ancient call to search and question—and was ejected for his efforts just as the Jews had been.

Meanwhile, Spinoza's reaction to the excommunication is at least as interesting as the act itself. He had a right to appeal it, but he did nothing. He seems to have treated it as a relief. "All the better," he was quoted by a contemporary as saying; "they do not force me to do anything that I would not have done of my own accord if I did not dread scandal. But, since they want it that way, I enter gladly on the path that is opened to me." He simply left. He said good-bye not only to the community as a whole but to his family and went off in search of new meaning. What is amazing about his attitude is that the *herem* put him in an almost unique position. Everyone, in the seventeenth century, belonged to a formal faith. Your church or synagogue was not simply a place you visited for services: it was your community; it was a basic part of your identity and your legitimacy in the eyes of society. After his excommunication, Spinoza didn't convert to Christianity or some other faith. As the philosopher Rebecca Newberger Goldstein says, "Instead, Spinoza was to offer something rather new under the seventeenth century's European skies: a religion of reason."

———

The year 1653 may have been for some in the Dutch Republic a bit like 1960 was for many Americans. There had been a great war, and people were anxious now to put both it and the postwar period behind them. There was a sense of something fresh and modern on the wind. And a new, unprecedentedly young leader stepped to the fore. Johan de Witt was a brilliant intellectual—a mathematician as well as a lawyer, who contributed to the development of linear algebra and whose work was admired by Isaac Newton—who was also strikingly attractive and, although the scion of one of the aristocratic Dutch families, an ardent republican. At the age of twenty-eight, he was named grand pensionary of the States of Holland, the closest thing the country had to a prime minister. De Witt took it as his mission to keep the nation on its course of representative government (though it should be noted that De Witt's idea of democracy was limited to the regent class: only they would hold power on provincial councils). As De Witt saw it, the new, enlightened political world would be one in which people who took over from kings and princes would not be "those who spring from their loins" but men chosen by "merits."

Here, many believed, were the fruits of the long war against Spain. The ascent of a leader like De Witt, surely, was what William the Silent had meant by his repeated refrain of "freedom." Spinoza and his fellow republicans were vividly aware of the remarkable experiment their nation was undertaking. Pieter de la Court, a prominent republican with ties to De Witt, wrote what became a best-selling book in which he outlined the benefits of an open, tolerant society. In it he linked Dutch liberalisms in politics, religion, and the economy and contrasted these with the historic situation in neighboring countries: "neither in France nor England was there any liberty of religion, but a monarchical government in both, with high duties on goods imported and exported." Whereas: "freedom or toleration, in and about the service or worship of God, is a powerful means to preserve many inhabitants in Holland, and allure foreigners to dwell amongst us."

Spinoza idolized De Witt, thrilled at the historic opportunity his nation had, and determined to devote his work to furthering the cause of Dutch liberalism. He had moved from Amsterdam to a Collegiant community in the village of Rijnsburg; now he moved to another village, this one on the outskirts of The Hague, so that he could be near the center of power. He would later express his euphoria and his mission in a form that serves to this day as a crystalline expression of the value of tolerance:

> Now seeing that we have the rare happiness of living in a
> republic, where everyone's judgment is free and unshackled,
> where each may worship God as his conscience dictates,
> and where freedom is esteemed beyond all things dear and
> precious, I have believed that I should be undertaking no
> ungrateful or unprofitable task, in demonstrating that not only
> can such freedom be granted without prejudice to the public
> peace, but also, that without such freedom, piety cannot
> flourish nor the public peace be secure.

It was a world in which the word *freedom* was often tied to looseness, laxness, immorality, and neglect and in which religion and religious rules and morality were almost universally seen as necessary to maintain basic order in society. Spinoza gave himself the mission to show that freedom was not a threat to order but rather necessary for public peace as well as for faith.

It was a heady challenge. People were not ready for it. It's tempting to draw parallels with our time. Then as now, society was divided into two basic factions. There were those who felt that the idea of liberalism contained promise for a better world. And there were others, probably the vast majority, for whom the idea of liberalism contained the seeds of destruction for everything they knew.

For a time, though, the republicans were ascendant, and they glowed. De Witt had entered office in a time of war. In the balance of power between England and the Dutch Republic, the Dutch had the larger trading empire while England had more military might. English ships had been harassing Dutch trading and shipping vessels for several years when in 1652 war broke out. The war was ruinous for both sides. For the Dutch, their global shipping network was all but strangled. In Amsterdam, merchants toted up their losses. The herring fleet was decimated; in all, they figured 1,200 Dutch vessels had been taken or destroyed.

Johan De Witt stepped into this quagmire and negotiated a treaty with Oliver Cromwell, the English regicide and revolutionary leader who was in the process of being named lord protector, that was breathtaking in its boldness and cunning. Despite their obvious nationalistic differences, De Witt and Cromwell had a common desire: to keep the House of Orange out of power. As far as Cromwell was concerned, the present Willem of Orange—the son of the Willem who had died following his attempted storming of Amsterdam in 1650, and the latest in the line that stretched back to William the Silent—was a threat, for he was the grandson of Charles I, the man Cromwell had recently ordered decapitated. For De Witt, the same Prince of Orange was even more of a threat: to his government, yes, but also to the very idea of republican government. That the person in question was three years old was a mere detail to both men. Orangist forces within the Dutch provinces were already lined up behind the young Willem III.

The boldness and cunning in the treaty consisted in a so-called secret annex, which was not published with the full treaty. According to it, the Dutch agreed that Willem III would never be named *stadholder*, or hereditary monarch. The secret annex worked because it applied only to the province of Holland. Officially, De Witt was the leader of that province only, and, officially, Willem III would, if nominated for it, become *stadholder* of that province. But, with Amsterdam in the fore, Holland had grown in power to such a point that its leaders dictated the course the nation took. Thus, Holland's republican leader colluded with the English enemy to dupe his opponents in other provinces so as to block the ascendancy of a new hereditary leader in his home province.

In pamphlets and pulpits Orangists around the country raged in protest once the secret provision became known, but the treaty was already signed and De Witt and his forces were, for the time being, unstoppable. With the end of English attacks at sea, fleets of Dutch vessels returned to the waters, and the mighty Dutch trading empire reached new heights. Seemingly everything under the sun now came sailing into the IJ and from there into the canals and warehouses of Amsterdam. The fact that you drink coffee and tea may be indirectly thanks to De Witt's secret annex to the Treaty of Westminster, for it was in the immediate aftermath of the treaty that Dutch coffee and tea imports reached such volumes that those commodities became permanently affixed to the European way of life. The VOC penetrated remotest Burma and extracted everything from tin to elephant tusks. Dutch traders became dominant in India and Ceylon. They began the colony that would evolve into South Africa and set up posts in Persia and Canton. It was during this period that the VOC became the largest and wealthiest company in the history of the world, with, ultimately, fifty thousand people in its service.

All of this wealth benefited Holland more than the other provinces, further strengthening its hand, and De Witt's. And it benefited Amsterdam most of all. The city's per capita income grew to four times that of Paris. Amsterdam completed its expansion, engulfing whole islands in the eastern harbor and building new walls around itself. And the wealth further transformed the city's social fabric, with more and more immigrants pouring in, to the wonder and disdain of many. The English poet Andrew Marvell reflected the envious scorn his countrymen felt toward the near neighbor that had outstripped their nation in economic might by dismissing the very physical being of Holland, which

> scarce deserves the name of Land,
> As but th' Off-scouring of the Brittish Sand.

Marvell singled out Amsterdam and its population of mixed races and religions and ideas for particular derision:

> Sure when Religion did it self imbark,
> And from the east would Westward steer its Ark,

> *It struck, and splitting on this unknown ground,*
> *Each one thence pillag'd the first piece he found:*
> *Hence Amsterdam, Turk-Christian-Pagan-Jew,*
> *Staple of Sects and Mint of Schisme grew;*
> *That Bank of Conscience, where not one so strange*
> *Opinion but finds Credit, and Exchange.*

The redoubling of trade translated as well into cultural advances. We can bundle these advances into one set of statistics. All the arenas of life that burgeoned in the period—physics, medicine, politics, art, industry, finance—reduce, ultimately, to books, for new achievements in every field were eventually transmitted through print. The number of bookshops in Amsterdam at this time has been estimated at a staggering four hundred, and at one point the city had roughly a hundred publishers. One of the most remarkable statistics I have ever encountered is the estimate by H. de la Fontaine Verwey (who then held the chair in "the science of the book" at the University of Amsterdam) that in the seventeenth century one-half of all books published *in the entire world* were published in the Dutch provinces. Factoring in another estimate would mean that about 30 percent of the world's published books in the seventeenth century came out of Amsterdam.

De Witt's opposition, meanwhile, was down but not out. It consisted of two factions: the Orangists, who believed (as did nearly all Europeans) that a country needed a monarch as its leader and figurehead, and the orthodox Calvinists, who believed (as did nearly all Europeans) that a country's government needed a biblical foundation. The Orangists got a boost from England in 1660 when, following Oliver Cromwell's death, Charles II (who had been sheltered for a time by the House of Orange in The Hague) was restored to the throne of England. Orangists were now able to turn back republican arguments that there was a movement toward democracy sweeping Europe and to claim instead that the flawed English experiment of government without a monarch had come to its inevitable end. Propagandists staged a play about William the Silent to remind everyone that the House of Orange had led the way in the war against Spain.

De Witt was undeterred. A second trade war erupted with England, and under De Witt's order Michiel de Ruyter, the great Dutch admiral, sailed up the Thames, into the Medway, and destroyed the heart of the English navy, in what has been called the worst defeat in English naval history. The attack brought a quick end to the war at terms that were favorable to the Dutch.

It was in this moment of world-historic growth, and amid consistent attacks from the Orangist/Calvinist party against the Dutch republicans, that Spinoza put aside the great, deep, and arcane work of philosophy he was embarked on (his *Ethics*) in order to write a frankly political book. His decision to title it *Tractatus Theologico-Politicus* somewhat obscures the fact that he intended it for a broad audience. While he called the book a "theological-political treatise," its real purpose was to separate theology from politics. The basis of politics, he declared, in what was truly a first in history, should be individual liberty. And, he went on, "democracy is of all forms of government the most natural and most consonant with individual liberty."

There it is: the basis of modern, Western, liberal society, expressed in sharp, declarative print. And where would Spinoza look to find a model for such a society and to use as proof that ensuring individual liberty actually brings gains to society? Not far. "The city of Amsterdam reaps the fruit of this freedom in its own great prosperity and in the admiration of all other people," he wrote. "For in this most flourishing state, and most splendid city, men of every nation and religion live together in the greatest harmony, and ask no questions before trusting their goods to a fellow-citizen, save whether he be rich or poor, and whether he generally acts honestly, or the reverse."

The book came out in early 1670 and circulated rapidly. And there for the first time people read, in black and white, someone arguing that the Bible was the work of human beings, that it contained errors, that it was packed with superstitions, that its purported miracles were nonsense since intelligent modern men and women knew that the laws of nature were inviolable, and that government should be founded not according to religious ideas (for "laws dealing with religion and seeking to settle its controversies are much more calculated to irritate than to reform") but rather on rational, scientific, secular principles.

"Reviews" came quickly. A spontaneous chorus of reactions rang from every level of church body in the Netherlands about the book and its contents: "blasphemous," "dangerous," "monstrosities," "obscenities." The provincial synod of South Holland used language that a publicist today might cherish for the attention it was sure to bring, calling it "as obscene and blasphemous a book as, to our knowledge, the world has ever seen." It might possibly have brought a wry smile to Spinoza that the response to his book arguing that religion and politics should be kept apart included religious authorities complaining to political authorities, political authorities agreeing with religious authorities and encouraging the States General to ban it, and political authorities calling the book (as the court of Holland did) "soul-corrupting."

It wasn't only church authorities that attacked the book. Gottfried Wilhelm Leibniz, the great German philosopher (who is often paired with Spinoza in undergraduate philosophy syllabi today), was appalled by its "astounding critique of Sacred Scripture." Even Dutch republicans, whose side in the political struggle Spinoza hoped to support with his critique, condemned the book. In 1674 the States General banned the Tractatus in the Dutch Republic.

Spinoza knew the book would be hot, which was why the title page not only did not include his name but gave a bogus publisher and even lied about the place of publication ("Hamburg") in order to deflect some of the rage. It took a few months, but word leaked out that the excommunicated Jew of Amsterdam had written what was perceived as an attack on all religion and on the foundation of every government in Europe.

Spinoza was stunned by the response. He had been naive enough to think that a nice little controversy roiled by this "popular" book might pave the way for his *Ethics*, which he intended as the complete statement of his philosophy. He quickly realized the storm surrounding the *Tractatus* had the opposite effect: his *Ethics* was published only after his death. Perhaps the bitterest moment for him came when Johan de Witt, his leader and hero, joined in the condemnation of his book.

In fact, even if De Witt had believed all the arguments of the *Tractatus* (which is doubtful: De Witt was a republican but not truly a democrat) it would have been political suicide to support the book. In a classic instance of political distancing, De Witt even refused to meet with Spinoza, lest such a meeting be used by his enemies. But De Witt's enemies still tried to link him to the book. One referred to the *Tractatus* as a book "forged in hell by the apostate Jew working together with the devil" and said (inaccurately) that it had been published "with the knowledge and complicity" of De Witt.

Spinoza may have hoped the *Tractatus* would help the grand pensionary, but it did the reverse. De Witt's time was at an end. Years of skillful diplomacy in the European theater—in which he had manipulated numerous heads of state—combined with the massive profits Dutch companies had garnered, had led to the buildup of black clouds of resentment abroad. They erupted in 1672, and the ensuing storm marked the end of the Dutch golden age.

As if in monarchic reaction to the boisterous republicanism that had flourished under De Witt, two of history's most exuberantly aristocratic kings—Charles II of England and Louis XIV of France—attacked the little Dutch Republic simultaneously. The causes of the twin wars were numerous, and included money, but among Charles's interests was seeing his nephew Willem of Orange put on a Dutch throne. De Witt was caught with his guard down. He had kept the

Dutch army weak, out of fear that Orangists would use it to install Willem as *stadholder*. Now foreign armies invaded on two fronts, and Dutch towns were all but defenseless. A combined Anglo-French fleet, led by James, Duke of York and brother to King Charles, quickly decimated Dutch shipping. More than 130,000 troops crossed from the east onto Dutch soil. Cities that had stood up to Spain for eighty years collapsed in a week. Thousands of townspeople were killed seemingly overnight. Rioting broke out; city councils, desperate to save their people, voted to capitulate.

Dutch popular reaction seemed to aim itself less at the English and French enemies than at De Witt. There had always been a tremendous amount of warmth toward the princes of Orange among ordinary people; republicanism was an abstraction for many, but a brave young hero whose image could be stamped on pamphlets and posters was something they could appreciate. That populist feeling could be kept in check as long as everything was going well, but now it came rushing to the fore. Why had De Witt colluded with foreigners to keep their young prince from power? Why had he dispersed the army, which should have been there to protect them? Would Willem have let this happen? To appease the people, De Witt gave Willem, who was now twenty-two, an honorary title: captain-general. But it was too late—everything changed in an instant. People woke up to find their country overrun, and they blamed the disaster on their elite, out-of-touch leaders, with their effete theories. De Witt became the object of instant ridicule. While other countries had monarchs who trained with their troops, De Witt had translated Descartes's mathematical principles into Dutch. What did a country need more in a leader: an intellectual or a soldier? Under extreme pressure, in July of 1672, just four months after the military invasion began, the States of Holland tore up the agreement to bar Willem of Orange from becoming *stadholder* and named him to that office.

The following month, Johan De Witt was attacked by a would-be assassin and wounded. Unable to function, he resigned. But the popular rage against him had reached explosive levels. A crowd in

The Hague set on him and his brother just outside the Binnenhof, the seat of government. They were cut with knives, shot, hanged, dismembered, and set afire. The popular account of De Witt's death ends with his roasted corpse being devoured by the insane mob. We have no way of knowing how much truth is in the cannibalism story, but it certainly says something about how deeply De Witt and other Dutch republicans misjudged the people's feelings for liberalism.

Spinoza was living in The Hague at the time of De Witt's murder. The German philosopher Leibniz (who had attacked him in print but now wanted to become his friend) visited some time later and gave a recollection of the dark day. "He told me that on the day of the murder of the De Witts he felt impelled to go out in the evening and exhibit in the neighborhood of the crime a poster with the words 'Lowest Barbarians!' But his landlord had locked the door to prevent his going out and incurring the risk of being torn to pieces."

Four years later, in 1677, Baruch Spinoza died at the age of forty-four, apparently from lung disease. His last years, following the murder of De Witt and the end of his dream of a democratic state, were introspective. He rethought his ideas and recast them in soberer terms. He still believed democracy the best form of government, but now he understood better its inherent problems. "Men are of necessity liable to passions," he wrote, and "prone to vengeance more than mercy."

De Witt, Spinoza concluded, had been naive. And so had he. The year 1672 lives on in Dutch memory as the *rampjaar*, "disaster year." The country was invaded and overrun. A whole portion of captured territory would never again be Dutch. Much of the land was intentionally flooded in an effort to block the invaders, leaving a sodden mess: a landscape in retrogression. The republican form of government had collapsed. The soaring Dutch economic miracle came to an end. In an astoundingly short time, Amsterdam's era as a prime influence on the world was over. The city's great philosopher of liberalism was dead and disgraced. And so, apparently, was liberalism itself.

Rembrandt's group portrait of the men responsible for monitoring textiles reveals two things: the artist's ability to bring mystery to a mundane subject and the importance that Amsterdam placed on quality control of products it sold. *Rijksmuseum*

In a sense, the Dutch in the seventeenth century invented the idea of home as a uniquely personal space. Pieter de Hooch made it his subject matter. *Rijksmuseum*

Rembrandt's painting of the renowned surgeon Nicolaes Tulp giving his annual anatomy lesson made the artist famous among Amsterdammers. *Royal Picture Gallery Mauritshuis*

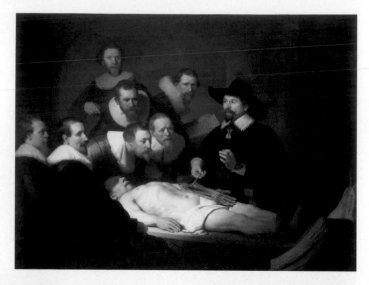

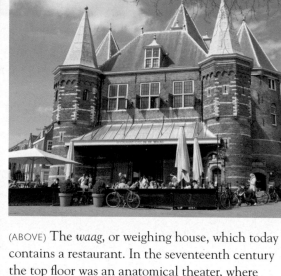

(ABOVE) The *waag*, or weighing house, which today contains a restaurant. In the seventeenth century the top floor was an anatomical theater, where Rembrandt painted *The Anatomy Lesson of Dr. Tulp*. *Photo: Miriam van der Meij*

(LEFT) Furniture maker Herman Doomer and his wife, Baertjen Martens, were among the many Amsterdammers who clamored for Rembrandt to paint their portraits. He seemed to them to capture not only what they looked like but who they actually were. *Metropolitan Museum of Art*

Movement was the innovation Rembrandt brought to the genre of the company portrait. Where before the guards were posed at rest, he chose to depict them in action. As a genre, the paintings were statements to the rest of Europe that said, in effect: Here we don't depend on kings or popes; this is our town and we take care of it ourselves. *Rijksmuseum*

Rembrandt's portrait of Jan Six has been called the greatest portrait of the seventeenth century. Six was one of the wealthiest men in Amsterdam and founder of a world-renowned art collection, the centerpiece of which is his own portrait. Six's direct descendant, Jan Six XI, is today a fine-art dealer in Amsterdam. *Photo: Stefan Korte*

Generational divide: the portraits of Andries Bicker, who was part of the generation that built Amsterdam's golden age, and of his son Gerard show a study in the contrasts of the era, from sober industriousness to excess and waste. *Rijksmuseum*

Willem Blaeu settled in Amsterdam in 1596, at the start of the golden age. He and his son, Joan, became the world's leading cartographers and part of the city's publishing industry, which was the biggest in the world. The Blaeu *Atlas Maior*, which included this world map, was the most expensive book of the seventeenth century. *Rijksmuseum*

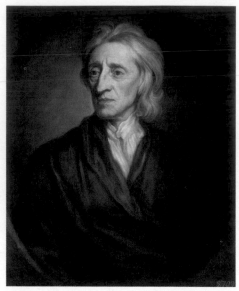

(LEFT) Baruch Spinoza, the philosopher of Amsterdam's liberalism. *Herzog August Bibliothek, Wolfenbüttel, Germany*

(ABOVE RIGHT) John Locke, the English political philosopher who began to publish under the influence of Amsterdam's Enlightenment circle. *State Hermitage Museum, St. Petersburg*

(ABOVE) A portion of a page from the Amsterdam betrothal registry showing the intention of Catalina Trico and Joris Rapalje to marry in 1624. Their marks are at bottom. Trico and Rapalje would sail to New Amsterdam, have eleven children, and in effect become the Adam and Eve of Dutch New York. Their descendants today have been estimated at over one million. *Courtesy Stadsarchief Amsterdam*

(LEFT) The landing of Willem III's army on the English coast. The "Glorious Revolution" was in fact an invasion, which resulted in the Dutch *stadholder* becoming King William. *National Maritime Museum, Greenwich*

(LEFT) Eduard Douwes Dekker, aka Multatuli, the Dutch writer who, by some reckonings, launched the anticolonial movement. *Multatuli Museum*

(BELOW) Karta Nata Negara, the Javanese leader whose abuse of peasants, which was tolerated by the Dutch colonizers, incited Dekker to write. *Universiteit van Amsterdam*

(BELOW) *Gedogen*, the unique Dutch word that means "illegal but officially tolerated" has long been part of Amsterdam's liberalism. Prostitution was legalized in 2000, but these prostitutes were openly exhibiting themselves in the red-light district in 1890. *www.stadsarchief.nl*

Part Three

SEEDS OF INFLUENCE

Very occasionally when you are researching the past and trying to perform the sleight-of-hand task of resuscitating people who are long dead, you get a bit of unexpected help from something as lifeless as a four-hundred-year-old piece of paper. Before me is a page from a bound volume in the Amsterdam City Archives. The book is the *ondertrouwregister*, the betrothal register, in which seventeenth-century residents of the city were required to record their intention to marry. At the top of the page, in a looping script that has faded to a pale brown, it says, in antiquated Dutch:

> the 13th of January 1624 Appeared as before Joris Raparlie
> from Valenciennes, borat worker, age 19 years, residing on the
> Walenpad, and Catharina Triko from ~~Parijs~~ Pris in ~~vrankrijck~~
> Wallonsland, accompanied by Mary Flamengh, her sister,
> residing in the Nes, age 18.

What lifts this bit of bureaucratic scribble up out of the fathomless black sea of past-tense minutiae and makes it possible to relive a scene from centuries ago are the crossed-out words, which I have left in the original Dutch spelling.

Before I set that scene I will restate the theme of this book to remind the reader of where we are going. As the city of Amsterdam grew to become, briefly, a world center, it developed a number of institutions and ways of seeing and doing that are elements of what we can broadly call liberalism: an ideology centered on beliefs about equality and individual freedom that is the foundation of Western society. The world's first stock market; a society focused on the concerns and comforts of individuals, one that is run by individuals acting together rather than by some outside force; the concept of tolerance, whether regarding religion, ethnicity, or other differences; art that is bound up with the experience of the individual human being and the desire to know just who each of us is; the family home as a uniquely special place: these are all parts of liberalism in the broadest meaning of the word. The second part of the book's theme is that Amsterdam's liberalism was exported in several ways and thus, from several directions, came to influence who we are today.

Of course, a city is an amorphous thing, and a city's influence is even more amorphous. Ideas can't be pinned down like butterfly wings. Yet I think there is a lot of truth in this theme, and value in pondering it. As an outsider who came to live in Amsterdam and was struck over and over by how these forces that govern our world today shaped and molded the city as they developed along with it, I had the idea that one could see Amsterdam as a template for understanding those forces and for reflecting on their value. That was my motivation for writing about Amsterdam and liberalism. Pretty much as soon as the city's golden age was over, its liberal innovations became less influential, at least until the twentieth century, when Amsterdam became synonymous with lower-case liberalism. But those innovations from the seventeenth century would spread outward in all sorts of ways. This chapter, then, leaves the city and traces some of its lines of influence. And one of the paths by which Amsterdam's liberalism moved out into the wider world involves these two Flemish teenagers.

We don't know when Joris Rapalje and Catalina Trico (to give the more often used spellings of their names) first arrived in Amsterdam. They were poor immigrants from the south who joined the thousands of people heading to the vibrant city in search of a better life. Apparently they did not find it on the canals of Amsterdam, and so they signed up for a colonizing expedition.

Following the extravagant successes of the early years of the VOC, whose theater of operation was the East Indies, some rich men in Amsterdam and other Dutch cities wanted to do the same thing in what is today called the Atlantic Rim. After all, there were also riches to be plundered in the Americas, the Caribbean islands, and western Africa. A sister company, the Dutch West India Company, came into being in 1621, and by 1623 it had raised seven million guilders: enough to fund any global enterprise. Like the East India Company, it received a government charter and a regional monopoly.

With the West India Company established, the exploratory trip that the Englishman Henry Hudson had made in 1609 while in the pay of the VOC, which failed to reach Asia by a westerly route but charted portions of the eastern seaboard of North America, took on new significance. The Dutch had claimed the territory Hudson had charted but had done little with it beyond a few more exploratory missions and some freelance fur-trading ventures. Now there was a reason to use it. The colony was given a name: New Netherland. And of course a colony needed colonists. In the midst of the golden age, finding young Dutch men and women who wanted to leave behind their highly evolved civilization and venture into a fathomless wilderness was difficult, but there were lots of recent immigrants who were willing. In particular, a large number of Walloons—French-speaking people from the region of the southern Netherlands known as Wallonia, which is today part of Belgium— had made their way to Amsterdam in recent years, and, by offering land in exchange for six years of their service, the West India Company managed to interest a few dozen of these to be its first settlers.

For some of them the prospect of a new life in the wilderness had a matchmaking effect: better to face the unknown as a couple than alone. Joris Rapalje and Catalina Trico apparently made it a condition of their going that the West India Company would help them bend the law, which stated that couples seeking to get married had to register three weeks before their wedding, so that anyone with objections could speak up. Their ship left port January 25, 1624, and the document in which the couple registered their intention to marry is dated only twelve days before.

The document tells us that Joris was nineteen and came from Valenciennes, a city that today lies in northern France, on the Belgian border. He gave his profession as "borat worker," that is, someone involved in the production of a cloth made from wool. Some maps of seventeenth-century Amsterdam show a little path called the Walenpad near the Walloon Church that he and Catalina would be married in eight days later—a sweet and plain little church that still exists, on one of the city's oldest canals, and still offers weekly services in French.

Catalina was a year younger than her fiancé. She brought her sister along as a witness and gave her place of residence as the Nes: the same street where Dirck van Os lived and where he opened up his home to those who wanted to register to become shareholders in the VOC. We know that the would-be bride and groom were illiterate, since they made marks at the bottom of the page in place of signatures.

It is the confusion over Catalina's place of birth—and the crossed-out words in the register—that brings the moment to life. So here is our little scene: The couple—nervous, surely, at the impending voyage into the beyond, not to mention at the prospect of marriage—stands in the sacristy of the Old Church in Amsterdam, which at this time was being used as an office by the *commissarissen voor huwelijkse zaken*, the commissioners for marital affairs. In response to one of the commissioner's standard questions, "Where were you born?" the young woman pronounces a syllable: PREE. Knowing her native language is French, the commissioner assumes that she is telling him she is from Paris and that she is pronouncing it in the French manner. He writes it, giving it the Dutch spelling, Parijs, and then says aloud, in confirmation, "Parijs," pronouncing it in the Dutch way: Pah-RAICE. Whereupon the girl realizes the mistake. "No, no," she tells him. "I'm not from Paris. I'm from a village called Pris." The commissioner crosses out "Parijs" and writes "Pris." He assumes this village is in France (which today it is, just over the Belgian border, though it is now called Prisches), and writes "in vrankrijck," the seventeenth-century Dutch spelling for France, and at the same time says it aloud. "No!" she must have said again. "It's not in France. It's in the Walloon country." So he crosses out "vrankrijck" and writes "Wallonsland." Thus the occasionally wonderful fact of human error gives us a window onto a quietly momentous scene: the coming together in Amsterdam of two illiterate teenaged peasants who would help set American history in motion.

Eight days later the couple were married, and four days after that they joined a few dozen other young Walloons who clambered aboard the ship *Eendracht*, or "Unity," riding at anchor off the North Sea island of Texel, and set sail into the icy hoar of a North Sea winter. After an ocean crossing that would become commonplace in the coming years but is scarcely imaginable today in its hardship— three months of pitching in Atlantic swells, with most of the time spent crammed into the between decks—they sailed into the grand amphitheater of a New World harbor, its shores bristling with pines, oaks, and hickories, the land beyond unfathomable in its scope and promise.

The colonists set about making the vastness theirs. The easiest way of doing this was by naming it. A point at the far southern extent they called Cape May, after Cornelis May, one of the first skippers to bring settlers. To the north, they gave a place the name Rhode Island because from the sea it looked red and like an island. Everything between those points was their colony, their New Netherland. Many of the other names they applied to their landscape would also stick, even if the spelling sometimes changed: Breuckelen (Brooklyn), Haerlem, Staten Island, Long Island, East River, Tappan Zee, Vlackebosch (Flatbush), Vlissingen (Flushing), Boswijck (Bushwick), Catskill, Conyne (Coney) Island.

The English had also recently planted colonies in North America, to the north and the south, so the Dutch were eager to establish their presence over their whole territory. A few families were packed off south, to what they called the South River, which in time became known as the Delaware River. Others went north, up the Hudson River, to found a settlement near the juncture of the Hudson and the Mohawk Rivers; from this place, they would trade with the Indians for beaver pelts. Joris and Catalina initially joined this group. There, at a place the Dutch would name Beverwijck (either after the Dutch city of that name or in honor of the animal that was the town's raison d'être), which the English would rename Albany, Catalina gave birth to a child, Sarah. It was an event with significance for the whole colony, for when she was a grown woman Sarah Rapalje referred to herself with apparent pride as the "first born christian daughter in New Netherland."

Relations with the natives were mostly good at first (the Indians were "all as quiet as lambs and came and traded with all the freedom imaginable," Catalina remembered in her old age). Then came an incident in which West India Company soldiers involved themselves in a dispute between two tribes, the Mohawk and the Mahicans. Four Dutchmen were killed. The news spread across the hundreds of miles of wilderness that separated the little clusters of colonists. It caused fear and led to a reorganization. A new leader was chosen, a man named Peter Minuit. One of his first orders was to bring the far-flung settlers together. The original thought was to make a small island in the harbor, today called Governors Island, the capital. Minuit chose a different spot and, following standard Dutch business practice, purchased the island where it was to be built, which the Indians called Mannahatta. Thus Catalina and Joris became Manhattanites.

The capital city of the colony, built at the southern tip of Manhattan Island, is commonly known as New Amsterdam but in fact its name was Amsterdam in New Netherland. It bore a genetic relationship to its parent. For one thing, it looked like a junior version of Amsterdam. The inhabitants built gabled town houses, dug a canal, and erected two windmills. There was a public weigh house, like the one in Amsterdam. Peace was kept by companies of guardsmen, like those that Rembrandt painted.

There were more important borrowings from Amsterdam. The genetic imprint of the parent city wasn't clear at the beginning because the West India Company initially tried to run the place along the lines of the VOC in Asia, as a military/trading post in which it had a monopoly on trade. The company wasn't prepared to establish a full settlement colony. Settlement colonies were a feature of the English empire, which is one reason English is so widespoken in the world today. The narrower Dutch system, in which forts were manned by soldiers and traders who sailed back home after their postings were complete, proved very good at building up a global empire in an astonishingly short time, but it would also be one of the reasons that empire did not last and why, when it collapsed, it did so very suddenly.

But New Amsterdam was different from Agra, Mandalay, Palembang, or the hundreds of other VOC outposts. Here, within a short time, people began buying land, marrying, setting up an orphanage and schools. In other words, they were forming a society. The archives of the colony, which are housed in the New York State Archives in Albany, are bewilderingly rich, some twelve thousand pages of court cases, council minutes, and correspondence that run from high politics (negotiating a boundary treaty with the governors of New England, which did not hold but which still defines the borders of several U.S. states) to low comedy (a prostitute measuring her customers' penis length on a broomstick). These records show Joris and Catalina fully participating as members of the growing community. They start modestly: renting a milk cow from the company,

borrowing sixty guilders from the deacons of the church, which they
promise to pay back at 5 percent interest. In 1637, Joris buys land for
a farm across the river from New Amsterdam, and in 1660 he and
his neighbors there request permission to form a hamlet: one piece
of the early development of Brooklyn.

The records show the development of a society and the foundation of a city—the city that would become New York. To the inhabitants of New Amsterdam, it wasn't an outpost; it became home.
And to make it home, they brought the home country to it. They
transported farm animals, cherry trees, clay pipes to puff in the evening, brandy to sip, lace, delftware pottery, stolid Dutch furniture.
They built their city with slender yellow bricks forged in Dutch kilns
that they used as ballast on the voyages over and that centuries
later turned up in building sites in Lower Manhattan. (Sitting on
my mantel in Amsterdam is one of these artifacts of the transfer-
ence of culture from old Amsterdam to new. The brick was given to
me by the historian Leo Hershkowitz, who as a graduate student in
New York in the 1960s knew what the ground held, befriended work
crews who were digging foundations for skyscrapers, and scavenged
the "junk" that they unearthed and tossed away. I take a strange
pleasure in having brought this small chunk of Amsterdam in its
golden age, which literally served as a building block of what became
New York City, back to where it was made.)

And the colonists brought other things, some of which they
were not even aware of transporting. They brought the approach
to trade that they had perfected. Amsterdam, the trading center of
the world, bequeathed to its offspring, New Amsterdam, its systems
of finance, making it a vital hub in the Atlantic Rim economy, so
that ships from the Caribbean and the English colonies in Virginia
and New England found it beneficial to put into port en route to or
from London and Amsterdam. The new city took from its parent its
sense that trade was something that was engaged in by individuals
for their own advantage. As in old Amsterdam, where all levels of

society had bought shares in the VOC, in New Amsterdam everyone was a trader; everyone had a piece of incoming and outgoing
shipments: beaver pelts, timber, salt, sugar, tobacco.

The immigrants also transported their mixed society. Because
Amsterdam was a melting pot, New Amsterdam became unprecedentedly cosmopolitan. A Jesuit missionary who showed up in the
little city on lower Manhattan in 1643 recorded that eighteen languages and dialects were spoken in its few streets—at a time when
there were probably no more than five hundred inhabitants. Truly,
New York was New York even before it was called that.

The colonists also brought their way of getting along—that is,
tolerance—which enabled the different ethnicities and religions
and languages to coexist. While tolerance was being debated as an
ideal among philosophers and theologians, it is probably safe to say
that most people in New Amsterdam did not think they were founding a society based on lofty notions of equality and justice for all.
It was simply part of their makeup to tolerate differences. It was
an aspect of *gedogen*, an official policy of looking the other way, as
when, a century earlier, the Holy Roman emperor decreed that the
city of Amsterdam must crack down on renegade Catholics but the
city officials gave little more than lip service to the order. Tolerance went back to the time of Willem and the fight against Spain:
the Dutch who made their homes on Manhattan knew from their
grandparents' era what happened when a power pushed its church
and God and justice and tax policy all as one package onto a people. They knew (some of them did, anyway; there remained a lively
orthodox party that was eager to impose its God and God-given
laws on all) that things worked better, people flourished and made
money, when they were left alone.

Ad hoc as it may have been, this tolerance eventually became
codified in New Amsterdam when colonists in the community of
Vlissingen, across the East River on Long Island, protested their
leader's attempt to bar a group of Quakers from settling among

them, citing the Dutch policy of tolerating religious differences, undergirded by biblical principles. These protesting colonists happened to be English, for the English were one of the many minorities in the colony—and their petition was written in English:

> The law of love, peace and liberty in the states extending
> to Jews, Turks and Egyptians, as they are considered sons of
> Adam, which is the glory of the outward state of Holland
> soe love, peace and liberty, extending to all in Christ Jesus,
> condemns hatred, war and bondage. . . . Therefore if any
> of these said persons come in love unto us, we cannot in
> conscience lay violent hands upon them, but give them free
> egresse and regresse unto our Town, and houses, as God shall
> persuade our consciences . . . for we are bounde by the law of
> God and man to doe good unto all men and evil to noe man.
> And this is according to the patent and charter of our Towne,
> given unto us in the name of the States General, which we
> are not willing to infringe, and violate, but shall houlde
> to our patent and shall remaine, your humble subjects, the
> inhabitants of Vlishing.

Vlissingen, or Vlishing, became the modern Flushing, and the petition, the Flushing Remonstrance, is considered the first statement of religious freedom in America.

As the colony developed, its residents began to insist on such rights. They wanted their settlement to be recognized as an official Dutch municipality. The matter came to a head when Willem Kieft, who became director in 1638, decided to deal with the problem of repeated skirmishes with local Indians by declaring war on them. The settlers protested: they knew they were outnumbered by the Indians, and what's more they were there to bargain with the Indians for pelts. Nevertheless, Kieft's War, as it became known, unfolded in a series of brutal attacks and reprisals. The war made the colonists realize they could not trust the West India Company leaders, far away in Amsterdam and other Dutch cities, to understand their situation. They began a campaign to convince the Dutch government to take direct control of the colony. A man named Adriaen van der Donck, who had trained in law at Leiden University before emigrating to the colony, emerged as the leader of what was in effect an opposition party. He wrote a series of legal petitions to present the case of the colonists before the government. The West India Company directors reacted to the turmoil in the colony by removing Kieft from his position and installing a new man, one who they hoped would bring order: Petrus Stuyvesant, a stern Frisian minister's son who had made the West India Company his career.

Stuyvesant arrived in the colony in 1647—his previous posting was the West India Company base on Curaçao; he'd lost his leg as a result of a naval encounter with the Spanish off the island of St. Martin—and clashed with Van der Donck. At the height of the clash an irate Stuyvesant arrested Van der Donck and threatened to execute him for treason. Stuyvesant was persuaded by his council to release Van der Donck, whereupon the opposition leader traveled to Amsterdam and The Hague to make a personal appeal to the Dutch leaders on behalf of the colony.

The colonists wanted the full force of their golden age civilization to apply to their faraway but bustling city. In particular, they wanted a system that copied that of the parent city: "as far as workable," they wrote, "according with the form of government of the laudable city of Amsterdam—name giver of this our new [city]."

Eventually they got it, or at least some of it. The Dutch authorities gave New Amsterdam a municipal charter that allowed for features that the Dutch had brought to the New World to become cemented into their city's foundation. The Amsterdam chamber of the West India Company created a court in New Amsterdam that was to base its decisions, as the directors wrote, on "the laws of this city." Rules for becoming citizens (burghers) and magistrates were copied from Amsterdam.

From the start, English settlers in New England had been

encroaching on the Dutch territory. Following the restoration of the English monarchy, Charles II determined that he would reorganize England's North American colonies. The New England colonies were Puritan strongholds and thus had supported Oliver Cromwell; they needed to be brought into line. And Charles wanted the colonies to be integrated so that they could become an economic resource. The problem of the Dutch colony, which occupied the choicest portion of the eastern seaboard and lay smack between New England and Virginia, now needed to be resolved.

The English took the Dutch colony by force in 1664. The Dutch got it back again in 1673, then lost it for good the next year. From that point, one might say, began the history of the "thirteen original" American colonies. But while the English changed New Amsterdam to New York, they kept many of its structures in place for the simple reason that the city worked. It continued to function as an important harbor and transshipping center, a New World version of its parent city, with the addition that it was now a node on both the Dutch and English trade circuits, allowing it to expand connections further still. And while the image of a takeover suggests a change of populations, in fact the people of New Amsterdam didn't go anywhere. Its immigrant communities remained, so that New York became distinctly different from Boston. Some of the first mayors of New York City were Dutchmen, who had been in the colony for decades and knew how it functioned. In 1674, ten years after the English takeover, New York's city hall still kept a copy of the bylaws of Amsterdam. Dutch remained a common language; in the mid-eighteenth century, English officials who wanted to negotiate with Indians had to find a Dutchman as interpreter, for the only European language the Indians knew was Dutch.

With tolerance and a free-trading sensibility in its foundation, New York City would grow into even more of a powerhouse of mixed ethnicities and faiths: indeed, it would become the ultimate immigrant city. In the nineteenth century, when the great waves of immigrants traveled from Europe to North America, they mostly made for New York, partly because its long-standing mix of cultures made for an easier landing. And as these Victorian-era newcomers explored Manhattan's mean streets, and heard its multiplicity of languages, smelled its wild stew of cuisines, and saw people from everywhere pushing ahead following an ethic that would later become known as upward mobility, they decided that what they were experiencing was "America." In fact, it wasn't America—not yet. It was New York. And it was New York because it had been New Amsterdam, and it was New Amsterdam because its roots were in Amsterdam.

Many of these nineteenth-century immigrants took up this strange New World mix of ingredients and made it their own. And some brought it with them along with the rest of the possessions packed into their wagons and train carriages as they headed farther west. They brought it to Ohio, to the Indiana Territory, and all the way to the Pacific Ocean. As they did so, they brought, all unknowing, pieces of a culture that had come into being in a far northern corner of Europe, where people had forged their identities in a struggle against the sea, had defied the medieval system of dominance by Catholic Church and monarchy, and created their own way of being.

Joris Rapalje died in 1662, while the Dutch still controlled the colony. Catalina long outlived him and became a matriarch of early America. We get another glimpse of her, in the last years of her life, from a religious leader who was traveling on Long Island in 1680 in search of a place to found a community. He came to a farm opposite Manhattan where he found "an old Walloon woman from Valenciennes, seventy-four years old." He describes her as "worldly-minded" and "living with her whole heart as well as body, among her progeny, which now number 145, and soon will reach 150." And he gives us a little sense of the personality that carried her across the ocean and through the decades of carving out a new life in the wilderness: we catch a glimpse of willfulness, of an individual. Despite being

surrounded by her progeny, he says, "nevertheless she lives alone by
herself, a little apart from the others, having her little garden, and
other conveniences."

The missionary isn't the only person to note Catalina Trico's
progeny; that has been a source of interest for genealogists ever
since. She and her husband had eleven children in total. Today their
descendants have been numbered at more than one million and
are spread across the United States and beyond, making Catalina
and Joris not only, as I said in my book about New Amsterdam, the
Adam and Eve of the Dutch colony but one of the founding couples
of America, a human link from seventeenth-century Amsterdam to
the America of today.

Catalina entered the historical record one more time. In 1684,
as she was nearing eighty, she was asked for information about
the founding of the Dutch colony to help settle a boundary dispute between Maryland and Pennsylvania, and in a deposition she
recounted some of the details of how she and Joris had traveled from
Amsterdam to New Amsterdam. Funnily enough, here in her last
historical entry, as in her first, there is the same mistake over her
place of birth. "Paris," the secretary wrote, interpreting her spoken
syllable the same way the official in Amsterdam had sixty years
before. But this time, it seems, no one read it back to her, because
the error was not corrected.

Lodewijk and Hendrick Trip were brothers and arms dealers
in golden age Amsterdam. Foreign wars were as good a business to
be in as shipping or the herring trade, and they got rich. (To the
English market they proudly broadcast themselves as "Purveyors of
Waepens, Artilleree, Shotte and Amunition of Werre.") But there
was evidently no strife between the brothers, for when they each
married they decided to live side by side. They bought a lot on the
Kloveniersburgwal, just steps from the weigh house where Rem-

brandt had painted Dr. Tulp giving his anatomy lesson, and commissioned two canal houses with a single facade so that, while each
family had its own living space, from the outside the Trip house
seemed a single imposing monument.

After Napoleon Bonaparte reorganized the Netherlands in 1806
as the Kingdom of Holland, his brother, Louis Napoleon, whom
he installed as king, took over the Trip house and turned it into
the headquarters of a learned institution that eventually became
the Royal Dutch Academy of Sciences. And so it remains. I ventured there one evening in late summer of 2012 to hear two key-
note addresses. The first speaker, Anthony Grafton, distinguished
professor of intellectual history at Princeton University, colloqui-
ally summarized the topic we had all come to hear about, and its
effect on centuries of European and world history, as "Hurricane
Spinoza." The excommunicated Amsterdam Jew who had died in
disgrace would come to revolutionize Europe with, as Grafton said,
an "extraordinary, shattering message."

The second speaker, Jonathan Israel, professor of history at the
Institute for Advanced Study in Princeton, has over the past few
decades done more than anyone else to change the way we think
about the Enlightenment. Intellectuals had come to regard the great
period of transformation in Europe in the eighteenth century as
a kind of bomb that had its epicenter in Paris. From France, the
shock waves of the Enlightenment spread outward, so that study of
it became subdivided by nationality: there is the English Enlightenment, the Scottish Enlightenment, the German Enlightenment,
the American Enlightenment. Of course, these are only categories:
conveniences for trying to comprehend vast and inchoate forces.
Over time, old categories become less useful and new categories,
new explanatory paradigms, are born. Israel and others have pushed
another way of understanding the fundamental change that came
over Europe, that launched the American and French Revolutions
and, for many of us, remains central to who we are. In this new
understanding, the transformations of the eighteenth century are

the visible outcomes of mental shifts that took place in the century before. And that change of outlook came about first and foremost in the Dutch provinces, with the city of Amsterdam in many respects leading the way.

In the latter part of the seventeenth century a word came into being that had an effect something like what the word *communist* had in the 1950s. In Paris, in Leipzig, in Rome and Naples, *Spinozist* meant subversive, radical, dangerous. *Spinozist* was a synonym for atheist. It signified a threat to civilization. Spinozists themselves wore the term as a badge of honor; for them it meant modern, rational, clearheaded, free from superstition.

Immediately after Spinoza's death, his friends arranged for the publication of his *Ethics*. The *Tractatus Theologico-Politicus*, which had been published seven years before, was banned in every country in Europe, but still it spread. Spinoza's friends had realized by now that what he had to say had a deep allure for all sorts of people. You don't need the church or the king to tell you right from wrong; you can figure that out for yourself, using the power of your own reason. Not only that, but the church and the king may be telling you lies; you need to develop your critical faculties, the way a soldier maintains his weapons, in order to fight through the walls of falsehood and deceit and confusion that hem you in.

These were heretical and treasonous thoughts, but lots of people harbored them. The Spinozists formed study groups, which spread. Many in Spinoza's immediate circle began publishing their own work. Doing that didn't require professional credentials. An Amsterdam basketmaker named Willem Deurhoff was one of the first to publish in Spinoza's wake, producing volumes in which he tried to bring a critical analysis to bear on the Bible. Lodewijk Meijer, an Amsterdam playwright and man of medicine, had been a close friend of Spinoza's—he was one of those who had taken charge of Spinoza's papers after his death and went about the dangerous task of editing and publishing the incendiary material—and even before Spinoza's death his own career began to flourish. Meijer believed the new approach to critical thinking could change the world. To do so, he was convinced, meant replacing existing infrastructures of knowledge. Language was a vital part of this project. He advocated using vernacular languages over Latin and published a dictionary of foreign words commonly used in Dutch. His masterwork, *Philosophy as the Interpreter of Holy Scripture*, which was published in 1666 in Amsterdam (which the title page called "Eleutheropolis," Greek for "Freedom City"), was a takedown of the Bible. Meijer didn't attack the Holy Book itself, though; he saw himself as a thoughtful Christian. His problem was with the existing translations, which he said had become so corrupted over time that the book that ordinary people cherished and worshiped from was an abomination to God. That argument might have gotten past church leaders, but the larger theme indicated in his title—that theology has to subordinate itself to reason—caused a furor that echoed around Europe; the book's theme resonated enough that it was republished a century later, in the very year of the American Revolution and at the height of the Enlightenment.

The *rampjaar*—the disaster year of 1672—began the decline of the Dutch empire, but curiously it also had the effect of helping to spread ideas outward from Amsterdam and other Dutch cities to Europe as a whole. For the next forty years, as power ebbed and flowed in new patterns around the Continent, the declining Dutch state was locked in a series of wars with its neighbors, and the chaotic times brought a steady flow of spies, diplomats, generals, merchants, and sailors into the city. Amsterdam slipped from its height as a European financial center, but its cultural infrastructure remained in place and came to serve in new ways. The city's tradition of allowing a free flow of information continued, the publishing industry remained strong, and authors came from afar to have their work published and to meet with other thinkers. Publishers responded by creating a new form of communication: the scholarly journal. Even as its golden age slipped away, Amsterdam, along with other Dutch cities, became, as historian Wijnand Mijnhardt puts it, "the undisputed focus of the cosmopolitan Republic of Letters and the center of an emerging European knowledge society."

The turmoil roiling Europe was due in large part to the convergence of two historic forces. The Reformation had fractured the unity that had existed under Roman Catholicism. People yearned for a new underlying unity. Many if not most of those who practiced the new critical thinking did so not to try to debunk Christianity, or religion itself, but to reconcile faith with the new philosophy. Christianity was a religion rooted in historical events; its founding figure was a man-God who had lived in a definable period, so that its foundational texts recorded events that took place alongside other historical events. The goal of many thinkers was to weed out inconsistency in the Bible, to reconcile its supernatural elements with natural philosophy, to solve problems of translation and untangle confused historical time lines: in short, to make the Bible make sense. The longing for this was palpable. And the debates about how to do it, or whether it was the correct strategy at all, raged, in large part, in Amsterdam's cafés and in journals and books that came off the city's presses. Its printers were willing to give voice to all sides.

One of the most vital questions was whether a state should tolerate churches other than its established one. The debate on this question reached a crisis in 1685, when Louis XIV revoked the Edict of Nantes, a ruling that had allowed Huguenots—Protestant French—to practice their faith. Protestantism was once again banned in France. As Protestant schools and churches were shut down, fifty thousand French Calvinists—including much of France's intellectual elite—migrated en masse to Dutch cities. The affair simultaneously reenriched Amsterdam's intellectual life and made the city the center of a renewed debate on the question of tolerance. The newcomers were alive to the fact that the tolerance the city practiced, which not only allowed them to settle but also gave them the means to disseminate their ideas, was itself a model of what they wanted for their home countries. Jean Le Clerc, who emigrated from Geneva and became one of the founders of the scholarly journal (he published three French-language journals in Amsterdam), was eager to acknowledge his debt. "May this Town ever remain a safe Sanctuary to the Innocent, and by it's generous Carriage draw down upon it's self the Praises and Blessings of all those who are Lovers of Virtue," he wrote at one point. And at another: "I confess had [I] lived any where else, [I] could not possibly have profited [my] Contemporaries so much by the printing of so many Volumes, because so many Books are no where so easily publish'd, and sold, as at *Amsterdam*."

The Huguenot émigrés took root in Amsterdam and helped to spread the city's liberalism. Maybe the most useful part of the recent recategorization of the Enlightenment is the idea of dividing this complex force into two streams: a moderate and a radical Enlightenment. The moderate thinkers were those who believed it necessary to make the new philosophy match up with Christian theology. They wanted not to tear down the existing foundations of society but to strengthen them. The radicals believed there was no choice but to rebuild from the ground up, on secular, rational lines. Each strain had its impassioned proponents, who did battle with one another for a century, in journals and books and from church pulpits. And the two strains each climaxed in a world-historic event. The French Revolution, which was a total revolution, against both the church and the monarchy, was the outcome of the radical Enlightenment. The patriot army of the American Revolution, which threw off a monarchy and made way for government to be rebuilt on a democratic ideal, did not ransack churches; the Enlightenment channel of Jefferson, Madison, and Franklin followed a more moderate course. To this day descendants of the radical Enlightenment equate religion with superstition and believe that religion is a vestige of Western society's childhood that it has yet to outgrow, while people who believe that faith and reason are mutually beneficial are under the influence of the moderate Enlightenment.

Both of these branches of the so-called High Enlightenment have roots going back to the Dutch Enlightenment of the seventeenth century. Seeds of both lines of thought sprouted in Amster-

dam's literary scene of the late seventeenth and early eighteenth
centuries. In many cases, figures of moderate bent were seen as dan-
gerously radical. Jean Frederic Bernard was born in Provence; his
father was a Huguenot pastor, and after Louis XIV's proclamation
made it illegal for Huguenots to practice their religion in France,
the family traveled to Amsterdam, where they registered as members of the Walloon Church (the same church where Joris Rapalje
and Catalina Trico were married). Bernard became a bookseller and
publisher. His abiding conviction, which surely was based in part on
personal experience as well as his reading of Spinoza, was that when
religion was a public matter, war and turmoil ensued. Therefore, he
argued in the first book he published, which he himself wrote, religion should be a strictly private matter: a tame-sounding pronounce-
ment today but it marked him as dangerous. Bernard's magnum opus,
produced together with an engraver named Bernard Picart, a fellow
Huguenot who had also fled to Amsterdam, was a seven-volume
overview of the world's religions, *Cérémonies et coutumes religieuses
de tous les peuples du monde*. It took the two men fourteen years
and encompassed 3,000 pages and 250 illustrations. The engravings
were intricate and the text was dispassionate. And it was revolutionary, for it applied one of the tools of critical thought—comparative
analysis—to religion. It set varieties of Christian worship alongside
"pagan" practices. A Chinese funeral procession, a marriage on
Java, a praying Turk, the Catholic ceremony of confirmation, Incas
worshiping the sun: all of these appeared together with scenes of
what would have seemed to most readers ordinary piety: a funeral in
Amsterdam, a service in the Walloon Church. The book was widely
criticized for lowering Christianity to the level of pagan worship,
but over time (and shorn of some of its radical Spinozist language) it
took root. It went through many printings and became one element
of the long, slow advance of the idea of religious tolerance.

One of Bernard's more radical colleagues—also a Huguenot
refugee—was Charles Levier, who in 1719 published what was pos-

sibly the most scandalous book of the early eighteenth century: *La Vie et l'esprit de Spinoza*. It was actually two manuscripts. The first part was the first-ever biography of Spinoza, the publication of which indicated that, more than forty years after Spinoza's death, he was an icon to radicals and freethinkers. The second part—the "spirit" of Spinoza—would eventually be retitled and go on to have a long life of dismaying the righteous. Its later title was *The Treatise of the Three Imposters*; the three imposters were the founders of the three great Western religions. The text—which appropriated a whole chunk of Spinoza's *Ethics* and mashed it together with writings by other radical thinkers, all done by an anonymous editor for maximum shock value—argued that Moses, Jesus, and Mohammed had deceived their followers and established their religions not as spiritual resources but as power bases. Levier published the book on behalf of a group of Dutch-based radicals; their purpose in putting out this incendiary text was, as one scholar puts it, "to construct and disseminate the first portable philosophical compendium of free-thought, at once anti-Christian and anti-absolutist." The little volume rankled and raged its way down the eighteenth century and became a kind of intellectual setup for the French Revolution: an aggressive screed that attacked the whole established order. Those behind it signaled their homage to Spinoza on the title page of its 1735 reprint by giving the same false place and fictional house of publication (Hamburg, Chez Henry Hunrath) that Spinoza had invented for his *Tractatus Theologico-Politicus*.

Through such works, as well as his own, Spinoza influenced both radical and moderate thinkers in the eighteenth century. One of his prime overall contributions to Western history, as Israel puts it, was "his denial of Satan and of devils in general." That may seem a bit narrow as an overall contribution, but it is in a sense the wedge between the medieval and the modern. Devils, hell, and sin, and for that matter miracles and heaven: these were seen by freethinkers as invented devices for controlling people, for keeping them chained to the will of the established authorities. The new philosophers promoted common sense and reason in ordinary life. Theologians saw at once what was at stake: if a system such as what Spinoza advocated took hold, society would not be rooted in church and monarchy; instead, people would insist that politics have as their guiding principles things like the promotion of individual life, individual liberty, and the pursuit of individual happiness.

The decades from the late 1600s to the early 1700s saw a remarkable change take place in the European debate. Where disagreement and even war had raged between different Christian factions, now the split was between faith and secularism. The whole of society shifted to the left, as it were. By the mid-1700s there were entire libraries of literature promoting science and secularism. And Spinoza's *Tractatus* remained a central text. In France the book was scary enough that police in Paris raided bookshops in search of copies. In Germany, Johann Christian Edelmann, one of the leading thinkers of the 1740s, said the *Tractatus* was the cause of his whole reconsideration of the Bible: "I went over and over again what I read, . . . used my own reason, asked the advice of other authors who had written either in favour of or against the reputation of the Bible. The more I searched the more I found what an ill ground it was." Like many others, he followed Spinoza in doing a historical-critical analysis of biblical texts and tried to tease the spirituality at their root from later political overlays. One of his arguments was that the Greek "Logos"—the term that the Gospel of John uses to characterize God's essence—was originally translated as "ratio," reason, but that this was changed to "word" in the third century to suit the Church's political agenda, since any individual could follow his or her reason, but following the word of God suggested obeying the word of the Church. By the early nineteenth century, the excommunicated Jew of Amsterdam had become so much a part of the foundation of German thought that Gotthold Lessing, one of the major figures of the German Enlightenment, responding to a reference to Spinoza's and various other philosophies in a debate, could remark drily, "There is no other philosophy than the philosophy of Spinoza."

The importance of Spinoza to both the radical and moderate Enlightenment strains is reflected in the continued division in how people think of him. For many even today he is the father of modern atheism, yet the German philosopher-poet Novalis called him "God-intoxicated" and Bertrand Russell noted that "his whole philosophy is dominated by the idea of God." The editor of a recent collection of essays on his philosophy observes that Spinoza has been considered the hero of "Conservatism, Liberalism, Materialism, Idealism, Secularism, Federalism," and other isms. That range, and its geographic root, is what strikes me. For many of the ideas that went into this philosophy that had such influence across the whole spectrum of modern liberal thought and that are so much a part of who we are sprouted amid the canals, winding streets, and gable-topped houses of the city in which the philosopher came of age.

In September of 1683 an Englishman sailed across the North Sea and took up residence in Amsterdam. Before he left England, he had made out a will and burned many of his papers, for spies were watching and he feared for his safety. He was fifty-one years old, a man whose interests extended from philosophy to medicine to science to government, but as yet he had published nothing and was unknown outside English elite circles. During and after his five years in Amsterdam and travels to other Dutch cities, where he would be influenced and encouraged by the international cast of thinkers he met there, he would write and publish what would become three hallmark texts of the Enlightenment, on democratic government, tolerance, and epistemology, books that would earn him the unofficial title of father of classical liberalism and that would shape modern political thought, especially in England and the United States. His name was John Locke.

In England, Charles II was ailing and his death would mean that the monarchy would pass to his brother James, who had converted to Catholicism. The idea of a Catholic's becoming King of England was so anathema that a vast movement had come into being to try to avert it. Extremists in the movement had gone so far as to devise a plot to kill both Charles and James. Although Locke seems not to have been involved, he was associated with people who were, and he was known to be an ardent republican. Thus, once the plot unraveled, he decided to flee.

Like thousands before and after him, then, Locke came to Amsterdam for refuge. The winter in which he arrived was one of the coldest in memory; the canals froze over, people took to their ice skates. Quite a few exotic animals, which the city as an emporium of the world regularly housed, didn't survive. It happened that a lion froze to death, whereupon men of science advertised a public dissection of the rare beast. Locke attended this event, and there a man named Philip van Limborch introduced himself. Van Limborch was a minister and a member of a group of scientists and theologians from a variety of backgrounds—French Huguenots, English separatists, and Dutch Remonstrants—who were committed to finding common ground between faith and the new philosophy and who were devoted above all to articulating a policy of religious tolerance. They exactly suited Locke's intellectual tastes, and Locke became a fixture at their weekly salons—so much that, in his fastidious way, he drew up rules, in Latin, by which the meetings should be run.

A main topic of these discussions was the Arminian-Gomarian split in the Dutch Reformed Church. This, Locke learned, was a defining feature of Dutch society over the course of the golden age. The founding protagonists of this debate had both been leading theologians. Jacobus Arminius and his followers preached a philosophy of tolerance of other faiths. They reasoned that the sufferings that the Dutch people had endured under the Spanish Inquisition showed that it was wrong for a government to push its religiously fueled will onto a people—that, in effect, no one should claim to know the mind of God. Arminius's contemporary Franciscus Gomarus had led the orthodox wing in insisting that the knowledge that theirs was the one true faith compelled them to reject other faiths and that to do otherwise was to invite Satan into society. The Arminians, or Remonstrants (who were so called after their petition, or remonstrance, to the States of Holland and West Friesland concerning reforms to the faith), became identified with the left wing of Dutch politics over most of the course of the century, and the Gomarians with the right wing.

The men Locke found himself in cozy company with were the leading lights of the Remonstrant movement. Under their sway he read books by Dutch writers, including Hugo Grotius, the legal scholar who is considered the founder of the concept of international law, and Spinoza. What Locke most appreciated from them, however, were their own moderate views on reforming society. Religious tolerance—what exactly it meant, what form it should take, what the stakes were in this war of ideas that their society was immersed in—was their primary interest. Van Limborch was himself a Remonstrant minister. He wrote a history of the Arminian-Gomarian controversy and also the first full history of the Inquisition, which he meant as a warning of the dangers of religious intolerance.

Van Limborch's right hand was Jean Le Clerc, the Swiss émigré who had founded three French-language scholarly journals in Amsterdam. Le Clerc was likewise a Remonstrant cleric, and a particularly impassioned believer in using the media to press the circle's ideas out into the world. It was he who began to urge Locke to publish. Thus it was that some of the great English philosopher's first published works appeared in Amsterdam, in French, for Le Clerc's *Bibliothèque Universelle.*

There was a natural connection between religious tolerance and

republicanism, and the Dutch thinkers were aware of Locke's political views. Locke had already written much of the manuscript of
what would later be published as *Two Treatises of Government*. This
he had written in England and kept secret (to avoid detection he
seems to have referred to the work in discussions as *De Morbo Gal-
lico*, "The French Disease," since he and his republican friends used
the common term for syphilis as a cover for the "disease" of autocratic government). In the midst of what many felt was a buildup
of autocratic power around the king, Locke constructed a two-part
political document. The first was a refutation of the then common
argument that the king's absolute power was justified by mankind's
descent from Adam and transferred from generation to generation
via a father's absolute power over his children. Locke dismantled
this tortured logic and put forth the proposition that humans are
born not into a state of subjection but rather a "state of nature" that
is also a "state of liberty." In the second treatise, he moved from the
proposition that "all men are by nature equal" to the argument that
a community is held together by "the consent of every individual"
and that government is legitimized by "the consent of the people."

These issues became even more topical early in 1685 when
Charles II died and his brother James became king of England. James
moved quickly to amass power, increasing the size of the army and
adjourning Parliament, and also installed Catholics in important
positions and otherwise acted to favor Catholicism over Protestantism. In France, at virtually the same time, Louis XIV revoked the
Edict of Nantes. Van Limborch urged Locke to write and publish
something on what was now the burning question of religious tolerance. Before he started work on the topic, Locke was able to get
some perspective from those in his circle. He read the manuscript
of Van Limborch's own book on Christianity and tolerance, which
summarized and added to the tradition of theological thinking on
religious tolerance that had developed from the time of the Spanish
Inquisition in the Dutch provinces through the golden age. Regarding the orthodox who insisted on intolerance vis-à-vis other Chris-

tian denominations, Van Limborch wrote (in the English translation that appeared in 1702):

> 'Tis necessary that they pronounce all, who err even in the least matters, to be guilty of eternal Damnation. They confess, if we mind the Rule of God's Word, that all Error is damnable; since whoever preaches any other Gospel than what is preach'd, tho it were an Angel from Heaven, is *Anathema*, or *Accursed*, and every Error is in their account a new Gospel: And thus they are under a necessity of damning all who dissent from them; which is not only repugnant to the very Genius of Christianity, but likewise barbarous and inhuman. 'Tis damning Men by whole-sale, and throwing the very Fathers of the Primitive Church, those Glorious Lights of the Christian Religion, into Hell, since they (as well as other Men) were not without their Failings and Errors in some lesser Matters. And what barbarous Usage is this?

Locke admired the depth of Van Limborch's perspective as well as his conclusions. He also read Le Clerc's newest work, *Sentimens de quelque théologiens*, which he found overly aggressive in tone. With these examples in his mind, Locke wrote, in the months of November and December 1685, his own statement of tolerance. He put it in the form of a letter addressed to Van Limborch, and it was published as *A Letter concerning Toleration*. He began by setting the concept of tolerance in a Christian context: "I esteem that toleration to be the chief characteristic mark of the true Church." But where Van Limborch's concern was tolerance between Christian denominations, Locke's main interest was in advancing an argument for the separation of church and state. It was almost universally held at the time that a state religion was an essential part of the stability of a society, but Locke declared, "The commonwealth seems to me to be a society of men constituted only for the procuring, preserving, and advancing their own civil interests," so that "it neither can nor ought in any manner to be extended to the salvation of souls." Locke—who was writing in a country that tolerated a plurality of faiths—argued that a mixture of religions was healthy for society and that the "magistrate ought not to forbid the preaching or professing of any speculative opinion in any church."

The fact that the *Letter concerning Toleration* was written by a man who was on the run from the authorities over his connections to a plot to assassinate a leader because of that leader's own faith may fairly be seen as a bit ironic. The ire against King James was due in part to his royal intolerance of Protestantism, but the plotters, many of them, were equally intolerant of Catholics. But such is the nature of the concept of tolerance. It evolves. Every generation puts its own limitations on it, and the clashes that define a given generation seem in many respects to be over the question of who and what that generation tolerates. Locke imposes limits when it comes to Catholics and atheists, arguing that the former would always be beholden to Roman authority and thus a danger to English society while the latter would be beholden to no authority. Put in a modern context, Locke's fears about Catholics and atheists might be analogous to the fears of those who, in the debate about immigration, argue that Muslims are by definition enemies of secular Western civilization and thus should not be allowed to settle in Western countries.

That said, Locke's overall approach in the *Letter* is one of moderation. He has no interest in a radical, anti-Christian rendering of the new philosophy. He stays firmly within a Christian value system, and, following on writers like his friend Van Limborch, he maintains that tolerance is part of that Christian ethic. His moderate perspective helped to give his work wide influence, especially in England and among the founders of the American republic, while at the same time it is precisely what caused French radicals to reject him.

The atmosphere could hardly have been a more dramatic one in which to craft what became a watershed statement of tolerance. Especially after James's wife, Mary of Modena, gave birth to a son, ensuring a Catholic dynasty on the English throne, English rebels began to gather in Dutch cities and plot a takeover of the government. Locke may have helped raise funds for an invasion; James's government ordered him to be "seized and banished." Locke now had to keep on the move. He lodged with different Dutch friends and took to using pseudonyms. Somehow during this period he found time to write his grand work of epistemology, *An Essay concerning Human Understanding*, in which he argued that the mind begins as a blank slate on which experience is written. The work has held a place in the syllabi of philosophy courses ever since.

Locke's writings on politics and tolerance sprang from a common notion: the fundamental value of the individual. There has been a lively debate in recent years about whether Thomas Jefferson relied on exact phrasings from Locke in writing the American Declaration of Independence: "We hold these truths to be self-evident, that all men are created equal, that they are endowed by their creator with certain unalienable Rights, that among these are Life, Liberty and the pursuit of Happiness." While there may be echoes of phrases Locke used a century earlier ("life, liberty, and estate," "pursuit of true and solid happiness"), more to the point is that Jefferson considered Locke's overall grounding of society on the individual and individual rights to be his starting point—that coupled with the fact that, in contrast to the more radical Enlightenment figures, the American founding fathers, like Locke, considered the "Creator" to be the ultimate ground. Jefferson acknowledged his debt when he asserted that he considered Locke "one of the three greatest men that ever lived, without any exception" (the other two being Isaac Newton and Francis Bacon).

Locke had begun working on many of his ideas while he was still in England, but it was in Amsterdam that they caught fire. As one scholar puts it, "in the vigorous and capable hands of Le Clerc and Limborch, in the city of Amsterdam where writing and printing were so natural to all good minds, Locke began to become Locke, and the obscure political exile turned into the philosopher *par excellence* of a new regime of thought."

Fifteen years before John Locke set foot in Amsterdam, a man named William Temple arrived in the Dutch Republic to serve as English ambassador. He took advantage of the posting to become a kind of official snoop in an effort to try to understand how the place worked. He roamed the polders, poked into canal houses, studied institutions and architecture, talked to soldiers, sailors, traders, preachers, farmers, and housewives. And he took careful notes. Such as this, recorded in 1668:

> In this city of Amsterdam is the famous Bank, which is the
> greatest Treasure either real or imaginary, that is known any
> where in the World. The place of it is a great Vault under the
> Stadthouse, made strong with all the circumstances of Doors
> and Locks. . . . And 'tis certain, that whoever is carried to see
> the Bank, shall never fail to find the appearance of a mighty
> real Treasure, in Barrs of Gold and Silver, Plate and infinite
> Bags of Metals. . . . The security of the Bank lies not only in
> the effects that are in it, but in the Credit of the whole Town
> or State of Amsterdam, whose Stock and Revenue is equal to
> that of some Kingdoms. . . . This Bank is properly a general
> Cash, where every man lodges his money, because he esteems
> it safer, and easier paid in and out, than if it were in his
> Coffers at home.

Amsterdam, Holland, and the Dutch provinces as a whole were a source of fascination for the English during much of the seventeenth century. The English couldn't get over the fact that the inhabitants of the tiny, water-logged strip of land across the Channel had done battle with the great Spanish empire, formed themselves into a nation, and risen to become the dominant financial power of Europe. Repeatedly the fascination boiled up into hatred. Competition between the two small Protestant countries on Europe's north-

western shoulder erupted into three trade wars during the course of
the century. The rivalry was so intense that English pamphleteers
competed with one another to come up with ever more lurid head-
lines about the Dutch. (My favorite of these: *The Dutch-mens Pedigree; Or, A Relation Shewing How They Were First Bred and Descended
from a Horse-Turd Which Was Enclosed in a Butter-Box.*) The vestiges
of the rivalry are embedded in the English language. "Dutch treat,"
"Dutch courage" (that is, alcohol: needing to get drunk to summon
the nerve to take a difficult step), "Dutch uncle," "going Dutch": all
are derogatory, and all date from the pamphlet wars of the time.

As much as they detested the Dutch, the English copied them.
William Temple's observations gave his countrymen a glimpse of
the mechanism that fueled the Dutch economic miracle—and in
time the English set about copying the Amsterdam Exchange Bank.
While the English monarchy was in exile in The Hague during
Oliver Cromwell's reign, Dutch art came into vogue among English
courtiers, who brought it, as well as the artists themselves, back
to England with them during the Restoration. Amsterdam's lens
grinders were Europe's best: by midcentury their methods had been
perfected by the English. English scientists went to Amsterdam to
attend public anatomy lessons. Architects brought innovations in
gables, windmills, and water management back from their Dutch
excursions.

Of course, the exchanges went both ways. But because the
Dutch Republic was the more advanced culture, it was the English
who benefited most. Beginning roughly at the time the English Pilgrims went to Amsterdam and Leiden for religious refuge in 1608
and continuing through the century, English refugees and visitors
imbibed Dutchness, and England slowly and steadily took on features of its neighbor. This, according to one theory, helps to explain
one of history's most stupendous examples of whitewashing: the so-
called Glorious Revolution of 1688.

A plot against King James II—which English Protestants and
antiabsolutists so longed for during John Locke's time in the Dutch

provinces—finally coalesced, but in a way that none of the English rebels gathered in Dutch cities, Locke included, could have foreseen. It brought to a climax a range of events going back decades. As we saw earlier, back in 1654, Johan de Witt, at the height of his diplomatic powers as the leader of the Dutch Republic, had negotiated a treaty with Oliver Cromwell to end the Anglo-Dutch trade war. The treaty contained a secret annex in which De Witt, and the States of Holland, promised that the toddler Willem of Orange would never be made *stadholder*. Both De Witt and Cromwell had antimonarchic reasons for wanting this—in Cromwell's case, the fact that little Willem was the grandson of Charles I and thus could one day conceivably claim title to the English throne. In the disaster year of 1672, as his power was collapsing, De Witt capitulated to monarchist forces within the republic and gave the now twenty-two-year-old Willem an honorary title; shortly after that, the States of Holland, facing invasion on multiple fronts, strengthened that by naming Willem to the position of *stadholder* in the hope that he would perform a miracle and save the country from ruin.

Willem took the title, and control of the country. Under him, the nation stepped back from republicanism toward autocracy. Willem was never loved, but he turned out to be a shrewd leader. He understood power. For one thing, he learned that he needed to treat the city of Amsterdam, which controlled the country's commerce, almost as a state within the state. By the mid-1680s, more than a decade after the disaster year, the VOC's business was booming again, which meant that Amsterdam had regained some of its former power. Willem tried to negotiate with the city regents for a buildup of the military, because he understood that under Louis XIV France had expanded ambitions. But the Amsterdam regents—who didn't like diverting their hard-earned cash to the military and knew that expanding the military meant expanding Willem's power—resisted. Meanwhile Willem set about forming alliances with other European powers to block the French king. One of these alliances took the form of marriage to Mary Stuart, daughter of James. Since Mary had been raised in the Anglican faith, Willem hoped that making her his wife would cement a Protestant alliance between England and the Dutch nation. But he had other designs as well. Once James became king, Willem knew the English monarchy was unstable. The fact that he was grandson of Charles I gave him some grounds for claiming title to the English throne. His marriage strengthened that case.

That would probably have been an unrealistic dream but for the fact that France—which had suffered severe economic hardship with the flight of Huguenots—unleashed a series of drastic trade restrictions that crippled Dutch business in everything from herring to tobacco. As tensions escalated, France and England showed signs of joining forces against the Dutch. The thought of reliving war on two fronts, when the disaster year was still a vivid memory, was harrowing enough that the Amsterdam *burgemeesters* came around to Willem's wishes. A rapid military buildup began. And now that Amsterdam's merchant leaders and the politicians in the States General were scared, Willem pushed onto them one of the boldest military plans of the era: not to go directly at France but to pivot and take advantage of the confusion in England and James's increasingly weak power base.

Observers of the massing of troops and ships in Dutch ports in late summer of 1688 assumed it was for an attack on Louis. But in October the English ambassador realized what was about to unfold: "an absolute conquest" not of France but of England, and he wrote, "such a preparation was never heard of in these parts of the world."

On November 1, 1688, a veritable ocean of sails put in to the North Sea and made south for the Strait of Dover. Those who saw the spectacle considered it the sight of their lives: the fleet Willem had assembled was four times the size of the great Spanish Armada that had been infamously defeated exactly a century earlier. The ships raced across the Channel thanks to what some called a "Protestant wind" and landed on the Devon coast without incident. The vast army—nearly twenty thousand soldiers and another twenty thousand support crew—then began to move on London. People lined the roads to watch and greet; there was little opposition. In fact, the invaders were cheered in places. People cried, "God bless you!" Peasants offered apples.

Willem sent troops into London ahead of his main army. They found no opposition and secured the city, so that Willem was able to ride in in state, dressed in white to signify the purity of his intentions. James, who had at first refused to believe an invasion was afoot, did not order troops to attack. He eventually fled to France.

History has called Willem's ascension to the English throne the result of an "invitation." There is truth in this, but it's misleading. It was Willem who had arranged for a group of English rebels—none of whom had any real power—to issue him an invitation to take over the country, as part of a spin campaign. For it was important to him that, facts notwithstanding, the takeover seem like a friendly helping hand. There was collusion on the part of some English rebels, but the events of November and December 1688 were, pure and simple, a Dutch invasion of England, involving one of the largest invasion forces Europe had ever witnessed. Its result was the naming of the Dutch *stadholder*, Willem, as King William III of England.

The bizarre turn of events—England's longtime foe marching straight into the capital unopposed, and even being cheered by ordinary people—succeeded partly as a result of the state of crisis that had built up in English society under James, whom people had feared was in the process of instituting a Catholic autocracy. It was also a result of the agitation of the antimonarchic rebel leaders whom John Locke had supported. But there was a broader reason, which had to do with the whole long century of English borrowing of Dutch culture, everything from grandfather clocks to religious tolerance to the development of a market for cheap genre paintings to decorate ordinary homes. As the British historian Lisa Jardine argues, "By 1688 England and Holland were already so closely intertwined, culturally, intellectually, dynastically and politically that the invasion was more like a merger."

The final step in this merger, prior to the invasion itself, was the careful groundwork Willem's people did in the months leading up to it. Willem laid in an elaborate propaganda campaign. The centerpiece was a document that Willem's agents spread in an unprecedented clandestine effort that consisted of tens of thousands of copies being printed in Amsterdam, London, Hamburg, York, and several other cities, shipped throughout England, and distributed en masse and on cue. The title set up clearly what was about to occur: *The Declaration of His Highness William Henry, By the Grace of God Prince of Orange, etc. Of the Reasons Inducing him to appear in Armes in the kingdome of England.* The surprise that the English leaders felt once the Dutchman actually did appear "in Armes in the kingdome of England," even after having thus been warned of it, speaks to the boldness of the plan and to the blinkered state of the English rulers.

In the *Declaration*, Willem seems to have followed self-consciously the model of his great-grandfather William the Silent, who blanketed the Dutch countryside with texts in which he communicated to his countrymen his own perspective on the ravages being done by the Duke of Alba on historic Dutch freedoms and liberties. Now, the great-grandson, pulling together Dutch and English notions of tolerance and liberty, wrote to the people of England: "It is both certain and evident to all Men, that the publick Peace and Happiness of any State or Kingdom cannot be preserved, where the Laws, Liberties and Customs, established by the lawful Authority in it, are openly transgressed and annulled." The declaration went on to enumerate James's abuses of power, highlighting especially the threat of a Catholic takeover in violation of the principle of religious toleration, and then got down to the real business: "since our dearest and most entirely beloved Consort the Princess, and likewise ourselves, have so great an Interest in this Matter, and such a Right, as all the World knows, to the Succession to the Crown . . ." It only makes all the sense in the world, Willem was telling the people of

England, that he, the leader of the rival Dutch nation, should sweep in with an army of tens of thousands and take over their monarchy and state.

Whether it made sense or not, he did it. And ordinary English people swallowed it. The *Declaration* was read out in town squares all over England. William and Mary were crowned. John Locke (who played no part in the invasion but returned to England on the same ship that carried Princess Mary across the Channel to take up her new royal position) expediently (one might say cravenly) chose, when he published his *Two Treatises of Government* less than two years later, to preface it with the bold remark that his grand statement of the social contract theory of government—a work that many consider to be part of the political framework of the modern world—was little more than a justification for Willem's power grab:

> These [pages] I hope are sufficient to establish the throne of
> our great restorer, our present King William; to make good his
> title, in the consent of the people, which being the only one
> of all lawful governments, he has more fully and clearly, than
> any prince in Christendom; and to justify to the world the
> people of England, whose love of their just and natural rights,
> with their resolution to preserve them, saved the nation when
> it was on the very brink of slavery and ruin.

William's Dutch invasion of England—which would be spectacularly rechristened as the Glorious Revolution—would go down as one of history's more consequential events. Among its legacies would be the financial modernization of Great Britain and the expansion of the British East India Company (during his complex reign, Willem/William would preside over not only rival nations but competing East India Companies). But historians say that its greatest legacy was the end of absolute monarchy in Britain and the beginning of a constitutional monarchy, with a steadily stronger Parliament. This is what Willem more or less promised in his *Declaration*, and, whether or not he actually wanted it, it's what England got.

It would be wrong to suggest that this vast transformation came about all because of the Dutch roots of the new English king. But it's fair to say that in 1688 Dutchness, in some degree, formally blended itself into Englishness, and the impossible-to-pin-down but sprawling legacy of Amsterdam achieved a foothold across the Channel. It was a process that had been taking place for some time: all through the seventeenth century features of the liberalism the city helped to spawn—fragments of things we collectively call capitalism, religious tolerance, secularism, pragmatic popular rule—were carried as ephemeral cargo on stout wooden ships that moved from the Dutch coast to the English and penetrated English consciousness. And especially after the Dutch leader became the King of England, the English set about employing those fragments, those ideas, those tools, as they constructed their own empire. And through the British empire they spread just about everywhere.

THE TWO LIBERALISMS

I began this book by describing how I start some of my days in Amsterdam. I leave my apartment in the Old South section of the city, bring my son to his Moroccan day care provider, then stop in for an interview session with Frieda Menco, who has lived all her life in Amsterdam except for two years in hiding from the Nazis in a nearby village and the two years she endured in the concentration camp at Auschwitz. I didn't mention my ultimate destination: my office. I am the director of an American culture center that is located in the West India House, a small and stylish mansion near the historic harbor that in the seventeenth century was the headquarters of the West India Company. A long, high-ceilinged room on the opposite side of the courtyard from my office was where the company's directors met. Here they organized their North American colony. This was, in effect, the place where New York City was conceived.

At some point while working on this book it occurred to me that as I move through this morning routine I am traveling backward through the stages of Amsterdam's liberal heritage. Chatting with Iman Mreqqi, my son's caretaker, I am in the city of the present, the city that not long ago was dubbed the most ethnically diverse in the world, with 178 different nationalities represented and all of the issues, questions, problems, and potential that that staggering diversity entails. As I sit down to coffee with Frieda Menco I rewind to wartime Amsterdam: the city under Nazi thrall, a city of oppression and resistance and heroism and perfidy. And as I walk through the archway of the West India House and encounter the statue of Petrus Stuyvesant in the courtyard, I'm in the shadow of the Amsterdam that ruled the world, the city that helped to invent so many of the constituent parts of liberalism and that broadcast its heritage like pollen on the wind.

The liberal heritage remained part of the city's DNA, though it was not always apparent in the years that followed the golden age. As the eighteenth century progressed, the United Provinces of the Netherlands fell steadily behind neighboring countries. The VOC suffered a string of losses in its global chess match against the rising British empire. Amsterdam slipped steeply from its height: poverty grew; disease became rampant; the canals reeked. Corruption became the hallmark of the city government. An example: one official gave an important and highly paid position to his son—who was fourteen. Taxes on food and fuel skyrocketed, and people knew that tax officials profited personally from money they collected.

One climax to this era came on June 25, 1748, when people gathered in a broad public square, rimmed by gabled buildings, in the city center. They were angry—angry enough that soldiers showed up to keep the peace. The square, where a century later a huge statue of Rembrandt would be unveiled and that since that time has been known as Rembrandtplein, was then called the Butter Market, because that was where dairy farmers from outside Amsterdam set up booths to sell tubs of the yellow essence of Dutch cuisine. It was also where tax officers showed up periodically to ensure that excise tax was being collected on the sale of goods, and it was these men who were the objects of the people's ire. The crowd began to throw trash at the tax men and the soldiers. The soldiers pushed back. Whereupon, in the words of an eyewitness, "A rude female several times hitched up her skirts, smacked her bare buttocks and told the militia that this was for them." A soldier fired—and hit the offered target. The place went wild. Four days of rioting ensued, with people raging through the city, storming into the houses of wealthy merchants, and tossing expensive furniture into the canals.

Despite the downturn, Amsterdam still had its pockets of wealth and luxury; intellectuals still gathered in the city, and its inhabitants, troubled as they were, considered themselves very much a part of the wider world. One feature of the era was a tendency for elements of the liberalism that the city had sent abroad to come ricocheting back to reanimate it. In 1776, news from across the ocean caught the attention of intellectuals and shopkeepers alike. Copies of a British pamphlet that had been translated into Dutch smacked down onto café tables and were eagerly opened and pored over. In his *Observations on the Nature of Civil Liberty, the Principles of Government, and the Justice and Policy of the War with America*, a Welsh minister named Richard Price pondered the sudden outbreak of war in America from a philosophical perspective. He analyzed the various meanings of the word *liberty*, focused his attention on the concept of civil liberty, spoke of self-determination as a right, and argued not only that the American colonies were in the right but that a moral right such as theirs was an unstoppable force, one that would continue to change history. What jumped out at the Amsterdam readers of Price's pamphlet was a bit of background he gave:

> The United Provinces of Holland were once subject to the
> Spanish monarchy; but, provoked by the violation of their
> charters; by levies of money, without their consent; by the
> introduction of Spanish troops among them; by innovations
> in their antient modes of government; and the rejection of
> their petitions, they were driven to that resistance which we
> and all the world have ever since admired; and which has
> given birth to one of the greatest and happiest Republics that
> ever existed.

Amsterdammers who read Price's glowing words knew full well that the greatness and happiness were things of the past. But the example of the American Revolution awakened something in them. What was the root cause of their own misfortune: of the economic collapse, the corruption of government officials, the degradation of life? Over the next handful of years Amsterdammers formed dozens of "reading societies"—in essence, revolutionary cells—that met regularly to trade political tracts and ideas. The big idea on people's minds suddenly was the accumulation of power at the top and the evils that flowed from it. As before, political battle lines were drawn between Orangists who supported the *stadholder* (currently, Willem V) and the house of Orange, along with their orthodox Calvinist allies, and the patriots, who wanted power to be held by the people. But this latter group was pushing something more than what those of Johan de Witt's time had championed a century before. The Dutch Republic had always been imperfect, as far as democracy went. It was an oligarchy, a rule by the merchant elites. Now, following the American example, the Dutch patriots were calling for actual popular representation.

The immediate influence was from America, but the Amsterdam patriots knew their history. The political upheaval roiling America and Europe had its roots, as Richard Price had pointed out, in their own soil. Homegrown pamphlets proclaimed that the setup to the events unfolding in America was the Dutch rebellion led by William the Silent against Spain—against Charles V and his son Philip II and the dreaded Duke of Alba. But while the Eighty Years' War had given the Dutch their own nation, it hadn't resulted in true liberty. And, as irony would have it, their new tyrant was the descendant of their founding father. "Our dear Orange princes," went one pamphlet, which seemed to copy the antimonarchic language of the American patriot press, "are princes just like others in the world. They are raised in the same perverted kind of courtly education; from their youth they suck up the same sentiments, the same arrogance, pride, ambition." Referencing the ongoing power struggle between the *stadholder* and the city of Amsterdam, the pamphlet noted that Willem "would like to see Amsterdam's trade flourishing, which is now perishing, if only that city would open its gates for the Prince's garrison and would leave the appointment of its governors to him." Patriot leaders even referred to Willem as the "new Alba."

Meanwhile, the Dutch state ensnared itself in the British-American war by shipping supplies to the American colonists, which led Britain to declare war on the Dutch: the fourth trade war between the two nations, and one that would truly end Dutch dominance in world affairs. The British captured hundreds of Dutch ships, took West India Company slaving forts in West Africa, and began dismantling the VOC infrastructure in India and Asia.

Amsterdam won its independence, so to speak, from the *stadholder* when, in 1787, following huge popular demonstrations on Dam Square, the members of the city council who had stayed loyal to the prince's party capitulated. A democratic revolution seemed to be unfolding. But Willem countered by engaging a Prussian army of twenty-six thousand troops. Faced with the threat of invasion, Amsterdam and other cities caved in. The *stadholder* regained control. He outlawed the reading clubs, forbade talk of democracy, and otherwise began to consolidate his power.

Then came the French Revolution. Dutch patriots got excited all over again as French aristos lost their heads. Once again, for the Dutch, what was happening in a distant land was the outcome of ideas and actions in their own struggle against Spain and over the course of the rise of the Dutch Republic. The French, like the Americans, were bringing liberalism to its logical conclusion: democracy. For Dutch patriots, the French Revolution was equally their own.

And, conveniently, it came right to their doorstep. As Europe's monarchs became alarmed by what was taking place in France, they took steps to snuff it out. The result was a messy sprawl of mayhem that is collectively known to history as the French Revolution-

ary Wars. As French armies did battle with those of neighboring
countries, in what amounted to a struggle over the idea of monarchic supremacy, they trudged northward into the Dutch provinces,
where Prussian forces were reinforcing the *stadholder's* men. Patriots
in Amsterdam papered the city with posters and pamphlets informing their fellow citizens that the French army was on their side;
they even decked out the canals with tricolored flags. When French
troops arrived, Dutch patriots were in command of the situation, so
that instead of an invasion there was a merger of two revolutionary forces. Amsterdam willingly let itself be swallowed up by the
French Revolution. Parades filled the streets. Democracy—a radical
new system in which each male citizen was entitled to vote—was
put into effect. Willem V fled to England. A new government—the
Batavian Republic, so called after the Latin term for the tribe that
inhabited the area in Roman times—came into being.

But it too was short-lived. The emergence of Napoleon Bonaparte
brought the liberalization—this round of it, anyway—to an end.
Nevertheless, Napoleon's reorganization of the Dutch provinces
resulted in several legacies, some worthwhile, that are still part of
the Dutch system. French and Dutch cultures contrast fairly sharply:
the French favor top-down systems, where Dutch society has always
functioned more as a collective of smaller power centers. Napoleon
brought the metric system and a national governmental bureaucracy. In Amsterdam, it was the French who established the picture
collection—with Rembrandt's *Night Watch* as its centerpiece—that
eventually became the Rijksmuseum, the national art and history
museum. And Amsterdam's City Hall, built in the height of the
golden age as a testament to the city's liberal glory, was transformed
into a palace that would be home to Louis Bonaparte, the brother of
Napoleon, who installed him as King of Holland in 1806.

But Louis didn't last long either. In the wake of devastating military losses incurred in their invasion of Russia (read all about it in
War and Peace), the French abandoned the Low Countries. In 1813,
in what was perhaps the final result of French rule and surely the

greatest irony for a supposedly democratic transformation, Willem V's son (also a Willem) stepped into the French monarch's shoes, became the first Dutch king, and took up residence in the palace. Thus, late in the day, after royal rule had effectively been drained of its meaning thanks to the liberalism that the people of Amsterdam had helped to usher in, they found themselves strolling, in their daily routine, past the palace of their very own king. There is no way of saying whether William the Silent would have shaken his head at the fact that the popular revolt he led would eventually result in his own family's being installed as the hereditary rulers of the Dutch nation. In common with other blue bloods who became patriot leaders (George Washington comes to mind), he had a pretty strong personal aristocratic sensibility, so perhaps he would have found it pleasing. The Dutch monarchy persists to this day, ceremonially speaking, and the building on Dam Square remains the Royal Palace. The current king, Willem Alexander, represents the eleventh generation from the era of William the Silent.

Napoleon, meanwhile, tried once again to invade the Low Countries. It was on this campaign, on June 18, 1815, that "meeting one's Waterloo" entered the lexicon, as he was defeated by the Duke of Wellington in the village of that name near Brussels and forced into exile.

The building is practically a dollhouse: a few tiny rooms stacked on top of one another, connected by a corkscrew staircase. It looks out onto a narrow street of similar toylike homes. It's called the Multatuli House, and my guess is that if you are not Dutch the unusual name probably means nothing to you. In the mid-nineteenth century, however, it was known in Europe and America, and in 2002 the Society for Dutch Literature declared Eduard Douwes Dekker, who wrote under the pen name Multatuli, to be the most important Dutch writer of all time. Dekker was born in this modest little structure in 1820, the fourth of six children. His father was a ship's captain; the house is just a few minutes' walk from the harbor. It is also just steps from the aforementioned West India House, where my office is, which makes me feel that this most quixotic of writers, whose work ignited international upheaval that echoes to our own time, is something of a neighbor.

The parents of young Eduard sent their boy to a Latin school in the neighborhood with the idea that, bookish and clever fellow that he was, he would become a minister. But he struggled against the church. He seems to have been a hothead and something of a neighborhood scamp. When he was eighteen his father got a commission to skipper a vessel bound for the Dutch possessions in the East Indies, which roughly correspond with the modern state of Indonesia. The parents decided that Eduard would sign aboard and see if he could make something of himself in the colonies.

Dekker's experience in the East serves as a bookend to another historic voyage from Amsterdam to the East Indies that was equally momentous: that of Cornelis de Houtman 243 years earlier. If De Houtman's was the first step in the formation of the Dutch East India Company, and the launching of an age, Dekker's would mark the beginning of the end of this phase of history.

In 1799, after the VOC's losses to the British, the Dutch government had taken over its East Indies possessions, thus turning a corporate empire into a colonial empire. As the Dutch economy faltered, King Willem I became desperate to squeeze income out of the distant possessions in order to finance his budget deficit. He commissioned a dashing general named Johannes van den Bosch, who had had long service in the region, to craft a system that would make money. Thus began the so-called culture system—culture meant in the sense of cultivation. Under it, beginning in 1830, East Indies peasants had to devote 20 percent of the land they cultivated to growing crops that the Dutch could ship to the European market. Van den Bosch, as governor-general of the East Indies, sat at the top of a vast pyramid of Dutch officials and island noblemen. The system depended on the almost religious fealty that local peasants felt they owed to their nobility; the Dutch tapped into this by paying off the nobles, who in turn enforced it. It was coercive, corrupt, and brutal. Peasants, for example, were forbidden from leaving their home districts, so that in times of famine or war they were trapped. At different times thousands died of starvation. But as a moneymaking venture, the system was breathtaking. Within three years it turned a profit; eventually, hundreds of millions of guilders' worth of goods came flooding into the Netherlands. Amsterdam sea captains, such as Eduard Douwes Dekker's father, got work shipping sugar, indigo, and tea. As profits filtered through the economy, the little uptick in fortunes was reflected in the Amsterdam skyline. Some of the canal houses that had been built in the glory days of the seventeenth century and topped with the pretty little step gables and bell gables that were then in fashion, got a face-lift: those old-fashioned gables were removed and replaced with sober modern cornices. Walking along any block of the canal district will give this sense of the different eras of Amsterdam's financial dependence on the East Indies.

When young Eduard Dekker arrived in the archipelago in 1838, he became a cog in the now fully functioning culture system. He had a lengthy career there, working his way up from a clerk in Jakarta to district officer in Natal, in western Sumatra. As he experienced the exploitation of peasants firsthand, Dekker developed a righteous ardor and evolved into a whistle-blower. More than once he took the side of a local against the Dutch. He seems to have been alternately intensely devoted to his work and wildly erratic in his behavior. He received commendations and promotions but also got into fights and was suspended for a year for irregularities in his accounting. In his free time he developed a passion for gambling, based on a (mistaken) conviction that he had concocted a foolproof system for beating the roulette wheel. He fell madly in love with a Dutch girl and converted to Roman Catholicism to appease her and her parents, but she broke the engagement at her father's insistence, writing to Dekker, "He has heard such bad reports about you." Later, on an R & R excursion in Europe, Dekker gave much of his money to a French prostitute to enable her to leave her profession, then lost the rest of his money at roulette, whereupon he went back to the woman and asked her to return his gift, which she did.

In 1856 Dekker was transferred to Java Island—in fact, to the province of Bantam, the very place where Cornelis de Houtman initiated the first Dutch encounter with the Indies. He took up the position of assistant resident, which meant he was second in command of the region. Reading through the paperwork left behind by his predecessor, who had died, Dekker discovered that the man had been documenting "the gross exploitation of the people" by their Indonesian overlords, with the complicity of the Dutch. Dekker's sense of righteous indignation was now fully inflamed. He threw himself headlong into his predecessor's work, and only weeks after arriving in the province (his haste seems partly to have been motivated by a belief that his predecessor had been poisoned and that he might be next), he launched a public inquiry into the conduct of the Javanese nobleman in charge of the area, a man named Karta Nata Negara, who in the Dutch system held the title of regent. He charged the regent with extortion and systematic abuse and demanded that the resident, his immediate Dutch superior, take action. When this man refused, Dekker went directly to the governor-general of the whole colony. He too refused to act, whereupon Dekker resigned his position and determined to return to the Netherlands and try to make the Dutch aware of the abuse taking place within their system.

Back in Europe, in a white heat of creativity (writing three hundred published pages in three weeks), Dekker produced the book for which he would become famous, *Max Havelaar*, a fictionalized account of his stay in the East Indies. He got the manuscript into the hands of a famous Amsterdam lawyer and writer named Jakob van Lennep, who was dazzled by it and found a publisher. Dekker chose the histrionic pseudonym Multatuli (Latin for "I have suffered much"), and it became a sensation.

On opening the novel, even today, you experience a rush of

delight. The prose is immediate, wild, almost bizarrely modern—as if it appeared not in 1860 but more like a century later. The narrator who opens the story, for example, an officious Amsterdam coffee trader, hands the reader his business card at one point. And in the latter stages of the book, Multatuli sets his fictional alter ego aside and enters the story himself in order to comment on all that he has just written. Which is not to say that the book offers a perfect reading experience. It has long, meandering passages typical of nineteenth-century novels. And Dekker's "self-portrait" goes on for a maudlin six pages, in which he compares the character based on himself to both Socrates and Jesus.

An instant best seller in the Netherlands, *Max Havelaar* was translated and read around Europe, and it echoed throughout the Dutch government. "There has been of late a certain shudder passing through the country, caused by *a book*," one politician intoned in the parliament, and he named the feeling it aroused: "indignation." For the first time, many Europeans saw that their relatively comfortable lives were built on the misery of people in faraway places. It must have occurred to some Dutch readers that, in milking a foreign populace to alleviate their own government's financial distress, they were now doing precisely what the beleaguered Spanish empire had done to them, which had led to their revolution and independence. British reviews took special delight in using the novel to highlight the inhumanity of the Dutch colonial system, though for the most part the feelings of guilt and indignation the book aroused seem to have been collective. The first English edition of *Max Havelaar*, which appeared in 1868, three years after the end of the American Civil War and five years after the Emancipation Proclamation, contained an introduction that compared it to *Uncle Tom's Cabin* for the way it awakened a society to its systemic abuse of a whole people.

Max Havelaar appeared at a curious moment in the development of liberalism not just in Amsterdam or the Netherlands but more broadly. Over the course of the nineteenth century, liberalism underwent a titanic change: it swelled in every direction, and then, like an amoeba, it subdivided. As kings and churches lost the dominance they once had as political forces, liberalism—meaning here a system that puts ultimate significance on the individual human being—became the new norm. This transformation became clear right in the middle of the century, when, in 1848, the so-called year of revolutions (and the year, not coincidentally, when Karl Marx's *Communist Manifesto* was published), at least a dozen countries experienced political upheaval, as old monarchic orders buckled under pressure from the new forces. The Industrial Revolution, further, put a motor behind liberalism and drove it in two different directions. New industry meant new potential to make money, and thus economic liberalism rose to the status of ideology. Economic liberals all over Europe pushed to end trade barriers and otherwise keep government out of the way of business. In the Netherlands, King Willem II, facing a threat of revolution, acceded in 1848 to a new constitution, which was crafted by a liberal lawyer named Johan Rudolph Thorbecke, who soon after became prime minister. Once it was in place, power shifted from the monarchy to the parliament and to the economic liberals.

But the other variety of liberals—social liberals, who believed government had to protect individuals and who saw peril in the way modern industrialized companies could devour workers—was also on the rise. *Max Havelaar* became a rallying point for both liberal camps. So did Multatuli himself. He immediately capitalized on the fame of his book by writing others that promoted issues he was passionate about, which were related to the social liberal causes that were just beginning to stir. In 1861 he took on voting rights. At the time, only male citizens who earned a certain income, and paid a certain amount of tax, could vote. Multatuli advocated universal suffrage, at first for all adult male citizens; shortly after, he expanded his appeal to include women. Then he championed workers' rights—he connected their plight to the colonial situation, calling working people "Europe's Javanese."

And he took on established religion. He was a passionate atheist who believed that education should have the objective of weaning people off religion and leading them instead to the use of reason. Echoing Spinoza, he rejected the standard view of God and held that "Nature is everything." Going beyond Spinoza, he called faith "a plague" and "a forced substitute for knowledge." A genuine secular movement was just then in its infancy in Europe, and Dekker's writings—so public and so insistent—gave it oxygen.

In the course of the 1860s, then, a host of activist groups adopted Multatuli as one of their own—indeed, as their champion—and he became a driving force in bringing their causes into the mainstream. And yet, Eduard Douwes Dekker was a very strange, complicated man who by and large disowned these associations. Once, as socialists were in the process of championing him, he took out a newspaper ad to declare that he was not a socialist. In fact, at a time of increasing focus on individual rights, he advocated strengthening the monarchy and weakening democracy, which he did not trust. One might wonder how someone who opposed democracy could advocate universal suffrage. It was the illogic of the then current system that irritated him: I don't like democracy, he argued in effect, but if you're going to have it then by definition it should include everyone.

Indeed, Dekker was a vital but contorted presence in virtually every important cause of his time, simultaneously exciting and then locking horns with one group of activists after another. This applied above all to the anticolonial cause that would slowly unfold, which *Max Havelaar* helped to launch but from which, true to form, Dekker quickly distanced himself. For, as it turned out, Dekker did not write the book to bring down the colonial system—he actually considered himself a colonialist. Rather, it was the failure of the Dutch overlords to implement the system fully that bothered him. Colonialism, he felt, had to follow and enforce Dutch law. Dutch law forbade the kinds of abuse that he had witnessed in the East Indies. Yet the Dutch administrators there had allowed that abuse to continue. Dekker wanted not to overturn the colonial system but to strengthen it.

This fact was completely buried by the tidal wave that the book helped to create (and it remains buried to this day, as Dutch socialists and other leftists continue to hold him up as their forefather). Dekker's odd, self-contradictory beliefs were pushed aside, as society took from his writing what it wanted. Indeed, both varieties of liberals used his work, particularly *Max Havelaar*, for their own ends. Economic liberals used the book to drive their insistence that overseas colonies be opened up to private companies. Social liberals pushed for ethical reconsideration of the whole colonial system. Both sides were involved in creating the new approach that came into being, which was named the "ethical policy." Companies would be allowed into colonial territory, but with certain guidelines in place, among which were obligations to build schools and roads, to provide irrigation and other technology to locals, and to establish a Westernized local elite. The ethical policy had the same basic flaw as the culture system—it was still colonial exploitation—but it did envision, way off in the future, independence for the lands that the Dutch now ruled.

Dekker's book was a prime force in bringing about this change of thinking. And it had another wave of influence in the early twentieth century, when a new generation of Indonesian leaders, who had grown up in Westernized schools and for whom *Max Havelaar* was required reading, decided it was time for independence. The Dutch in the 1940s, however, were not so ready for it, and on top of this resistance was the complication of the Japanese occupation of the archipelago, so that Indonesian independence came only after years of warfare and tens of thousands of deaths. But it did come and, according to the celebrated Indonesian novelist Pramoedya Ananta Toer, Dekker/Multatuli was thus doubly, or even triply, influential. "The Indonesian revolution not only gave birth to a new country," he wrote in 1999, "it also sparked the call for revolution in Africa, which in turn awakened ever more of the world's colonized peoples and signaled the end of European colonial domination." In Toer's reckoning *Max Havelaar* is nothing less than "the book that killed colonialism."

———

My first act after reading *Max Havelaar* was to ask my friend Virginia Keizer to meet at an Amsterdam café. Among the book's many indirect legacies was the eventual rooting of a substantial Indonesian community in Amsterdam, which became the foundational layer of the intensely diverse immigrant population the city has today. In 2005, when I first arrived in Amsterdam, immigration was the big issue in the city, and in Europe as a whole. After years of relative openness, Amsterdam, and Europe, now wanted to close the doors. People with white skin were talking bluntly and angrily about the unwillingness of nonwhite newcomers to integrate. I noticed, however, that they made an exception for Indonesians. When I pointed this out, I always heard the same response: "Oh, but they're Dutch." People saw them as fully assimilated. The problem these same people had with other immigrant groups, then, did not have to do with skin color. The anti-immigrant talk has since died down, but the underlying issue—how and to what extent Western societies should welcome immigrants—remains. So, I wondered, what was different about the Indonesian influx that made their integration successful?

Virginia was thirty-three and lived in the Watergraafsmeer section of Amsterdam. She worked for British Telecom, where she managed the company's outsourcing to Budapest and São Paulo. She was born and raised in the Netherlands and is ethnically Indonesian.

Or not: the first thing she did was correct me. "We're not Indonesian," she said. "We're called *Indisch*, or Indo-European." Or Indo: that is the most common English term for people of mixed Dutch and Indonesian ancestry. After the Indonesian revolution, hundreds of thousands of such people, who held Dutch passports, were given a choice: renounce Dutch citizenship and become Indonesian or go. Most left Indonesia and settled in the Netherlands. Virginia's grandfather was an Indo: half Dutch (hence the name Keizer) and half Indonesian. Her grandmother was Indonesian. Both were born on Java and became part of the mass migration. In the Netherlands, they raised their family as Indo: that is, they were fully Dutch— speaking Dutch at home, celebrating Dutch holidays, keeping a picture of the queen on their wall—but also Indonesian. "Most of all, *Indisch* means food," Virginia said. When she was growing up her mother would make "normal" food during the week—*stamppot* (mashed potatoes mixed with vegetables), pea soup, spaghetti—but weekends would be all *rijsttafel*, the Indo version of an Indonesian multicourse feast.

The Indo experience, in Amsterdam and elsewhere, contrasts with that of other immigrant groups from former Dutch colonies. People from Suriname and the island of Curaçao, for example, have had a harder time: they have been less likely to integrate, and, they would say, the Dutch have shown more prejudice against them. My thinking was that this had to do with timing: the first Indos came into an overwhelmingly white, European society; they stuck out, but at the same time they had no choice but to learn the language and customs. Virginia saw it differently. In the case of Indos, she said, both the Dutch in the Netherlands and they themselves were ready to think of them as Dutch. "At the start, on the street they'd hear, 'Hey, *Bruine* (Brown)!' But that was that. They didn't let it escalate because they felt like they belonged here too." What mattered was not skin color or language skills but the fact that both the ethnic Dutch and the newcomers themselves were ready to see them as "Dutch."

Since Indos are of mixed ancestry, many look European; a lot of well-known and typically Dutch-looking Dutch people—actors, artists, politicians—are in fact Indo. One that stands out is Geert Wilders, the golden-haired far-right politician who has led the anti-immigrant, anti-Islam movement in the Netherlands in the early part of the twenty-first century. Wilders infamously compared the Koran to *Mein Kampf*, called for it to be outlawed and for anyone caught with a copy of the Muslim holy book, whether "in the household or in the mosque," to be punished. The fact that someone who claims to speak on behalf of "real" Dutch people, and against would-be infiltrators, is himself of a mixed-race, immigrant background says something about both the success of integration and some of its downsides. For one thing, with assimilation, ethnicity fades. "What upsets me is we are a dying subculture," Virginia said. "My kids won't have the feeling of the culture that my grandparents brought here." Then too, maybe this is an ironic benchmark of how well a country processes immigrants: you know you're succeeding, at least in some ways, when someone of a mixed-race, immigrant background becomes your culture's self-appointed defender of purity who preaches a gospel of intolerance of outsiders.

———

The group of thirty people who got off the train at the Willemspoort station in Amsterdam, together with another twenty who had been waiting for them on the platform, walked peacefully along the Haarlemmerdijk—"not in a procession," noted the policeman who had been assigned to keep an eye on them, "but in small groups." The date was September 7, 1872. Had I been around then I could have watched from my office window in the West India House, for they walked right past. I would have seen, in their midst, a man with a great bush of gray-white beard that met his shock of white hair. He was fifty-four years old, looked older still, but possessed the vigor of a man who had the world's attention. The Amsterdam police had gotten word from their colleagues in The Hague that, following the conclusion of the congress of the International Workingmen's Association there, Karl Marx would be heading their way. Agents were assigned to shadow his every move; the police wanted no trouble.

The next day, Marx spoke at an Amsterdam dance hall. He

started by explaining the choice of the site for the workers' congress: "In the eighteenth century, the kings and potentates were in the habit of meeting at The Hague to discuss the interests of their dynasties. It is precisely in this place that we wanted to hold our workers' meeting, despite attempts to arouse apprehensions among us. We wanted to appear amid the most reactionary population, to reinforce the existence, propagation, and hope for the future of our great association." He expressed solidarity with "our emissaries in Amsterdam . . . workers, laboring sixteen hours a day," and concluded with a vow that the movement and its ideas "will lead to the world domination by the proletariat." After the meeting, another police officer filed a report on it, which sounded a bit bored: "The speakers all argued to the same purpose: exaltation of the worker, destruction of capital, reminder to cooperate to achieve their goals." When it was over, the people sang some songs, then everybody went home quietly.

Marx may not personally have taken Amsterdam by storm, but the overall message of social liberalism was hitting as forcefully there as elsewhere. The economic liberals who had come to power in the 1850s, with a vow to keep government away and let private business run things, were now looked on by young people with anger: their laissez-faire approach had brought the city roaring into the industrial age—trade to the East Indies was resurgent, the city's diamond processing industry got a new lease on life as new mines opened up in South Africa, the harbor was being modernized to accommodate steamships—but with virtually no thought given to its social effects, this activity had brought the city to the brink of chaos. The population was in the process of doubling in less than forty years. Slums on the outskirts of the city center had swelled. There was no building code in the slums, families of eight lived in airless one-room apartments without running water. Roads there were unpaved, there were no streetlamps, human waste was carried in buckets and dumped into the canals. Cholera epidemics were routine. One public health official, on his first tour of the city slums, fainted.

As a result, trade unions had formed and became hugely popular in a short time. The concept of individual rights began to be taken up by ordinary people, as the title of the newly launched social democratic newspaper, *Recht voor Allen* ("Rights for All"), indicated.

It was indeed now a city of work and workers, a city of the industrial age. Another transformation came in 1876, when the massive new North Sea Canal opened. It had involved years of herculean effort—millions of cubic yards of sand dug by men with shovels, resulting in a six-mile-long trench that ran straight west from the IJ and connected Amsterdam directly to the ocean. The city was ready for globalization, nineteenth-century style.

A young man of twenty-four who came from the southern part of the Netherlands moved to Amsterdam just as the canal was finished and got a room in his uncle's house with a view of the harbor. Shortly after arriving, he picked up a pen and described the old-and-new mix spread out before him: "in the distance the masts of the ships in the dock" and in front of them a brand-new coal steamer, called the *Atjeh*, or *Aceh*, named for one of the provinces in the Dutch East Indies colony, "completely black, and the grey and red gun turrets." Another time, he witnessed a predawn scene in the harbor and sent an evocative description of it in a letter: "A terrible storm blew up here this morning at quarter to five, a little while later the first stream of workers came through the gate of the dockyard in the pouring rain. . . . The poplars and elders and other shrubs were bent by the strong wind, and the rain pelted on the wood-piles and the decks of the ships, sloops and a little steamboat went back and forth in the distance, near the village on the other side of the IJ, one saw brown sails passing quickly and the houses and trees on Buitenkant and churches in more vivid colors."

Indeed, it was a city of work and, at the same time, as it had been ever since the miracle of Amsterdam more than five centuries before, a city of churches. And that was what had drawn this young man. He had come to study for the ministry. Between his lessons in Latin and Greek, he made his way from church to church, sampling.

He went to the St. Olof Chapel, where, in the late 1500s, merchants had gathered to buy and sell shares of VOC stock before there was a stock market. He went to the French-speaking Walloon Church, where in 1624 Joris Rapalje and Catalina Trico had gotten married before they ventured off to America. He compared the sermons in all of them. These days preachers, as much as politicians, were speaking up for the rights of workers. A sermon he heard at the Walloon Church "consisted mainly of stories from the lives of factory workers." A preacher in the Noorderkerk spoke about the parable of the sower and drew from it the lesson of working and earning just rewards.

This preacher, Eliza Laurillard, struck the young man deeply. He equated God and nature. God, he suggested, was in all things; to find God, you didn't look in the Bible or in church—you looked at life. The young man was thrilled by this insight, and even as his own studies were foundering—he couldn't master the arcane languages, and increasing the intensity of his study drove him toward a hallucinogenic breakdown—he seemed to rediscover God, in himself and in the city around him. "It's a beautiful city, this," he wrote; "one finds it everywhere, the world is full of it, may our own heart be filled with it and become so more and more." It was in a cemetery where he went walking, "especially in the evening when the sun shines through the leaves." It was in the streets of Amsterdam: "those old, narrow, rather somber streets with chemists' shops, lithographers and other printers, shops with sea-charts and warehouses for ships' victuals." He saw it as he walked past the massive sand mountains on the waterfront where man-made islands were being created, on which the new central train station was about to rise: "the moon was shining, . . . from there it's such a wonderful sight across the city and towers, with lights here and there, . . . and everything was so deathly still." It was in a burning barge that lit up the sky one evening: "the black row of people standing there watching, and the little boats going back and forth around the blaze also appeared black in the water in which the flames were reflected." It was in "the people working with sand-carts," in the "narrow little streets with gardens full of ivy," along "a canal lined with elm trees," in "the old tar-yards" and the "gnarled undergrowth and the trees with their strange shapes." Most of all, it seemed, *it* was in the sky: "Today was stormy, on my way to my lessons this morning I looked toward the Zuiderzee from the bridge. There was one white stripe on the horizon with dark grey clouds above it, the rain pouring down from them in slanting lines in the distance."

Yet despite this expansive insight, he suffered: "Why art thou cast down, O my soul?" he quoted desperately from the Psalms. "And why art thou disquieted within me? Hope thou in God; for I shall yet praise Him, Who is the health of my countenance, and my God."

Vincent van Gogh stayed only a year in the city. When he left, a failure at the ministry as he had been a failure several times before, he was still far from being, as it were, Vincent van Gogh, far even from the decision to devote himself to art. Yet in a sense devoting himself to art was precisely what he had been doing. Everywhere he went in the city, he thought of Rembrandt; street scenes and faces and landscapes reminded him of the master. Rembrandt was the artist of the interior life. Van Gogh would be as well, but he would impress the interior life onto the outer world: onto tree trunks and cornfields and starry skies. Spinoza said God and nature were one: or rather, that God was a name for all, that God envelopes and unites what is inside us and what is beyond. Van Gogh's Greek lessons were painful, but he loved his teacher, a Portuguese Jew named Mendes who lived in the Jewish quarter, which was both Spinoza's and Rembrandt's old neighborhood and which Van Gogh loved to explore. Van Gogh was haunted by Rembrandt in Amsterdam, and finally he found him. In the last letter he wrote to his brother Theo before leaving Amsterdam, he expressed his delight that Theo had moved to Paris, and he also told him that he had discovered something he had been looking for. "I found the house in Breestraat where Rembrandt lived," he wrote. And he added, as if as a bittersweet premonition for himself, "It can be so glorious in Paris in the autumn."

Somehow, Amsterdam was simultaneously a hard-bitten, conservative place whose narrow streets were crammed with people who eked out livings as engine stokers and corn carriers and sawdust sellers, who bowed their heads in cold, echoey churches as hell and brimstone rained down, and also a place that exalted the individual, where people pushed for the spread of individual rights and nurtured an awareness of their city's historic role in the development of liberalism and wanted to show it off. Seven years after Karl Marx made his appearance and a year after Vincent van Gogh gave up on the city, an international conference on advances in medicine was held in Amsterdam. At a break in the proceedings, a tableau vivant was staged for the amusement of the guests but also to call attention to one particular advance. In this performance piece, which was entitled *The Future*, the Amsterdam hosts staged for the benefit of their foreign medical guests a reenactment of Rembrandt's *Anatomy Lesson of Dr. Tulp*, using actors in period costume, but with one difference: all the parts were played by women. Everyone got the point; everyone knew that the actress at the center of the living canvas was meant not only to represent Dr. Nicolaes Tulp, the seventeenth-century Amsterdammer who pioneered surgery, but also one of the physicians present, who was easy to spot because she was the only woman among them. The audience broke out in applause, which she acknowledged.

Her name was Aletta Jacobs. She was only twenty-five years old—almost exactly Van Gogh's contemporary—but already famous as the first Dutch woman to receive a university degree, the first ever to become a medical doctor, and one of only a handful of female doctors in the world. The idea that a medical school would accept a fully qualified female applicant had been so outrageous that she had appealed to the prime minister, Thorbecke, to intervene on her behalf so that she might gain admittance. (He approved, after first checking with her dad.)

Jacobs had become awakened to the subordinate status of women at an early age. She read, and was inspired by, Multatuli's protofeminism, and at fourteen she read *The Subjection of Women*, a pamphlet arguing for equality of the sexes that was written by John Stuart Mill, perhaps nineteenth-century Britain's most influential proponent of individual rights. "As a child I was obsessed with freedom and independence," she later wrote, "and so it was no wonder that I was alternately inspired, depressed, and terrified by the title of the Dutch version: *The Slavery of Woman*. It became my personal touchstone, intensifying everything I saw, heard, or discovered. Girls did not become doctors. I was told that universities were only for boys. When I thought about all this, I realized that men not only made laws; they also had the power to reserve every privilege for themselves and to perpetuate women's subordinate role. I knew that this had to change, but as yet I had no idea how."

After receiving her medical degree, Jacobs set up a practice on the Herengracht, one of the chic areas of the city center. But she had the heart of a social liberal and came into contact with Bernardus Heldt, a furniture maker who had become head of the General Trade Union. Through him, she got to know workers and their families and became aware of the poor level of understanding among them about reproduction and basic health and hygiene. Heldt helped her to open a free clinic. Eventually she moved it to the Jordaan, the working-class slum just outside the canal ring.

There, she identified a recurring cycle that kept women in a downward spiral: families that were already poor and struggling to stay alive kept having more babies, dragging them down still further. In the 1870s she became the country's first advocate for contraception, and one of the first anywhere. In the midst of a society and a medical profession that were rigorously Victorian in their attitudes about sex, she had patients conduct trials of contraceptives and concluded that the pessary, a kind of diaphragm, was the most effective birth control device.

She got more vocal in suggesting that it could help not only women but families and society as a whole, and she received in return, as she said, "the wrath of the entire medical establishment." That establishment was, of course, entirely male, and some of her colleagues took her championing of contraception as evidence for why women—weak, naive, not understanding the complexities of the world—should not become doctors. As the condemnation raged she took to walking in the Vondelpark, the city's new central park, wondering if maybe the prevailing arguments against contraception had validity: "Could the availability of contraception ultimately lead to a world without children?" she asked herself. "Would it cause adultery? And, if the birth rate fell, would the country's economic position be threatened?" She emerged from her period of doubt with her conviction reaffirmed, and she voiced it in practical modern language: "contraception would certainly lower the number of unwanted pregnancies and hence should be welcomed for many social, sociological, and individual reasons." Her office in the Jordaan became what some feminist historians have called the world's first birth control clinic. In time, criticism faded, and she was sought by people around the world for advice on what she called "planned motherhood."

As her fame grew, Jacobs became simultaneously a hero for many Amsterdammers and a source of confusion for her colleagues, the press, and the Dutch in general. She was a small, thin woman who would rail against injustice in what was considered a very unfeminine manner. In her bearing she remained dignified, yet in her personal life she chose a nonstandard path. She called marriage an economic trap for women, and when, at thirty-eight, she nevertheless married a radical politician named Carel Viktor Gerritsen, they crafted a modern partnership, with separate incomes and bank accounts and equality in their decision making. She led a campaign for shopgirls' rights (at the time, shops were open from eight in the morning until eleven at night and female workers were required not only to work the entire time but to stand at attention, which resulted in physical problems) and became an internationally renowned pacifist leader, eventually meeting with President Woodrow Wilson to implore him to keep the United States out of World War I (he politely rebuffed her).

Early on Jacobs came to believe that women's problems were all linked by what she considered to be the nonnegotiable matter of individual rights, and she became more strident in voicing her conviction that there was no moral justification for denying women the same rights and privileges that men had. She stepped from the birth control controversy directly into women's suffrage. In 1883 she asked the mayor and city council of Amsterdam to put her name on the list of eligible voters, basing her argument on the fact that the Dutch constitution did not specifically deny women the right to vote. The matter went to the Supreme Court, which rejected her, using logic that further incensed her. The court argued first that women "do not have full citizenship or civil rights" because "they lack the right to vote." "Ludicrous" was Jacobs's response. The court further reasoned that "husbands and fathers pay taxes for their wives and underage children, a fact that unequivocally proves married women are excluded from enfranchisement." Two years later, the Dutch constitution was revised to state explicitly that only men had the right to vote.

Jacobs took the fight abroad. In London in 1899 she participated in the first International Women's Conference, where she befriended Susan B. Anthony. With another American suffrage leader, Carrie Chapman Catt, she toured the Middle East and Asia observing and writing about the plight of women, amplifying the issue in the echo chamber of the early twentieth-century media. She lived to see women in the Netherlands get the right to vote in 1919 and in America in 1920.

By the early 1900s, Amsterdam was in the midst of a renaissance, thanks to the coming together of the two liberalisms, and with considerable help from the global economy. It was a kind of mini–golden age, and if this one did not influence the wider world as the earlier one had, it allowed the city to fashion itself into a showpiece of twentieth-century urban life: prosperous, fair, comfortable, stylish, striving. Capitalism (a word that Marx himself made famous, and he meant it to sting, but economic liberals took it to their bosoms) brought new wealth. New or revitalized industries, many of which had their origins in the East Indies, flourished. Factories in and around the city had long churned butter; in the 1870s they began converting copra (coconut) into margarine and started a related industry. The discovery of oil on Sumatra led to the founding, in 1890, of Royal Dutch Petroleum, which later merged with Shell and as of 2012 was the fourth-largest company in the world. The next year, Gerard and Frederik Philips opened a plant in Eindhoven to produce lightbulbs, and Philips went on to become a leader in nearly every new technology, from radio tubes to video cassette recorders. But Amsterdam's economic engine was multifaceted, rooted in dozens of industries. Metalworking, shipbuilding, printing, coffee brewing, diamond polishing, and tobacco processing were mainstays; Gerard Heineken started brewing beer in the city in 1864.

Of course, the economic explosion came at a price. As factories got larger and competition increased, owners slashed wages and lengthened workdays, shredding the fabric of working people's lives. Daily existence became harder to negotiate. Households came undone under the new strains. Parents were forced to send children to work; girls became prostitutes; boys stole; and when either were caught they were punished with a severity that convinced many people that the liberal government was little more than an enforcer of the capitalists' system. Trade unions and socialist parties thus grew further in stature, because they held out the promise of making life fairer and less harsh, but also because with their regular meetings and newspapers they offered a new kind of community to replace lost comforts and traditions.

All of the above was true in many places, but the social and political struggle took on a different aspect in the Netherlands. Marxism and socialism had the goal—the dark and fearful goal, as many saw it—of outright revolution. The Dutch moved faster than others away from that ideology and toward the more pragmatic project of working within the system to improve the lives of workers. The debate between doctrinaire Marxists and social reformers came to a head in the 1890s. One of the leaders of the orthodox Marxist camp was a firebrand named Herman Gorter, whom I feel compelled to talk about for a couple of paragraphs because I find him such a rich personality: the sort of person you would fall into deep friendship with in one all-night conversation during college, then spend the rest of your life trying to avoid. Gorter studied classical languages at the University of Amsterdam and launched into a career as a poet of nature. At age twenty-five he published what would be his best-known work, *May: A Poem*. Then he collapsed in depression. What brought him out of it, besides his mother's nurturing, was Spinoza, whom he took up as the final arbiter on truth and nature. He published a Dutch translation of Spinoza's *Ethics* and also a collection of "Spinozistic poems."

Then Gorter became smitten by socialism. Spinoza was out the window; Marx was his man. Gorter had never really worked himself—he tried teaching but found students to be an annoyance—but he became convinced that Marx's revolutionary theory about society and economic justice had a mystical, absolute truth. He became a popular public speaker on the plight of the working class and the coming revolution. He joined the Social Democratic Party, forerunner of the Dutch Communist Party, and became the editor of its journal. He grew into a revered figure, though he also seems to have been a bit of a joke to the metalworkers and pipe fitters and printers who attended party gatherings. Gorter seemed oblivious to the contrast between his take-no-prisoners revolutionary rhetoric on the one hand and his personal appearance on the other—he favored a straw hat and pince-nez—and his bourgeois private life, which involved playing tennis and cricket. As it turned out, Gorter's personal interest in Marxist revolution was equally contradictory. He wanted to turn Marx's truths into a new form of mystical poetry. He published a collection of verse that took the reader through the aesthetic stages of mankind's economic awakening, climaxing with rapturous communism. The Bolshevik Revolution in Russia propelled him to even greater heights, resulting in poetry that, to say the least, has not aged well. His last collection is entitled *The Workers' Council.*

On the other side of the social liberalism debate stood a man named Henri Polak. Polak had grown up in a family of eleven children squeezed into an apartment on Amsterdam's Butter Market, one of those workers' families that had been battered by unchecked economic liberalism. Despite being a brilliant student, he was forced to leave school at age thirteen to work in a diamond polishing factory in order to help keep the family together. At eighteen, he went to London and at Hyde Park rallies became entranced with the ideas of Marx. When he returned to Amsterdam, he joined the doctrinaire Socialist Party, but he grew tired of its ideological fervor, which he felt was too far removed from the real world, and began to work toward a practical form of social liberalism.

The evolution of Polak's ideas had a great deal to do with the fact that he was a Jew. Like Jews elsewhere, those in Amsterdam kept a low profile; they were predominantly workers, and so they were attracted to the socialist program of fairness and decency. But they were deeply repelled by the idea of revolution. They knew from centuries of experience which group would become the scapegoat if things turned out badly. Polak read widely and while in England was influenced by the Fabian Society, which promoted a moderate path between socialism and capitalism. He cofounded the Dutch diamond workers' union (whose members were overwhelmingly Jewish) and became its chairman. From that perch he was able to put his ideas into practice. He wanted not only decent housing for workers but something more: beauty, a genuinely good life. Under him, the union provided health insurance and offered classes for personal improvement; workers had access to a library; they got instruction in personal hygiene and even suggestions on how to furnish their homes. Polak commissioned a new headquarters, designed by Hendrik Berlage, the most sought-after architect of the day. Berlage conceived of it as a modernist version of a medieval Italian palazzo, a palace for the people, and so it was called The Citadel. Today the building is a small museum; touring it offers a sense of the exquisite, handcrafted care that went into this effervescent idea of turning the top-down capitalist system on its side and giving workers a sense of the good life. The building incorporates stained glass, sculpted brickwork, art nouveau murals, and an inscription in which the workers thank their board for introducing the eight-hour workday, which took effect in the Netherlands in 1919.

The diamond workers' union became the model for the city's other trade unions, and Polak went on to head both the national federation of trade unions and the international federation of diamond workers, exerting a huge moderating influence on the prevailing social liberalism.

For a time, hard-core Marxist leaders and those advocating social reform without revolution battled it out in Amsterdam, while much of the working class sat on the sidelines. The argument over which direction social liberalism should take was carried out in union halls and newspapers, but the center of it was a café along the Amstel River called the Ysbreeker (Icebreaker), which still exists and which was the watering hole of leaders of both groups.

When the shouting was over, Herman Gorter and the hard-core socialists did not hold sway in Amsterdam; they faded. Instead, something else was born. The features of the city of today were coming into focus—and they had an already familiar look. The Amsterdam that emerged out of the early twentieth century would be a capitalist place, a place of business and money, but it would at the same time wholeheartedly commit itself to the "social" path: to providing a blanket, a safety net. How, outsiders may wonder, could it do both? The short answer is: by having the capitalists themselves join in the commitment to social welfare. You can trace this commitment back to the seventeenth century, when the regents who ran the city— the merchants who were principals in the VOC—created (often, it must be said, after intense battles) some of Europe's first orphanages, homes for the elderly, and an urban structure in which rich and poor were not segregated but lived in the same neighborhoods.

But you can go further back than that in looking for the roots of this dual identity: to the very founding of the city, and the battle against water. Early in this book I highlighted the curious notion that the struggle to reclaim land and then to protect it from the sea involved two seemingly contradictory factors: it was both a communal project and one that fostered intense individualism. Imagine a group of people in the Middle Ages standing on a shore, looking out across the water, and deciding that they would reengineer what they were looking at, make land where now there was water, and do it entirely with sweat and backbreaking labor. The degree of cooperation required would surely be a powerful binding force for a community, as would the long-term project of maintaining a system of dams and dikes to keep the water at bay. And once they had reclaimed the land, it was not, as was the case elsewhere in Europe, the property of a church or king: it was *theirs*. Individuals were free to buy, sell, or rent it. That protocapitalist power excited an individualistic sensibility. Yet it was only possible because of the underlying social bond. This combination, which seems in many other places to be a contradiction, became an essential part of the city's identity.

The combination was personified in one man. As socialists advanced, they gained a powerful leader. Floor Wibaut had been raised in a Roman Catholic household and considered becoming a priest, but at age seventeen he came into contact with Multatuli's progressive antireligion writings and abruptly dropped his faith and went into the timber trade. He became highly successful—selling as far as Russia and the United States—and rich. At the same time, he was deeply affected by the ideas of class and fairness that were in the air. He joined the socialists and won a seat on the city council.

From that perch, he oversaw the biggest expansion in the city's history. As it had during its early golden age, Amsterdam annexed a vast semicircle of land on its outskirts, tripling its size, and sketched out new neighborhoods for its growing population. Wibaut determined to imprint Henri Polak's social vision into the city's geography: "The point of departure for raising the culture of the working class," Wibaut said, "must lie in the improvement of housing conditions." Hendrik Berlage—who had designed The Citadel for the diamond workers—crafted the layout for the new areas, and dozens of young architects filled in the blanks on the map. The new area would complement the seventeenth-century canal zone without trying to duplicate it. That earlier expansion, which brought the Amsterdam canal house into its own, was a kind of response to the monumental architecture of cities like Paris and London, suggesting, in effect, that the greatness that this city would herald was not in institutions but in its people, its families, their ordinary lives. The city's new zone would be a recommitment to that notion, but in a style that spoke to the modern age. The town houses that went up—block after block of them—followed a few common design principles: they were made of brick, not too high, and fairly uniform in width. But beyond that the architects let themselves play. They sculpted in brick, created curves and turrets, wove animals and small children into the masonry, incorporated glazed tiles and stained glass, riffed on the gables of the seventeenth-century canal houses located just a few minutes' walk away. Their immediate aesthetic influence came from Germany, but the style was distinct enough that they became known as the Amsterdam School.

The town houses were to be sold, but the apartment buildings were intended as social housing. Even more loving attention went into these. The most famous is called The Ship: a block-long apartment complex near the waterfront, built of brick, seemingly ready to sail away. (Today it is a museum devoted to Amsterdam School architecture.) In all, thirty thousand dwellings were created in the six-year period between 1915 and 1921. Wibaut was aided by a personality that was by turns domineering and cajoling—the press took to calling him The Mighty—and by good fortune: he had the tailwinds of history with him. The fortunate convergence seemed to carry right down to his name. His political campaign slogan was "Wie bouwt? Wibaut!" The question and answer are pronounced the same in Dutch; the question means, "Who builds?"

But Wibaut had something more going for him. He was not the stereotypical socialist city planner, oblivious to and indignant about larger economic realities, but an experienced, savvy businessman who made this massive real estate project work by overseeing a novel approach. Private developers did the building, and made profits, but, together with an economic liberal in the city government named Willem Treub, Wibaut fashioned something called *erfpacht*, or "ground rent," which gave owners long-term rent of the land their building stood on rather than ownership of it; this arrangement avoided the kind of speculation and corruption that had defined the seventeenth-century expansion. Social housing complexes, meanwhile, were run by housing corporations, which allowed for both private investment and government oversight. The system has been altered many times since the early twentieth century, but its basic feature—mixing capitalist incentive and a commitment to the public good—is still the goal.

The sensibility that brought social and economic liberals together in Amsterdam in the early twentieth century is captured in a single structure, which foreshadowed Wibaut's era. In 1903, a new "church" of economic liberalism was christened, which had also been designed by Hendrik Berlage: a modern stock exchange, just up the road from where the original seventeenth-century one had stood. Berlage created a fortress of a building that mixed traditional, even ancient, stylistic references with new elements, festooning it with terra cotta and gold tile murals. Its relief panels and poems convey a bewildering hybrid of signals about capitalism, socialism, society, and where it should be going. One relief shows paradise in the form of a matriarchal society; another shows people from all walks of life with the motto beneath declaring rather confidently that

> the earth will soon be one; its people as groups
> all forming one great union the wide world round.

The building was all about capitalism, but its facade, its message, was social—and its design was an attempt to bring the two forces together.

A strange thing about journals and personal correspondence of Amsterdammers in the period from 1914 to 1918 is that they just hum along; ordinary life carries on. It's strange because there was a world war going on. The Dutch government managed to maintain a position of neutrality based on the belief that the war was a struggle for world dominance by major powers, which their little country had no part in. (As one Dutch writer later put it, "Our self-esteem told us that we were too good to fatten other people's ambitions with our blood.") So while the Dutch army was on continual maneuvers during the Great War, the city of Amsterdam trundled along, pausing its expansion plan but not halting it.

As soon as the war was over, the development continued. A stadium went up amid the apartment complexes—and became the centerpiece of the 1928 Olympics. As far as the city's leaders in the 1920s were concerned, the expansion offered an opportunity not only to tear down slums and provide new living spaces but to change the social dynamic. Henri Polak was a devotee of the Enlightenment, and he wanted to encourage workers to loosen the chains of their traditions, particularly religious traditions, and to become versed in science and art. He had in mind particularly his fellow Jews. Amsterdam's relative tolerance of Jews, so novel in the seventeenth century, had by this time resulted in a community of eighty thousand, 13 percent of the total population. But of course the tolerance had always been limited, and ever since the time of Spinoza Jews had kept themselves largely in the old Jewish neighborhood. Polak encouraged them to move out, to mix with the wider community.

And they did: thousands left the cramped quarters of the old ghetto and moved into the new neighborhoods on the southern perimeter. Apartments and houses there were modern, with larger rooms, clean white walls in place of fusty wallpaper, and broad and inviting avenues to stroll along outside the windows. People moved into new jobs as well, and intermarrying between Jews and non-Jews became more common. Certainly discrimination existed, but there was a fresh wind blowing, a feeling that the twentieth century was going to be different from everything that had come before.

The stories of three families may give a sense of this hopeful, newly expansive, but brief moment of the city's history. Of course, many of the Jews who moved into the new district were diamond workers. A cluster of streets preserves the memory of the time in their names: Topaz Street, Diamond Street, Emerald Square. One couple in particular moved to Sapphire Street. Another moved a few blocks up the river. The boy from the one family, whose name was Joël Brommet, fell in love with Rebecca Ritmeester, the girl from the other. They married, and the young man, who had an artistic sensibility, began to work with fabric and window design for shops. In 1925 they had a daughter whom they named Frieda, and the little family moved to the Zuider Amstellaan, or Southern Amstel Avenue, one of the wide boulevards that Berlage had laid out. Frieda spent her girlhood in the embrace of her extended family, living a few blocks from both sets of grandparents. She had an easy life, she tells me. Her parents doted on her.

Meanwhile, another son of a Jewish diamond cutter, whose

name was Bernard Premsela, fell in love with a girl named Rosalie, married her, and moved with her to an address just across the river, in what is now called Spinozastraat. In the same year that they married, 1913, Bernard Premsela got his medical degree. He came under the influence of Aletta Jacobs, and in this expansive, liberal era he became consumed by thoughts of sex: that is, he realized that gender differences, sexual urges, and the act of sex constituted a large portion of what it meant to be human, and yet society had caged and perverted this vast and undeniable force. He decided to specialize in something that almost didn't exist. He chose to become a sexologist.

Following Aletta Jacobs, he focused first on birth control. As a socialist, he saw it initially as a way to help lift people out of poverty, but as his ideas expanded he concentrated more on women. He believed that equality between the sexes should be a goal of society and that birth control was a tool to achieve this, for it helped protect women against, as he said, the "excessive procreative demands" of men. After Jacobs's death in 1929, Premsela helped to found the Aletta Jacobs House, a family planning clinic, and became its director. The next year he held a public event at the American Hotel—one of the big new structures that architecturally defined the city's new golden age—at which people discreetly submitted questions about sex to him in writing. For by now he was interested not just in birth control but in sex as a means of personal growth and liberation. He began a radio show about sex. He wrote a series of books with titles that sound more like they were written in the 1970s than the 1930s: *Sexual Education for Our Children*. It was all quite shocking to the prevailing conservative culture, but Bernard Premsela maintained a serious, dignified persona, and he pulled it off. It also helped that he enlisted the aid of Floor Wibaut, whose advocacy of sexual reform and women's rights dated from his reading Multatuli in his early years.

At home, meanwhile, Bernard and Rosalie had three children, and when the time was right Rosalie taught them frankly about sex using her husband's books. Benno, the youngest of the three, later remembered being aware in the schoolyard that he knew colossally more than his classmates knew about the human body and what people did in their bedrooms. Overall, he said, the atmosphere in their household was secular and progressive, which matched that of many Amsterdam Jews. "We may have been Jews," he said, "but we were not religious at all. Socialism and humanism were of much greater importance."

Jews were also emigrating to the city from other parts of Europe. Amsterdam was now, as it had been in different eras in the past, a famously liberal place: tolerant, relatively speaking, and a city whose planners had adopted quality of life for ordinary people as part of their program. Otto Frank was a German Jew, born in Frankfurt and raised in wealth: his father was the president of a bank that bore his name. At Heidelberg University, Otto became friends with a German American named Nathan Straus, whose family owned Macy's department store in New York. Straus got him a job at Macy's, and Otto crossed the ocean and threw himself into the adventure and whirl of midtown Manhattan. His father's death, however, forced a change to his plans. He returned to Germany and took over the task of rescuing the bank. Then World War I broke out; he served in the German army. After the war, he married Edith Holländer. The two struggled through the painful postwar period, when Germans suffered economic depression, hyperinflation, humiliation, and poverty. It was a lousy time to be in the banking business. Otto tried to keep the bank afloat by moving it to Amsterdam. It didn't work; he returned to Frankfurt and eventually the Michael Frank Bank went bust.

The Wall Street crash of 1929 set off depression in European cities starting the following year. Germany was hardest hit; as unemployment reached six million, the national socialists grew stronger. By 1933, Otto and Edith Frank had two daughters: Margot, who was seven, and Anne, who was four. The collapse of the bank coincided with the appointment of Adolf Hitler to the position of chancellor. Otto Frank was prescient, and he decided that for the foreseeable future Germany was not going to be a comfortable place for Jews.

The Franks moved to Amsterdam, which they knew to be a refuge, as well as a place where Otto had connections. He got a job as the Dutch distributor for a company called Opekta, which marketed pectin, the gel that is the basis for making jam. The Franks took an apartment on the Merwedeplein, right around the corner from Frieda Brommet.

Amsterdam by now was suffering as well from the global down-turn: 20 percent of the population was unemployed, and out-of-work men stood in lines to be transported out of the city to labor camps. For kids, though, at least according to the memories of people I have interviewed, it was still a haven. The 1930s unfolded like a languid dream. Frieda's parents rented a beach house in nearby Zandvoort every summer. For her birthday, her father hired a band that would show up at her doorstep to serenade her. Neighbors soon discov-ered that Anne and Margot Frank had rather opposite personalities. Anne was outgoing and opinionated. According to one story, when she was four and got on a crowded streetcar with her grandmother, she called out, "Won't someone offer a seat to this old lady?" Margot, three years older than Anne, was quiet and bookish but still a part of things. Jaap Groen, who was the same age as Margot and now lives in Atlanta, Georgia, remembers playing baseball with Margot on the square in front of her house. Frieda remembers skipping rope with the Frank girls.

Frieda and Anne were precocious when it came to boys. Frieda, who was four years older than Anne, had several boyfriends in her teens. Two of them were named Andre. "But my great love," she said to me one day as she reminisced in her apartment, and I think she meant really the great love of her life, "was Bob de Jong." Bob combed his blond hair straight back and had a calm, patient face. She showed me a picture of herself with Bob, with both of them looking into the camera. He looks earnest and has a slight smile. Frieda looks a bit moody. "The eternal couple," she said as we stud-ied the picture together.

Bob's family lived near Frieda's, close to the Olympic stadium.

"I never went to his house," Frieda said. "He would come here, and then we'd walk. Through the Maasstraat to the Zuidelijke Wandelweg, then to the left. There was a café called The Calf. We'd go to the upstairs room because it was usually empty. We'd have hot chocolate if we could afford it, and if not we'd get coffee, which we hated. Then we'd sit in the empty room and cuddle."

Bob and Frieda were still carrying on their teen love after Nazi tanks had appeared on the streets. For a short time, people in their neighborhood behaved as they had before: strolled along wide boulevards, while overhead the branches of the young trees that had been planted following Berlage's design swayed under spring breezes. But a thickness was gathering in the air. Bob felt both it and his swelling heart. He wrote a poem:

> But despite the sadness I see
> While I wait for happier times,
> One thing shines out above all.
> That is Love, the little rogue,
> Who gave me the prettiest thing he had,
> A small precious treasure
> Who looks at me so happily
> And seems like a little princess.

A few months later, Bob was among the first Jews to be taken by the Nazis, one of the first to go to Auschwitz. Frieda heard later that Dr. Josef Mengele had singled him out for a place in the ward reserved for subjects for his human experimentation program. Liberalism, the evolving attempt to fully express the human, was about to face an inhuman threat.

CHAPTER

9

"WE INFORM YOU OF THE ACTION OF A POWERFUL GERMAN FORCE"

If you go online and search "Anne Frank video," you will find a twenty-second snippet of black-and-white footage. It was shot in Amsterdam on June 22, 1941, right around the time that Bob de Jong wrote his poem to Frieda Brommet and just before the Nazi presence in the city became a horror. A couple on Merwedeplein got married on this day, and a friend captured the bride and groom leaving their apartment. Three things stand out in this simultaneously remarkable and humdrum bit of film. First and most obviously, as the camera pans upward for an instant you see Anne Frank, just turned twelve, pop her head out the window of her apartment to watch the couple step out into the daylight in their finery. What is striking is not only that we have here the only existing film footage of her but that this quick flash actually gives a sense of who she was. Nearly everyone who knew her remembered Anne Frank as fidgety and quick-witted, the kind of girl who could be a handful for her parents. Watch the film and you see her give one sharp turn of her head to say something to someone inside, presumably her mother or father. It's a sassy motion; it brims with attitude. It fits precisely what we know of her.

The second thing the little film shows is the new section of

Amsterdam, whose construction Floor Wibaut oversaw. It's all fresh and clean looking and, most of all, modern. This is not the city of Rembrandt. It's not even the city that Vincent van Gogh wandered during his sojourn in the 1870s. It's recognizably a place that any of us today would feel at home in: you can almost hear the flush toilets flushing, and you know that, come evening, electric lamps will be snapped on.

The third thing that stands out is how normal life looks. At the end of the clip the camera pans down the street. We see people strolling, people on bicycles; two cars turn a corner. It's a calm, sunny day and a couple are heading off to their wedding while others take casual note.

Over the previous year or so, as Nazi Germany made its first moves to swallow chunks of Europe, the Dutch had remained astoundingly at ease. They believed that history would repeat itself: as they had twenty-six years before, they declared themselves neutral, and most Dutch people thought that, as before, the combatants would respect the declaration. Indeed, Hitler vowed in a speech to the Reichstag that he would honor the Dutch stance. Then the next day he ordered the invasion of the country—saying, with some accuracy, "Nobody will question that after we have conquered." Even after numerous indications of an imminent attack, on the evening of May 9, 1940, the editors of the newspaper *Algemeen Handelsblad* were sanguine enough to lay out a story with the headline "Tensions Defused. Expected Events Not to Occur." In the predawn, within hours of the paper's hitting the stands, people all over the country ran outside in their pajamas to watch heavy aircraft lumbering overhead. A couple of hours later, a man named Count Julius von Zech-Burkersroda, who was the German ambassador to the Netherlands, met with the Dutch foreign minister, Eelco van Kleffens. The count was a very old-school diplomat whose service had begun in the aristocratic twilight of 1909. He had been as duped by Hitler as had the Dutch. His job now was to read a declaration-of-war telegram to

Van Kleffens, but in his shame and confusion words failed him, and the Dutchman took the paper and read it himself: "We inform you of the action of a powerful German force. Resistance is completely senseless."

The Dutch military mounted a vigorous but brief defense, which may have been worse than immediate capitulation. After troops battled Germans to a standstill outside Rotterdam, Colonel Pieter Scharroo, the Dutch officer in charge, refused to surrender even when told an air strike was imminent. Ninety German planes proceeded to drop more than one hundred tons of bombs, setting off firestorms that destroyed the city center. Five days after German planes crossed into Dutch airspace, and after the Germans threatened to do to Utrecht what they had done to Rotterdam, the Dutch commanding general surrendered. The Nazi occupation had begun.

Amsterdam suffered little outright war damage. A German plane that had taken a hit in the skies above unloaded two of its bombs, one of which landed at the corner of the Herengracht and Blauwburgwal, destroying a building and killing forty-four people. Four days later, on May 15, 1940, a long column of German soldiers rode unimpeded into the city to take possession. Members of the Dutch Nazi party, the NSB, who had been getting thuggish in public for several years, lined the streets and gave the Nazi salute. Everyone else just watched.

The Germans ensconced themselves throughout the city. The dreaded Sicherheitspolizei, the Security Police, which included the Gestapo, set up shop in a school on the Euterpestraat, in the new Zuid district created by Wibaut. The Reichskommissar chose as its headquarters a mansion on Museum Square, in what, curiously enough, is today the American consulate. A building on Vijzelstraat that was the headquarters of the Dutch Trading Association was taken over by the Luftwaffe. The building today is home to the Amsterdam City Archives, repository of the documentary remains of every Amsterdammer going back to the city's founding. If you are invited into the office of its director, you can see a clock on the wall

(ABOVE) Frieda Menco's family gathered at her Amsterdam apartment just before the Nazi invasion. Frieda is in the back on the right, standing behind her grandparents. Of the seventeen people pictured, twelve would die in the war, most at Auschwitz. *Courtesy Frieda Menco*

(RIGHT) Frieda Menco in 2013. *Photo: Russell Shorto*

(BELOW) Anne Frank (center) walking next to her father and with others en route to the wedding of his employee Miep Gies. The crucial thing to note is the date: June 1941. The city had been under Nazi occupation for more than a year, but, at this point, Jews in Amsterdam could still smile. *Courtesy Anne Frank Family*

(ABOVE) A Nazi show of power in Amsterdam, March 1941. *Courtesy Beeldbank WO2–NIOD*

(RIGHT) Walraven van Hall, the banker who led the Dutch resistance. *Courtesy Aad van Hall*

(BELOW) After World War II, a huge crowd turned out as Euterpestraat—a street that had been hated as the location of the Nazi SD and Gestapo in Amsterdam—was renamed in honor of slain resistance leader Gerrit van der Veen. *Courtesy Beeldbank WO2–NIOD*

Dutch designer and gay rights
pioneer Benno Premsela, who
hid from the Nazis and emerged
with the conviction that he would
never again hide who he was.
He is pictured here during one
of the groundbreaking television
interviews in which he declared
homosexuality to be normal.
Courtesy Stadsarchief Amsterdam

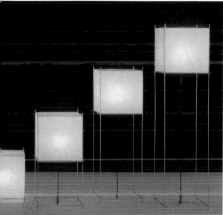

Probably Benno Premsela's most famous and
enduring design was the "Lotek lamp."
Courtesy www.hollandslicht.eu

Robert Jasper Grootveld leading a
happening at the *Lieverdje* statue:
the center of Amsterdam's 1960s
counterculture movement.
Photo: Cor Jaring

The cover of the first issue of *Provo*.
Courtesy Roel van Duijn

The wedding procession of Princess Beatrix and the German nobleman Claus von Amsberg was successfully marred by Provo smoke bombs, despite the heavy police presence. *Courtesy ANP*

The "white bicycle plan," which was to make bicycles available free of charge as a way to counter automobiles, failed. But in time it would spawn a new approach to bicycles in cities worldwide.
Photo: Cor Jaring

(RIGHT) John and Yoko's bed-in for peace, at the Amsterdam Hilton, helped cement the city's image as a global counterculture center.
Courtesy National Archief

Theo van Gogh, whose murder in 2004 led to a crisis point in the Dutch experiment with multiculturalism. *Courtesy Hollandse Hoogte*

(ABOVE) With 178 different nationalities, Amsterdam tops even New York in diversity. *Photo: Miriam van der Meij*

(RIGHT) Contemporary Dutch photographer Hendrik Kerstens riffs on seventeenth-century portraiture, using his daughter and a plastic bag. © *Hendrik Kerstens, courtesy Nunc Contemporary*

(BELOW) Amsterdam's bicycle network leads those of all other cities. There are two-way bike lanes, bicycle parking garages, and bicycle streetlamps. According to city statistics, 40 percent of every mile of human transport in the city is via bicycle. *Photo: Miriam van der Meij*

The horseshoe curve of the seventeenth-century canals,
wrapping around the medieval center, still defines Amsterdam.

Courtesy Hollandse Hoogte

With its groundbreaking orientation on the individual family and on the concepts of private space and *gezelligheid*, or coziness, the Dutch canal house of the seventeenth century became, in a sense, the first modern home. *Photo: Tim Killiam*

Modern canal houses in Amsterdam still employ traditional themes. They are built on the water, each made for a family, each with its own boat mooring. *Photo: Miriam van der Meij*

that has a small hole near the numeral 1. The story goes that the Luftwaffe commandant told the head of the trading association that he had to be out by one o'clock; when the man began to hem and haw, the commandant pulled out his pistol and aimed a bullet at the relevant numeral to underscore the deadline.

For the most part, though, things were calm in the months after the occupation set in. Look again at the snippet of Anne Frank film while holding in mind a backdrop of recent events. The Germans had just taken Crete by aerial invasion; a pogrom in Baghdad had resulted in hundreds of Jews being murdered, some of them hacked with swords; Croats had rampaged against Serbs in Croatia; Allied forces were conducting an invasion of Syria. Mass executions of Jews in Poland had begun shortly after the Nazi takeover of that country, nearly two years before. How, then, could peaceful, normal life be carrying on in the Jewish section of Amsterdam, a city that was under Nazi occupation and in a world that was being engulfed by the flames of war?

The disconnect points ironically to the subtitle of this book and the concept of liberalism. If you look at Nazism from a great enough distance, it seems like something that would undergird a bad science fiction or fantasy novel: a philosophy of racial purity based on the theory of a master race of warriors who swept down in chariots from their idyllic northern European homeland into India and Iran, where they spawned the philosophies of Hinduism and Zoroastrianism but over time became degraded by mixing with lesser races, while their northern remnants valiantly kept the bloodline pure. As if to accentuate the cheesy pop fiction image, Alfred Rosenberg, the chief architect of Nazi racial theory, argued that the original home of the Aryan race was none other than the lost city of Atlantis.

Silliness aside, the racial purity philosophy that powered Nazism—or, for that matter, "purity" as a goal in any social context—pretty much defines the opposite of liberalism. The Netherlands, and Amsterdam in particular, was historically a seedbed for liberal ideas: for tolerance of differences and for empowering the individual. It's all the more curious, then, that the Nazis had a special plan for the country. For they did the Dutch the honor of believing that "pure" Dutch descent was on a par with "pure" German descent—both groups were held to be part of the same Aryan stock. They planned to incorporate the Netherlands into a greater Germany after the war. The Germans hoped therefore to occupy the country and quietly neaten up its racial situation—to separate the good genes from the bad—without causing the chaos and turmoil that ensued in Poland, for example. That explains the calm that Anne Frank and Frieda Brommet enjoyed in 1941. The plan, in other words, was to turn the homeland of liberalism into a place governed by a polar opposite philosophy: a totalitarian, lethally intolerant, radically anti-individual ideology.

In many ways, the Dutch obliged the Germans in their quest to sort out the country's racial situation. Dutch society had, over the preceding decades, dealt with the increasing complexity of its social makeup by introducing something it called the pillar system. Pillarization was an effort to keep peace by giving different groups their own social space. The main pillars were Catholic, Protestant, socialist, and liberal. Each group had its institutional structures: its own newspapers, radio stations, schools, even banks. The pillar system had the advantage that it subdivided Dutch society into groups. Jews fell under the socialist pillar. Like everyone else, they were also cataloged; their addresses were on file. All of this made the Nazis' work easier. Beyond that, at the slightest prompting from the Germans, a Dutch bureaucrat named Jacob Lentz took it upon himself to create a nearly counterfeit-proof personal identity card. Lentz was so proud of his handiwork that he traveled to Berlin to show it off, and he wrote a little book about it. The Germans loved it and ordered every Dutch citizen to have one; those issued to Jews were stamped with a large J. Nothing like it had ever existed before. This little device became, in the words of Loe de Jong, the preeminent historian of World War II in the Netherlands, "an indispensable aid to the persecution policy of the German occupation."

The helpfulness of the Dutch points to one of the darkest statistics of the war. Jews in the Netherlands had far and away the lowest survival rate of Jews in Europe. Where 75 percent of Jews in France lived through the Nazi period, for example, only 27 percent of Dutch Jews did. Of approximately 80,000 Jews in Amsterdam at the start of the war, an estimated 58,000 were dead by the time it was over, most of them in concentration camps. The Dutch themselves aided, inadvertently but with great efficiency, in a systematic effort at eradicating their country's liberal heritage.

Jews too were instrumental in the assistance they gave the Germans. The Nazi occupiers ordered two prominent Amsterdam Jews, Abraham Asscher, a diamond merchant, and David Cohen, a professor, to form a Jewish council that would transmit instructions to the Jewish population. Asscher and Cohen did as they were told. The council published a weekly newspaper through which it passed along orders such as the decree that all Jews wear yellow stars, and when deportation orders began to come, it advised people to obey them. Of course, at the time no one had any idea that those being deported were headed to death camps; Asscher and Cohen convinced themselves that they were making the best of an impossible situation. But as Loe de Jong writes, "The path of collaboration . . . is a most slippery one." The Nazis slowly enmeshed the Jewish council into their system, by first asking its members to issue deportation notices only to German Jews living in the Netherlands, then broadening the decree to include all Jews, then "suggesting" that the council itself make the lists of those to be deported. Finally, after most everyone had been rounded up, Asscher, Cohen, and the other members of the Jewish council received their own deportation notices. While all the other members of the council died in concentration camps, Asscher and Cohen survived; in 1947 they were found guilty by a "Jewish Council of Honor" of abetting the Nazis.

Via the Jewish council, the Nazi overlords of Amsterdam steadily tightened the noose around the neck of the city's Jewish population. First, Jewish teachers were dismissed from their positions. Then

Jews on the city council were forced to resign. As NSB members caught on to what was happening, they brought the aggression out in the open, committing group assaults on Jews in public. In February of 1941 a vast meeting was held on the Noordermarkt, at which a general strike was proclaimed to protest what was transpiring. The strike was organized by the Communist Party and the call was taken up by the socialists. Striking was a tool that workers had become familiar with, and it seemed a rational move, but of course it was against an opponent that was playing a game of an entirely different order from that of factory owners. The strike was remarkable in that, despite the existence in Amsterdam of the same pervasive anti-Semitism that was prevalent in every other European city, it was held overtly in sympathy with Jewish fellow residents, as well as in support of Dutch workers who were being shipped to forced labor in German factories. It was a remarkably daring citywide action. De Jong calls it "the first and only antipogrom strike in human history."

The February Strike brought the city to a halt. And it got the Germans' attention. The noose was now tightened more assertively. Jewish doctors were forbidden to practice. Then Jews were barred from city parks, from concert halls, from libraries, from restaurants, from public buses. As of March 1942 it was against the law for Jews to have sex with non-Jews. In May came the ruling that all Jews had to wear a yellow star when they went outside. At some point during my series of weekly interviews with Frieda Menco, who in 1942 was the teenaged Frieda Brommet, I asked about the stars. She described the ritual around them. "Everyone got several of them. They were made of cotton." "Did you pin it on your coat?" I asked. "No, my mother would sew it on. I remember when we were going out she would say, 'Do you have your star on?' Like she was asking if I had my hat on. Do you want to see one?"

I was taken aback. "You have one?"

She rummaged in a drawer and laid a small piece of fabric in my hands. It was very thin; its yellow had a faintly metallic sheen; the lines of its intersecting triangles looked childish, as if they had been drawn by marker. I noted, however, that it said *Jude*, the German word for Jew, rather than *Jood*. "This one wasn't mine," Frieda said. "I got it from an old German Jewish woman. After she died, a friend of hers invited me to look at her things, to see if there was something I wanted to have. What I wanted was the star."

Frieda's mother felt the heaviness of those feathery bits of cloth. The heaviness was reinforced by the next order: Jews were not allowed outside after 8:00 p.m. "Now we are trapped," Rebecca Brommet said at the time. "Now we have fallen into their hands."

The deportations began in July. When Frieda's name appeared on one of the first lists of Jews to be sent to "work camp," her father made her scrub her whole body with sandpaper. Such a strange decree from her father somehow frightened her more than the Nazis did. She did as she was told, scarring herself to the point of bleeding, then stood shivering naked in the bathroom feeling shame and confusion as her father studied every inch of her sixteen-year-old body. He then went to the authorities and played his gamble: he told them his daughter had contracted scarlet fever. The deception bought the family time; Frieda was ordered to report later.

On his way home from this modest victory, Joël Brommet got caught in one of the *razzias*, the random raids on Jews that were now being carried out as an intimidation tactic, and was taken into custody by two German soldiers, along with about twenty other Jews. But he escaped: he took a chance when the soldiers weren't looking and made a break for it, tossing his white raincoat and running a zigzag pattern in an effort to avoid gunfire.

The whole neighborhood was now in a panic. Jews who had not already thought or been able to go into hiding were suddenly desperate to do so. But locations were hard to find. Frieda's uncle Louis, her mother's brother, said he knew of a place. Her father didn't trust Louis, whom Frieda described to me as the black sheep of the family, but they didn't have much choice. Louis knew of a man named Jaap Schrijvers who lived with his daughter in a quiet village called Warmond, twenty-four miles away; Schrijvers had a small space above his bicycle shop that he was willing to make available for *onderduik* Jews (the Dutch word for going into hiding literally means "diving under"). Like most others who provided haven, Schrijvers wanted to be paid.

It felt wrong from the start. When the Brommet family arrived, Schrijvers greeted them with: "Are you Jews? You look like ordinary people."

———

The Nazi occupation essentially channeled society into four categories. There were the hunted: Jews, Gypsies, and other "undesirables." There were collaborators, who out of either conviction or self-preservation aided the occupiers. There was a small section of society, numbering probably in the tens of thousands, who formed the active resistance: assassinating notable collaborators, transporting guns, running underground newspapers. The most daring and wide-ranging resistance operation of the war was run by two brothers, Walraven and Gijs van Hall. They had been raised in a patrician family of bankers. When the war broke out they joined the *Nederlandse Unie*, or Dutch Union, which tried to find a middle ground between collaboration and resistance. As the war progressed the Van Halls figured out ways to help those who were most financially distressed, including widows and others who had had welfare payments stopped, as well as Jews in hiding. Wally van Hall used his position at the Amsterdam Stock Exchange as the base for a secret operation that collected money from wealthy Dutchmen and distributed it to those in need. The Van Halls communicated with the Dutch government in exile in London; an agreement was worked out whereby the government would repay all donors after the war. Wally van Hall concocted a bookkeeping mechanism that involved dummy stock certificates. Donors would get certificates of, say, Java Petroleum Society, which they would eventually exchange for reimbursement.

As the war progressed and life got more desperate, the Van Halls and their team grew more daring. Their efforts climaxed with the robbery of the Dutch National Bank in Amsterdam, under the noses of both the Nazis and the bank leadership, which had been infiltrated by the NSB. They stole 50 million guilders from the bank's vaults, the equivalent of half a billion dollars today, by substituting false treasury bonds for real ones, which they then cashed in at other banks, and distributed the money throughout the country to those in need. The other end of the Van Hall organization involved regular payments—envelopes of cash—being delivered by two thousand couriers.

Wally van Hall was a thin, calm man who had the physical aspect of a young Jimmy Stewart. He regularly began meetings of resistance leaders by telling jokes, for he held that in order to loosen themselves for the work they were doing they had to have five minutes of laughter. The Nazi effort to get him—they knew only his code name, "Van Tuyl"—climaxed as the war did; in late January 1945, three months before the Nazis fled, he was captured, and executed by firing squad. For a long time his role in the resistance was not widely known, supposedly in part because banks did not want to advertise the breach of their system. In 2010, the city of Amsterdam erected a monument to him in front of the national bank he had patriotically plundered.

But most people under occupation were neither collaborators nor resistance figures. Loe de Jong writes of how in 1944 the Dutch reacted uncomfortably when Queen Wilhelmina, from her refuge in England, described her people in a radio broadcast as "a nation of heroes." As De Jong notes, "Nations of heroes do not exist." Rather, he observes, "Most people, however anti-German their feelings, tried to protect themselves, their families, and their property, adapting themselves to the increasingly difficult circumstances of daily life." Some Dutch people today belittle the resistance, saying the extent of collaboration and the number of people who betrayed Jews show Dutch tolerance was a sham during the war, maybe always was a

sham. I think what they mean to highlight is the fact that throughout Dutch history tolerance has been less an ideal than a practicality. It was more expedient, given the circumstances, to organize their
society so that different people could live and work together. And
if expedience is the rationale, then when circumstances change, so
can the notion of tolerance.

Those who provided places for Jews to hide did not all fit into
the same category. Some were part of the resistance. Others were
extortionists. Jaap Schrijvers was an extortionist. Frieda and her
parents, along with her uncle Louis and four others—eight people in
all—spent two years living in a single room above Schrijvers's bicycle shop, rarely setting foot outside. Frieda's father paid Schrijvers a
thousand guilders a month (in today's money, about seven thousand
dollars), and still the family was given so little to eat—mostly meat-
less stew—that they were kept close to starvation, and when they
complained Schrijvers threatened to turn them in. In addition, Joël
Brommet had to pay twenty guilders a week of outright extortion
money to a friend of Frieda's uncle who had helped them get to the
hiding place, to keep the man from giving them up to the Germans.

The story of Anne Frank and her family weaves in and out of
the story of Frieda and her family. The two girls lived around the
corner from each other in Amsterdam and interacted in their everyday lives. They went into hiding within a week of each other. The
Franks didn't have to deal with extortionists because Otto Frank
had arranged a hiding place for them himself. His pectin company
was located in the city center, on the Prinsengracht, just a few steps
from the Westerkerk and its great tower. It was a canal house, built
in the seventeenth-century heyday of the city. Above the warehouse
and behind the company offices was the *achterhuis*, the back extension, which happened to be hidden from the view of the houses surrounding it in the courtyard, and the entrance to which was easy to
conceal. This would be the family's secret home.

The reason the diary that Anne Frank kept in hiding became
famous is that it exquisitely highlights what was under threat during

the city's occupation, and what, in a sense, Amsterdam's history is all about: the freedom of the individual human being. Her pages reveal a complex, rounded individual, defiantly discovering herself even under the most stifling conditions. The diary is filled with sharply expressed anguish, with resolve, with freak bursts of joy. Even her bitterness is alive: her analysis of her mother's coldness ("She's not a mother to me—I have to mother myself. . . . Father's not in love. He kisses her the way he kisses us") was later excised by her father when he edited her diary and prepared it for publication. The diary contains bits about the Germans and what is going on in the city outside ("Night after night, green and grey military vehicles cruise the streets. They knock on every door, asking whether any Jews live there"), but mostly it's a small, intimate story she tells—it's a story of interiority, as much as a Rembrandt portrait of a seventeenth-century Amsterdammer is. But hers is made even more intense by the claustrophobic conditions, by the world-historic force threatening to come crashing in, and by being centered on an adolescent in the process of self-discovery: "It's funny, but I can sometimes see myself as others see me. I take a leisurely look at the person called 'Anne Frank' and browse through the pages of her life as though she were a stranger."

Both the Brommets and the Franks were in hiding for about two years, and both periods ended with betrayal. No one knows who turned in the Franks. The Brommets were undone by Rebecca's brother Louis. In the spring of 1944, when the family members had reached the limits of their endurance, Schrijvers's daughter told Joël Brommet that she knew a man who could get them to Switzerland. Brommet (who had built up savings in the early days of the war by speculating on diamonds) paid a total of fifteen thousand guilders, or about a hundred thousand dollars in today's money, to the supposed guide, a man who went by the name of Gerritsen. But instead of Gerritsen, Otto Kempin, the head of the Security Police in Amsterdam, showed up at the door and arrested all the Jews that had been in hiding together. It later turned out that Frieda's uncle

Louis had had an affair with a woman in Amsterdam named Adriana Valkenburg. She was the wife of the man who went by the name Gerritsen, whose real name was Joop Bom. Louis, knowing that his brother-in-law had diamonds in a safe-deposit box and that he had a friend who could bring them to him, had apparently worked out a scheme with the couple whereby Bom would bilk Joël Brommet out of a large sum of money in return for a bogus offer of escape. But Louis did not know that Adriana Valkenburg was also an informer for the Security Police in Amsterdam. Valkenburg, the mastermind of the scam, had wide experience of this sort of thing. After the war she would be found guilty of informing on dozens of Jews who then died in concentration camps. She was sentenced to death, though the sentence was later commuted to life in prison.

Frieda and her parents, along with her uncle Louis and the others they had been living with in hiding, were brought to the Security Police office on the Euterpestraat. And here I have to pause my narrative to focus on Frieda as she sat with me in our interview sessions. We conducted them in her apartment, her calm, bright apartment filled with modernist furniture and art. It sits on Gerrit van der Veenstraat, which after the war was named for one of the heroes of the Dutch resistance. But it was formerly the Euterpestraat. Just a few doors down the block from her apartment is a hulking structure, moody in its deco darkness, with a foreboding tower. It's a school now, but it was, during the war, the headquarters of the Gestapo and the Security Police. The SP was the intelligence arm of the SS, and it was from here that Willy Lages, the German head of the SP, ran, under Adolf Eichmann's supervision, operations to ferret out and round up Jews in the Netherlands and send them to concentration camps. Its basement was infamous as a place of torture. It was to this building that Frieda and her parents were brought once their hiding place in Warmond had been breached. How, I had to ask Frieda, when she sought an apartment in the early 1990s, and could have found one anywhere in the city, could she have chosen to live in the very locus of her family suffering?

She answered by saying that she had simply liked this apartment, liked the light, felt happy here, and by that time in her life she was able to put the past in place. Plus, in the curious way the mind works, while she has always remembered vividly the moment she and her parents were taken from hiding—she remembers a little black-and-white cat watching them as they got on the train with the Security Police—she has no memory of the other end of that journey: being brought here, to this street.

Frieda and her parents were sent first to the transit camp of Westerbork, in the northeast of the Netherlands, as were the Franks. It was a processing point; from here, Jews were shipped off to Auschwitz, Bergen-Belsen, Sobibor, and Theresienstadt. Frieda told me she had been outraged a few years earlier when she was quoted in a documentary as saying "how great it was in Westerbork." What she said had been taken out of context. Compared with the death camps, and with the two years in hiding, Westerbork was a place of some light. Jewish prisoners were allowed a bit of freedom; they put on a cabaret. There was a hospital; they had enough to eat. So after two years of cramped starvation, she arrived at this Nazi camp, an eighteen-year-old who was not aware that death awaited nearly all of them, and was relieved to hear laughter and have her stomach full. During the stay at Westerbork, Frieda Brommet and Anne Frank both put on weight and regained color.

Everyone at Westerbork knew the plan was to send them farther east, to "work," but there had been rumors that the war might end soon, so they hoped it wouldn't happen. But in August 1944 what would be the last trainload of prisoners was packed off to Auschwitz; it included the Franks and the Brommets. As soon as they arrived at the Polish camp Frieda was separated from her father; she would never see him again. The nightmare of Auschwitz began. They were beaten, starved, shaved, stripped, frozen. People were led away for gruesome medical experiments. People collapsed from hunger. They were made to stand for hours holding heavy stones. They were terrorized by *kapos*: fellow inmates who were put in charge of barracks.

People were shot at random. Frieda came down with acute diarrhea and was sent to a barracks full of women in the same condition. ("The diarrhea barracks at a concentration camp: can you imagine the smell?") A Czech woman warned her, in French, to get better within five days because in the night the Polish women who oversaw the patients strangled the ones who lingered. Frieda told me she remembers, after she had contracted scarlet fever (for real this time) and was sent to the barracks for victims of that disease, seeing the dreaded Dr. Mengele, who has gone down in history with the moniker "Angel of Death," enter the ward.

Later, her health failing, she was put in the scabies ward, where she encountered Anne Frank, who was in equally poor condition, skeletal and covered with a rash. At this point Rebecca Brommet and Edith Frank, in a primal effort to save their daughters, set to work as a team. Their children were starving; they dug a hole in the wall of the barracks and, as one mother stood guard, the other crawled in and fed their girls whatever they had managed to scrounge or steal. Frieda Brommet and Anne Frank had become twinned by horror.

By late October, Anne was well enough to leave the sick ward. Her improvement cost her her life. She and her sister, Margot, were sent to Bergen-Belsen, where they died. Frieda's multiple ailments— typhoid, pleurisy, scarlet fever, diarrhea—saved her by keeping her in the sick ward until the Germans abandoned the camp in January 1945. There was a confused rush one day as SS soldiers stormed into the ward and ordered all the patients to get outside and start walking. *Jeder der zurück bleibt, wird erschossen!* All who stay will be shot. She staggered to her feet, made it a few steps, fell to the ground. She closed her eyes in talking to me at the memory of being trampled by her fellow inmates. The choice, she and they all thought, was to march or die, and she could not march. But again her weak condition saved her. Those who trudged off into the January snow were the ones who died. She and her mother stayed, huddled together for warmth, foraged for turnips, hung on for nine days amid the decaying bodies and the ruins of the concentration camp.

Then, like apparitions, came huge men, all in white, on skis. Russian soldiers. The Second World War was over.

———

You can see the thousands of joyous and expectant people who filled Dam Square on May 7, 1945, in another snippet of black-and-white film, which is viewable on the Web site of the Amsterdam City Archives. The German surrender had come two days before, and now the news said Canadian forces would arrive shortly to take over the city on behalf of the Allies. The square that had seen so much history, from William the Silent to Napoleon, was packed with people wearing their spring finery: women in dresses and coats, men in suits and ties. But then something happens. The film is silent, so we don't hear what was to everyone in it a dreadfully familiar sound: the crackle of gunfire. People start to run. Within seconds, the square is empty, except for individuals hiding behind poles, a few sheltering under a barrel organ that had just been playing, and sprawled bodies.

In fact, German troops had not yet left the city. They had previously taken over the Grote Club, a private club that looked out over the square; a group of German soldiers had sat there getting drunk as the Amsterdammers came out of their long wartime hibernation and began to celebrate. The Germans set up a machine gun and opened fire. Twenty people were killed in this grisly coda to the city's wartime suffering.

The Canadians did come at last. The real celebration began, and people set about the task of creating a new city and a new world.

Frieda and Rebecca Brommet made their laborious way back to Amsterdam in the latter part of 1945. They had a brutal homecoming. Strangers now lived in their old apartment; all their belongings were gone. Frieda spent time recuperating in a hospital. Later, her mother stole mattresses from the hospital to furnish an apartment. ("Organized," Frieda corrected me. "In the camp we didn't say you stole some food—you organized it.") They tried to find out what family members were still alive. The answer was: almost nobody. Of Frieda's extended family, two cousins and three aunts had survived. Three cousins, three uncles, one aunt, both of her grandmothers and one of her grandfathers had died in Auschwitz, as had her father. Her other grandfather had been shot to death during a raid, and an aunt had committed suicide.

Otto Frank made the same unimaginably sorrowful return to the city. Miep Gies, an employee of his company, one of those who had cared for the Jews while they were in hiding, took him into her apartment. He learned that his wife and daughters were dead. Then Miep handed him something. He recognized the diary, with its checked cover, that Anne had scribbled in during the long months. After some months, he got it into the hands of a historian named Annie Romein. On April 3, 1946, nearly a year after the war's end, her husband, Jan Romein, also a historian, wrote an article that appeared on the front page of *Het Parool*, Amsterdam's daily newspaper, under the headline "Child's Voice." It began:

> By chance I have in my hands a diary that was written during
> the war. The Royal Institute for War Documentation contains
> about two hundred such diaries, but I would be astonished if
> there was another so pure, so intelligent, and so human as this
> one, which caused me to forget everything I was going to do
> today and to read it in one sitting. When I had finished, it was
> night and I was surprised that the light was on, that there was
> bread and tea to be had, that I heard no planes roaring and
> no soldiers' boots resounding in the street, so intensely did the
> reading capture me and return me to the surreal world that is
> already almost a year behind us.

The diary was published the next year in the Netherlands, and in 1952 in the United States and England. It is one of the most widely read books of all time, having sold thirty-one million copies in sixty-seven languages. It is universally and rightfully admired. But the Dutch have had a hard time with it. Many sympathize with the Holocaust survivor who called the book "a public relations exercise" by the Dutch to gloss over the fact that the vaunted tolerance of the Netherlands, and of Amsterdam in particular, was, during the war, only sporadically to be found. For every Walraven van Hall there had been many Jaap Schrijvers and Adriana Valkenburgs. While people elsewhere see Anne Frank's writing as an example of the buoyancy of the human spirit, for the Dutch it has been a thorny reminder and a cause for soul searching.

———

If there had been a moral collapse during the war, a failure to live up to their liberal heritage, some Dutch people in its immediate aftermath also believed that the rebuilding task ahead of them was an opportunity to improve their society. In effect, the Dutch asked themselves: "Who are we, what do we want to become, and how can we use this crisis to arrange our society to advance our goals?" At issue was the tension that existed between the two liberalisms that over the centuries had become part of the Dutch identity. Why did they have to be in conflict? Maybe in Germany or France it was inevitable, because of the structure of those societies, that workers and capitalists should be at odds. But Dutch history had different roots. Where in neighboring countries society in the dim past had broken down into nobility and peasants, the Dutch landscape had produced a different dynamic. The need to battle against the sea had ingrained a group ethic so elemental the Dutch have a term for it that they use on an everyday basis: the *poldermodel*, so called for the patches of land collectively reclaimed from the sea and hemmed in by dikes. The striking thing about this communalism is that from the start it was tethered to individualism. When medieval Dutchmen banded together to reclaim land from the sea, that new land was not owned by a king or church; it became *theirs*. They chose not to own it collectively, however, but to divide it up into individual parcels. So while feudalism held sway elsewhere in Europe, people in these low-lying provinces were protocapitalists: landowners who set about buying, selling, renting, and making profits. Yet at the same time they recognized that their individual economic interests lay in keeping the group bond strong, in working together. Could they not, then, use the historic commitment to both individual and social freedom—to economic and social liberalism—to rebuild in the aftermath of world war?

A kind of nationwide debate on the topic ensued in the war's wake. It had several results, one of which was the founding, in 1950, of something called the Social Economic Council, or SER, to use the acronym for its name in Dutch. The SER has been a feature of the Dutch landscape ever since. There is no equivalent to it in the American, British, or most other systems. It is a panel comprising three groups: labor leaders, industry leaders, and experts appointed by the government. On a given topic, the panelists will consult with their constituencies, then convene as a group and hash out the issue until they reach unanimous agreement on how it should be handled. Then they lay their finding before the government. Alexander Rinnooy Kan was the head of the SER from 2006 to 2012. He told me that the government almost always adopts the SER's position because "it's not just the position of the members of the council, but of all of their constituencies, whether employers or trade union members. That equals 80 percent of the economy."

In other words, after World War II the Dutch crafted a system that brings the forces behind their two vaunted liberalisms—social and economic—together. Or, put even more simply, they created a social welfare state that is fueled by capitalism. Instead of corporations and unions clashing and lobbying government from opposite perspectives, they work out a problem themselves and then lay their solution before the government. "The miracle, by Anglo Saxon standards, is that it's possible to arrive at this kind of unanimity," Rinnooy Kan said. "In Anglo Saxon countries the relation between employers and employees is adversarial. But in the Netherlands we've learned that there is a joint interest for employers and trade unions to get together."

By means such as this the country rebuilt itself after the war. Amsterdam was a part of the effort, of course. But then too, Amsterdam is not the Netherlands. I have been guilty in this book of sometimes seeming to equate the two. Every Dutch person who is from outside the city will be ready to counter that notion. Indeed, people from elsewhere often question whether the city is even part of the Netherlands. The Republic of Amsterdam, they derisively call it.

How is it different? If liberalism is part of the historical development of the Netherlands, that is even more the case in Amsterdam. In tolerating behavior, celebrating diversity, empowering individuals, the city almost always goes far beyond what the country as a whole would do. It has perennially argued with the national government in The Hague; it sometimes regards developments in other cities and provinces only vaguely, as if they were parts of another country. Most of all, for better or for worse, it has gone probably further than anyplace on earth in seeking to expand individual freedoms. One reason for this—for Amsterdam being the city it is today—has to do with the war. In maybe no other city was the connection between World War II and the countercultural and civil rights revolutions of the 1960s as clear as it was in Amsterdam. In one sense the connection is obvious: the city was actually under Nazi occupation. Beyond that, the fact that a larger percentage of Jews here were killed than almost anywhere else created a deep wound on the psyche, one that cried out for healing. And because of the city's liberal heritage, both before and during the war activists of various stripes had fled Germany and other places under Nazi thrall and set up shop here, so that those still surviving after the war helped to give the city a renewed commitment to that heritage. The horror of what had happened was as real here as anyplace else, but the conditions for acting, and bringing change, were in place as they were nowhere else.

The new era in Amsterdam's liberalism came about via several trajectories. I'll follow one of them by backing up to one of the individuals I focused on in the previous chapter: Dr. Bernard Premsela, who built on the work of Aletta Jacobs and became one of the first sexologists and a pioneer in the realm of sexual and reproductive rights and freedoms. He and his wife raised their three children in a secular, progressive atmosphere. They exposed them to culture and encouraged them not to be hemmed in by society but to follow their interests. When the family moved to a new house in Amsterdam, the couple had its interior done in Bauhaus style, the new, clean, modernist school of design then prevalent in Germany. Their thirteen-year-old son, Benno, was captivated by it and decided on the spot that he would become a designer.

But his ambitions were delayed. As Jews, the Premselas were forced into hiding during the Nazi occupation of the city. As it happened, Benno did not stay with his parents but took shelter in a house in Oud Zuid with an actress who had befriended the family years before. It was a fortunate choice, for the other hiding place was breached, and by the war's end his parents and sister were dead, all of them swallowed up by Auschwitz. Benno and his brother survived.

After the war, Benno Premsela began working in design and landed a job at the Bijenkorf, Amsterdam's premier department store. He was given charge of the store's display windows. Window display was a utilitarian affair at the time: show the product and the price. Premsela turned these windows into something else, a means of self-expression and a way for the city to interact with itself as it wrestled with the forces of change swirling within it. His mannequins were modern people, assuming aggressive poses; there were no price tags in sight. It was as if passersby were meant not to buy but to see, to have an experience. Premsela was friends with people throughout the city's art world, and he commissioned paintings and huge blowups of photographs as dramatic backdrops. Crowds began to gather on Friday evenings at the store's location on Dam Square, waiting for the new windows to be unveiled. Avant-garde art was meeting urban consumerism, and people were beguiled.

Premsela left the department store and founded his own interior design company, which in time made everything from furniture to clothing and gained worldwide renown. Probably his most famous design is the Lotek lamp, an ultramodern, pre-Ikea assemble-it-yourself lamp with white cubes for shades and steel rods as supports. As the decades went by Premsela became the Amsterdam node of an international circle of artists and designers that included people like Edward Albee, Philip Glass, and Robert Mapplethorpe; he became, as he liked to say with self-deprecation, "world famous in Holland."

But his real importance would not come from design. During his years in hiding, Premsela realized that he was homosexual. Being gay in the 1940s meant existing in a netherworld. It meant shame and secrecy. For most gay people, there were no safe places, public or private, to be together. (In Amsterdam, more than one street was known at night as Rue de Vaseline.) Hiding the truth had always been a part of what homosexuality was. But after the war, in Amsterdam, that would change. Benno Premsela later said that he had spent the war years hiding because of his identity, and once the city was liberated he vowed that he would never hide again. He had as an example his father, who had devoted his career to breaking down sexual prejudices and taboos.

Other Dutch gays felt similarly; in 1946, they formed the world's first organization to advance gay rights, whose original name, the Shakespeare Club, indicates the caution with which its members proceeded. It later became the Cultuur en Ontspanningscentrum, or Culture and Leisure Center, and is now known as the COC. Premsela was one of its first members and eventually its chairman. As was the case elsewhere, gays and lesbians in the Netherlands were divided on how to advance their cause, or even what it should be. Should the organization look inward and act as a place of refuge and support for its members? Or should it go public? Premsela wanted to go public. Homosexuality, he argued, was not the moral or physical deformity that society had cast it as; thus the COC had a responsibility to correct that view. Gays, in other words, were entitled to civil rights, and the COC, under him, would become an advocacy organization.

Many of the organizations' members were appalled at the notion of going public. They were respected members of society who knew perfectly well that society's recognition of homosexuality as normal would come, if ever, only after long struggle; in the meantime they had careers and families to think of.

Premsela effectively ended the debate by appearing on a television news program in 1964. Until then, membership in the COC was an incognito affair; if members were quoted, they didn't use their real names. Premsela's appearance on *Achter het nieuws* ("Behind the News") on December 30, 1964, marked the first time that a homosexual appeared openly on Dutch television giving his real name. In a professorial performance—at forty-four, he was mostly bald and rather severe of demeanor, and he wore a three-piece wool suit with a tie—he explained to an interviewer that the goal of the organization was to promote public awareness of the reality and normalcy of homosexuality, much as his father, three decades earlier, had appeared on the radio to make heterosexual sex a topic of public discourse.

The appearance turned out to be a landmark not only for recognition of homosexuality but for Dutch television and for the postwar advance of civil rights. Amid the upheaval of the 1960s and through the next two decades Premsela probably helped his cause by maintaining a sober, almost fatherly, above-the-fray manner. When he spoke publicly, the tone was businesslike but the message could be oracular. He seemed to echo what was already a long line of Dutch civil rights figures, going back to Multatuli and the nineteenth-century uproar over the exploitation of Javanese peasants under the East India Company. Multatuli, after all, had influenced Aletta Jacobs, who in turn had influenced Bernard Premsela. And Benno Premsela was aware of his father's values as well as of what the fight against Nazi ideology had meant. "The problem of homosexuality," he once said, in an apt encapsulation of the whole civil rights movement, "is the problem not of the homosexual but of society. Just like the problem of anti-Semitism is in the end the problem not of the Jews but of non-Jews. And it's the same with the problem of women's emancipation, where it's actually men who are the problem."

Another promoter of civil rights in the postwar period was the woman into whose home I ventured at regular intervals while writing this book. Like many other Jews who had been in concentration camps, after Auschwitz Frieda Brommet simultaneously renounced belief in God ("if God exists and he allowed that to happen, then it's better that he doesn't exist") and connected with her Jewishness for the first time. She married another Auschwitz survivor, Herman Menco, and followed him in joining the Progressive congregation. Over several years, while her body remained fragile from her camp experience, she found, especially after hearing fellow Auschwitz survivor Elie Wiesel discuss his experiences, that she had a voice. She became an international activist, speaking about the Holocaust and women's rights issues from Miami to Nairobi, and broke new ground of her own by becoming the first woman to head the Dutch Union of Progressive Jews. At the same time she turned herself into a radio journalist and made radio documentaries on the Holocaust, Jewish survivors, and the evolution of life in Amsterdam through the 1970s and 1980s.

Frieda's husband worked for a time at the Bijenkorf department store, and it was there, through him, that she met Benno Premsela. She and her husband eventually divorced, but she and Benno remained fast friends, bonding over their parallel drives to advance civil liberties but also over their shared sense of humor, which tended toward the gallows. In the early 1980s, Benno proposed that the two of them, along with his partner, Friso Broeksma, drive to Berlin to see an exhibit on "Jewish identities." Frieda was uncomfortable. "I've never been to Germany," she said. Whereupon Benno shot back, "How did you get to Auschwitz and back?" So they went. Soon after crossing the Dutch border into Germany, they stopped at a café. Frieda ordered mineral water, and the waitress asked if she wanted "gas or no gas." Frieda turned to her friends and deadpanned: "I never wanted anything to do with their gas."

The friendship of the two civil rights figures whose trajectories were forged in Amsterdam's Nazi-occupation era continued through the Day-Glo sixties and the art-scene seventies, until Benno's death in 1997, and culminated when both received knighthoods for their work to expand individual freedoms. At Benno's ceremony in 1995, his partner, Friso Broeksma, noticing that he and Benno were seated next to Queen Beatrix and her mother, Juliana, gave about as pithy a summary as you could get of how far Amsterdam, and the Western world, had come since the darkness of the Nazi era, when he whispered wryly into Benno's ear: "Four queens in a row."

CHAPTER

10

THE MAGIC CENTER

Look at a photograph of Gijs van Hall from 1957, the year he became mayor of Amsterdam, and you might well consider it a generic image of any politician in the Western world in the 1950s: white, male, middle-aged, besuited and bespectacled, hair slicked back, in every sense an establishment figure. Although mayors are appointed rather than elected in the Dutch system, his selection probably pleased the vast majority of residents, for beneath the image lay substance. Van Hall was a genuine war hero, who together with his brother Wally van Hall had been the heart of the Dutch resistance. And—useful in a time of rebuilding—he was a banker with contacts in the financial world in the United States. Moreover, politically he was a social democrat, so he embodied the dual-liberalism ideal. When he became mayor, Van Hall set about an adventurous building campaign in the city. His goal was to give businesses room to grow while maintaining the city's commitments to its citizens via the welfare state programs that had come into force. The 1950s were about casting off the wartime era and pushing toward the future. The city needed to expand. It had to finance new housing and roadways. It lashed itself to the forces that were coming into their own: cars, television, advertising, consumerism. There

was an ecomomic boom: industry took off; wages nearly doubled in
the course of the decade.

Van Hall's program worked for a while. And then it crashed. And
the crash—the story of a good man's fall, which is also the story of
how Amsterdam became what it is known for today—mirrored the
difficult trajectory that the whole Western world followed from the
postwar era to the latter part of the twentieth century: from black
and white to color, from double-breasted suits to bell-bottoms.

If the distinguished, decorated establishment figure of Mayor
Van Hall represented one side of what would become a colossal culture clash, then in the other corner was a seventeen-year-old boy
from The Hague named Roel van Duijn. In 1960, on learning that
the government was going to allow American nuclear weapons to be
stored on Dutch soil, Van Duijn and a couple of his friends sat down
in the middle of a busy intersection and blocked traffic. "I thought,
we just finished the Second World War—we don't need a third world
war, with even worse bombs," Van Duijn, now seventy, told me as
he reminisced in his neat little garden apartment in Amsterdam's
Slotervaart section. He and his friends were arrested. When he got
out of prison, he headed to Amsterdam, protested there, and got
arrested again. Why Amsterdam? "Amsterdam was still very much
wounded by the war," he said. "So it was the center of critical thinking about racism and fascism."

Indeed, in Amsterdam, an artist named Robert Jasper Grootveld was already involved in related activities, though on the face of
it the connection may have been hard to see. Grootveld's father was
an anarchist who had instilled in his son the evils of the consumerist
system. Grootveld focused his attention on the cigarette. Tobacco,
he believed, was the root mechanism through which global corporations made slaves of ordinary people. (The fact that he was himself
a chain-smoker apparently enhanced his zeal.) In a space near the
Leidseplein in the city center that had been donated by a local businessman who liked his message, Grootveld started doing what today
would be called performance art. He dressed himself like a kind of

mad twentieth-century version of an American Indian, painted his face, and pranced around a fire. Students and others came to watch and participate. Grootveld led them in a chant that went something like "Ugge-ugge-ugge!" It was meant to sound like a smoker's cough.

Where Van Duijn was personally shy and bookish, Grootveld was a flamboyant exhibitionist, but there was an overlap in what they believed. The victory of capitalism over Nazism had transformed society in fifteen-odd years into a herd of "despicable plastic people," as Grootveld said. This was true throughout the West, but in the Netherlands the irony was that the blending of the two strains of liberalism had helped to turn the capitalist-labor conflict, which at least had had some spice in it, into a bland mono-class, all the members of which ended their workday vacantly gazing into the blue light of their televisions, then went to bed dreaming dreams of the products they saw advertised there.

Van Duijn, the theorist, got his initial inspiration from late-nineteenth-century anarchists, writers like Mikhail Bakunin, but he was disappointed to find their philosophy out-of-date. He got a job at the Amstel brewery, hoping to pick the brains of workers in order to jump-start a proletariat revolution, but learned that they were not interested in revolt. "I realized that the working class and their employers all had the same aim: economic growth, nothing more," Van Duijn told me. "We thought, we need to look beyond, to a politics of freedom and creativity and playing. So I started looking for which class would support a revolution in society." He found it, and a new word was coined: *provotariat*. The provotariat were young people who had come of age since the war, who had no vested interest in the system that had come into being, who saw it as a threat to individualism and creativity, and who wanted to provoke a change of consciousness.

There is an odd little statue in the middle of the Spui, a public square in central Amsterdam. The skinny bronze image is of a young boy; it's called *Het Lieverdje*, "The Little Darling." It was cast as a monument to Amsterdam's street urchins and unveiled in 1960 by Mayor Van Hall's wife. In 1964, after Robert Jasper Grootveld had, on one particularly rambunctious night, burned his antismoking temple to the ground (and been arrested for it), he moved his happenings, as they quickly became known, to the square. The fact that *Het Lieverdje* had been built with donations from a cigarette company made the statue, for him, the logical new center of his theatrical world. Every Saturday at midnight, beginning in June 1964, Grootveld performed at the statue's base. First a dozen or so people watched. Eventually the crowd grew into the thousands.

Roel van Duijn showed up at one of the happenings with copies of an alternative magazine he had typed and printed himself. It was long and skinny, and the cover showed a brick wall with the name scrawled on it graffiti style: *Provo*. Provo was short for provocation. Van Duijn's experiences with the authorities reinforced what he and others had already understood: while officially there were such things as civil rights in the Netherlands, in practice the authorities were like the regents who ran the city in the seventeenth century: they could do more or less as they pleased, and they did whatever it took to maintain their society and their power. Such was the case elsewhere, of course. This was precisely the time of the Selma to Montgomery marches in Alabama, where state troopers used clubs and tear gas on civil rights marchers. In Amsterdam the reaction to abuse of power had its own local inflection, which had to do with the disconnect between what young people believed to be the Dutch heritage of liberalism and the reality of sometimes brutal police action, including arrests, beatings, and searches without due process. The authorities had to be provoked to show their true nature. That was the thinking behind *Provo* the magazine and Provo the movement.

For it quickly became a movement, blending with Grootveld's happenings. Saturday, midnight: University students gathering around the statue—and he appears, headdress, war paint, a wig, a woman's fur coat; he dances, starts to sing about the nicotine hell god. The kids laugh, chant: Ugge-ugge. Someone is pounding a drum. And here come the police, slowly rolling in on motorcycles, nightsticks at their sides. Kiki Amsberg, my former landlady, took part along with her husband. They watched from the terrace of Café Hoppe—one of the oldest in the city, dating to the seventeenth century. "We stood there watching and laughing at the police," she said. "They had no clue how to deal with this. Then suddenly, the police went into action. They turned and went into the crowd and started lashing people with a bullwhip, and people ran in panic."

Upstairs at his house, in his tiny library, Roel van Duijn slid something out of a plastic sleeve to show me. It was the first number of *Provo*, which he had pounded out on his Erika typewriter, dated July 12, 1965. If someone were to compile a top ten list of 1960s artifacts, this first edition of Van Duijn's homemade rag might well be on it. Its narrow pages are packed with angry, playful, absurdist rant. Van Duijn turned to a page and showed what I had asked to see. In every copy of the first number he had taped a couple of toy gun caps—the little strips of paper with pellets of explosive that make a pop when struck. "Grab a hammer and start the revolution in your own life with a bang!" his text said. "That got me arrested too," he informed me.

The authorities did not understand the happenings, which of course was the point. People were beaten and hauled off to prison for such nonoffenses as laying flowers at the foot of the *Lieverdje* statue. One of the most famous provocations involved a female coconspirator handing out raisins to people in the crowd. She went to jail. Grootveld played other games, too, to provoke the authorities. He scrawled a giant letter K (for cancer) on cigarette posters around the city. He substituted packs of faux-marijuana cigarettes for regular ones in Automat machines. He invented something called the Marihuette game, one version of which involved having participants in his happenings roll cigarettes that contained something other than marijuana or tobacco and smoking them in front of policemen; the objective was to get arrested for doing something legal.

While Grootveld ran the show and drew crowds, Van Duijn

sought ways to harness the energy. *Provo* announced a series of "white" initiatives. The most famous was the White Bicycle plan. The automobile having been declared tobacco's demon twin, *Provo* decreed that the city of Amsterdam should banish cars and make a fleet of white bicycles freely available to all who wanted to use them. They would be available, unlocked, at points around the city; residents would hop on one, ride it to their destination, and leave it there for the next person. The Provos purchased the first fifty, painted them white, and presented them to the city. Whereupon the police confiscated them.

As a pointed follow-up, the Provos declared their White Chicken plan. *Kip* (chicken) was Dutch slang for a police officer; the plan called on the city to make the police into true servants of society by providing them with supplies of condoms, Band-Aids, and fried chicken drumsticks to distribute on their rounds. (The White Chicken plan did not fly.)

By the summer of 1965 the Provo phenomenon dominated Dutch news. *Provo* declared Amsterdam "the Magic Center," the place from which a new consciousness would come into being. And Spui Square was the center of the Magic Center. Curiously enough, the square sits just in front of the Begijnhof, a little courtyard nunnery that dates to the period of the city's first fame, in the aftermath of the so-called miracle of Amsterdam, so that testaments to the two periods of the city's international renown—medieval piety and flower-power revolt—stand side by side.

The crowds at the happenings had by now grown exponentially. "Youngsters started to show up in Amsterdam from other parts of the country," Van Duijn said. "All of a sudden they had long hair. It was so surprising to see. This was 1965—you didn't see this sort of thing in Berlin or Paris until 1967. It still surprises me, because after all there were only ten or twelve of us doing this."

As the happenings swelled and the international press swept in to report on the curious youth movement under way in Amsterdam, the participants—who included members of the still small antiwar and anti–atom bomb movements as well as anarchists, beatniks, artists, and droves of generally disaffected young people—were more vigorously attacked by the authorities. Some spent a month or more in prison for nonexistent offenses. The police violence led the Provos to focus their attention on the mayor. "*Van Hall ten val!*"—Bring down Van Hall!—became a Saturday night chant. Steadily, Gijs van Hall, the hero of the resistance, was sucked into a cross-generational vortex.

No one knew at the time that Van Hall was to some extent caught in the middle; like Amsterdam officials of earlier centuries, he was trying to mediate between free expression in his city and distant superiors—in this case the national government in The Hague—who wanted the nonsense to end. And few of the young people knew or cared about Van Hall's valiant past. "In fact, he was a brave man," Van Duijn told me as we chatted in his apartment. "But I didn't know this then. I didn't know his part in the resistance. It was probably good that I didn't know because then I would have had respect for him. And the fact was, as mayor, he was patronizing, he considered us to be evil, trash. He was like the father and he wanted us to shut up."

One of Robert Jasper Grootveld's chants was *Klaas komt!* Klaas is Dutch for Saint Nicholas, the forerunner of the modern Santa Claus, who has his own holiday in the Netherlands. "Klaas is coming!" started appearing as graffiti around the city. It prophesied, apparently, that the end of the corrupt establishment was at hand and a time of peace and love and magic would soon follow. The crowds loved the chant, and may have believed it, but people were stunned when Klaas actually did arrive. In 1966 young Princess Beatrix announced she was marrying. Her fiancé was Claus von Amsberg, a German nobleman who had been in the Hitler Youth and served briefly in the Nazi army during the war. Grootveld's happy-times prediction seemed to flip upside down. Provos considered the Dutch monarchy the epitome of the reactionary old guard; that the princess was going to marry a onetime member of the occupying power, and that his name collided with that of their supposed magical savior, was a provocation of the Provos. Something had to be done.

The White Rumor plan went into effect as the royal wedding neared. People heard that the Provos were going to put LSD in the drinking water prior to the ceremony; they were going to spread lion dung along the parade route to make police horses bolt. The wedding was going to showcase Amsterdam, and the Netherlands, to the world. Mayor Van Hall and the authorities in The Hague couldn't afford trouble. They lined the route with twenty-five thousand police officers.

There were also rumors of Provo bombs being set off. These rumors turned out to be true, but they were smoke bombs. Many of the police were from outside the city; in the confusion, and with their edginess, as white plumes of smoke went up they started clubbing people seemingly at random. The pictures on TV were less of the royal couple in their gilded coach than of street chaos.

The wedding marked a turning point in the Provo movement: a critical mass of Amsterdammers in effect joined Provo. Many had understood the feelings of anger at the idea of the wedding in a city that had suffered so much at the hands of the Germans. Eighteen city council members had voted to boycott the ceremony. Now on television people saw the official overreaction.

Gijs van Hall—who had been considered a tyrannical beast by the Provos and a timid nonleader by officials in The Hague—was forced out of office soon after the wedding. With him went the old order. In a flash, Provo had won a strange kind of respect. "There came a breakthrough," Van Duijn told me. "People started to get the joke. The smoke bombs were not to hurt anybody but to make the TV picture go white so people couldn't see the royal wedding. They understood the nature of Provo. Suddenly we were getting invitations to speak, in London, in Paris, in Prague. I gave a lecture in Ljubljana on Provo and ecology. It started to spread."

It spread most decisively in Amsterdam itself. Historian Hans Righart calls 1966 the *rampjaar*, the disaster year, echoing the term for 1672, when war brought the golden age crashing down. In the *rampjaar* of 1966, Provos won five seats on the city council. One of the nation's still existing political parties, D66 (as in "Democrats 1966"), came into being on a platform to bring a truer form of democracy. Every institution felt its foundations tremble. Journalism had previously been staid and self-stifled; seemingly overnight, it changed, became aggressive, investigative.

The decade culminated in Amsterdam with two events in the spring of 1969, one that shook the city internally while the other rebranded Amsterdam globally as the liberal capital of the world. The first began with students of the University of Amsterdam demanding a say in all university matters; when the president rejected the demand, seven hundred students staged a sit-in at the Maagdenhuis, the central administrative building of the university (which happened to sit directly opposite the *Lieverdje* statue). As was the case with similar sit-ins elsewhere, the action brought home to many the starkness of the generational divide.

The second event took place in Suite 902 of the Amsterdam Hilton. In the three years since the wedding of Beatrix and her German beau, the rest of the world had caught up with Provo Amsterdam. The assassinations of Martin Luther King Jr. and Robert F. Kennedy, the My Lai massacre, and the crushing of the Prague Spring had shaken the foundations of things. The Summer of Love had come and gone. The Beatles had produced *Sgt. Pepper's Lonely Hearts Club Band*, *Magical Mystery Tour*, and the so-called White Album.

Beatles fans started to get nervous when John Lennon diverted his attention away from the group to focus on atonal musical projects with Yoko Ono. After their marriage in Gibraltar, in March 1969, John and Yoko began their honeymoon in Paris, where they had lunch with Salvador Dalí (they played a screechy song for him, and he turned the tables by biting the head off a grilled bird) and met a Dutch record producer named Hans Boskamp. Vietnam, war, and peace were on their minds; they wanted to harness the international media attention their wedding had attracted. Boskamp suggested that Amsterdam, the city of Provo and the happenings, was the place to demonstrate. "That's a good idea," Boskamp remembered Lennon saying. "You look for a good hotel and we will do the rest." So Lennon and Ono hopped in their white Rolls-Royce and drove to Amsterdam.

From March 25 to 31, they occupied a suite at the Amsterdam Hilton. They taped handmade posters to the windows—BED PEACE, said one; HAIR PEACE, said another—and announced that a happening was going to happen in their bed. Whereupon the Amsterdam police, fearing this might involve a public display of lovemaking, issued a notice: "If people are invited to such a 'happening,' the police would certainly act."

But that wasn't the plan. Instead, John and Yoko reinvented the sit-in by stitching it to the honeymoon concept and inviting the world press corps. Jan Donkers, then a young correspondent for VPRO radio who would go on to become a renowned Dutch pop journalist, remembered getting a call from someone at EMI Records: "We told them we had a radio program every Friday evening. Could we broadcast live from their bedroom for a whole hour? They said yes! Incredible." Thus Donkers found himself not quite in bed but sitting on the bed with the newlyweds. In his answers, Lennon said the bed-in concept was "the most effectual way of promoting peace that we could think of." But people didn't seem to want to dwell on Vietnam. A listener asked if Lennon had seen the musical *Hair*. "I thought it was crap, but I thought the idea was all right," Lennon replied. "We walked out after the nude bit." Someone else asked, "At what frequency are you vibrating in Amsterdam right now?" He shot back breezily, "Oh, about two million frequencies per second. Watch out!" Donkers told me his main impressions during the hour were of how insistent Ono was to be heard and how relaxed and funny Lennon was. Lennon held himself back while Ono gave a long, windy statement about peace and cosmic energy; he waited a beat and said with his Liverpool twang, "She's foreign, you know."

A month later, Lennon enshrined it all in the lyrics of "The Ballad of John and Yoko," which the Beatles released as a single a month after that.

The bed-in, which brought journalists from all over the globe, didn't do much for world peace but it may have been just the thing to cement Amsterdam's reputation as the center of the new liberalism. The energy of the 1960s got fused into the city even as the decade itself was passing. By the time John and Yoko checked in to the Hilton, the Provo movement was already officially dead. Provo's purpose had been to irritate the establishment. By 1967 both the police commissioner and the mayor had lost their jobs amid controversy over their handling of the provocations, leaving the Provos bereft of their antagonists, and, as a kiss of death, some establishment types were now signing on to the Provo program. (After a former government minister openly offered his support, Van Duijn said that if the minister had really wanted to support the movement he would have cracked down on it.) The leaders held a meeting to dissolve Provo. Within months after the bed-in, meanwhile, Paul McCartney announced that the Beatles were breaking up and everyone turned the page on their wall calendars. The 1960s were over.

———

But in Amsterdam, the 1960s didn't end. Roel van Duijn became a member of the Amsterdam city council in 1969; he remained in city government for the next thirty years. Other colleagues from the time also joined the establishment. Some former Provos accused them of selling out, but Van Duijn said he wanted to be part of "the mechanism for change." Indeed, it's not too much of a stretch to say that rather than former Provos becoming establishment, the city's establishment became Provo. Hans Righart argues in his aptly titled book *The Endless Sixties* that the Netherlands changed more after the 1960s than it did after the Second World War. Put slightly differently, the 1960s extended and sped up the process of change that the war had brought about. And that was especially the case in Amsterdam. In the 1960s, as Jan Donkers said, "The counterculture became Amsterdam's dominant culture. And it's still that way."

Symbolic of this, because it is part of the city's structure, was the Provos' White Bicycle plan, which spawned what is today probably the most sophisticated urban bicycle system in the world, with bike lanes, bike traffic lights, bike parking garages, and an elaborate system of cyclist etiquette (which, Provo style, many Amsterdammers ignore). The implementation of the White Bicycle plan can be traced to one man: Luud Schimmelpennink, a former Provo who conceived of the plan and went on to become a member of the city government. His ideas and effort also helped to initiate urban bicycle programs in cities around the world.

Other ideas that were radical when Provo floated them have since become commonplace in Amsterdam and elsewhere. The White Chimney plan sought to impose fines on polluters—which is what the emissions trading or "cap and trade" system for managing pollution does in a more sophisticated way. In the 1970s, Roel van Duijn rose to the position of alderman responsible for energy policy; he proposed that the city explore the possibility of using windmills to create energy. "People thought I was mad," he told me. "They said, 'Do you want to take us back to the Middle Ages?' But this is exactly the spirit in which society is working today."

Then, too, Amsterdam's late-twentieth-century liberalism did not spring whole cloth from its homegrown 1960s counterculture movement. It came out of the city's entire, unique history: its battles against water, the protocapitalist culture that developed against the backdrop of feudal Europe, the nonideological brand of tolerance that took hold at least as far back as the sixteenth century, when the city became a magnet for people from a variety of new religions whose chants and rants and dances would have gotten them burned as witches in other places.

Indeed, by the later twentieth century, that kind of religious freedom was itself able to evolve in the direction of freedom *from* religion. Maybe the most profound post-1960s transformation in the city was in the role that religion played in people's lives. In the city of the miracle of Amsterdam, in what had been one of Europe's most devout societies, people simply stopped going to church. A single set of statistics tells the story. In 1900, more than 45 percent of Amsterdammers identified with Dutch Protestantism, the Christian denomination for which their ancestors had fought a war of independence against the Spanish empire. By 1971, only about 18 percent considered themselves part of the faith. In 2000, the number was 5 percent. If liberalism is, as many of its adherents and detractors alike have said through the centuries, a force that ultimately stands in opposition to religion, or as an eventual replacement for religion, then here too Amsterdam seems to be leading the way.

The implementation of the social welfare state after World War II also brought sharp and nearly instantaneous changes. People suddenly got subsidies: unemployment payments, sick leave. Jobs came with built-in pensions. There is a relationship between the rise of the welfare state and the steady unchurching of the city and the country, as the welfare state took over some of the security-blanket functions that churches had provided. And many people found this to be a positive development. Jan Donkers, for example, told me how throughout his childhood in North Amsterdam his devout Catholic grandmother kept three statues of saints on her living room mantel. Then she started getting welfare checks of forty guilders a month. The next time he went to her house, he said, he saw the statues outside next to the trash. "She said, 'What has the church done for us, apart from anointing German tanks when they came? Churches didn't buy bread for us. The Labor Party did.'"

Whether via the countercultural revolution, secularization, or the social welfare state, Amsterdam came out of the 1950s and 1960s with a renewed commitment to its liberal heritage. The Dutch American historian James Kennedy argues that this was due less to a full-throated avowal on the part of the city leaders of what the new liberalisms meant than to a historic willingness to compromise, to allow alternative voices to be heard. In other words, the politicians who ran the city in the aftermath of the 1960s were not all leftist radicals; rather, thanks to the polder model that was part of their makeup, they somewhat passively allowed their city to be a breeding ground for causes and ideas that were still anathema elsewhere.

Of course, this passive allowing implies the existence of those who were being allowed, those who were forcing the new: the Benno Premselas and Roel van Duijns. The city has always had a rich array of radicals and rights promoters. But the passive character of Amsterdam's tolerance remained apparent in the period from the 1960s to the 1990s, when it continued to unfurl the liberal banner, extending rights and freedoms on a scale unequaled in other cities. Its drug policy evolved against a backdrop of passive allowance: when marijuana first came to prominence in the 1960s, there was no built-in moral condemnation of it on the part of the government, as there was in many other places. As Provo gave way to the wider hippie culture, radio show hosts began to list prices of various types of marijuana and hashish available in the city. With drugs becoming more prevalent, the Dutch Department of Justice employed *gedogen*, the uniquely Dutch approach to tolerance: hard drugs like heroin were seen as an intolerable danger, but officials started to float the idea of decriminalization for soft drugs like marijuana. In 1973, three political parties, including D66 and the Labor Party, ran on a platform that advocated treating marijuana in the same way as alcohol.

The problem with legalizing pot turned out to be less local public opinion than the fact that the Netherlands had neighbors: the country would face censure from international organizations. (Plus there was some fear that hippies from around the world would come flocking in, which of course they did.) So *gedogen* held sway. Since police cracked down on drug dealing in the streets, another way was found. Every Amsterdammer or visitor to the city knows the difference between a coffee shop and a café. Historically, the distinction was that cafés had licenses to sell alcohol. Because coffee shops basically just sold coffee, there was no reason for police to pay attention to what went on in them. Thus, the pot trade moved indoors, and the Amsterdam coffee shop developed its own hazy mystique. The first coffee shop, according to some, was Mellow Yellow, a former bakery on the Weesperzijde, which was started in 1973 by a twenty-three-year-old named Wernard Bruining. Thirty years later, he told a reporter that Mellow Yellow wasn't about profit but about "clear and fair trade, and bringing people together through a joint. We were hippies. The world would be better if people were smoking dope."

The coffee shop idea worked, as far as the city leaders were concerned. Liberalism as an ideal—allowing people free exercise of their rights to pleasure themselves—did not feature much in official deliberations on the topic. The coffee shop concept was an expedient: it managed the inevitability of soft drugs; it contained their use; it provided for a measure of control. Technically, pot was still illegal, but provided coffee shops didn't advertise and didn't permit hard drug use, *gedogen* ruled. Thus came the golden age of ganja Amsterdam, the spliff center of the universe, the place to which latter-day hippies would flock to sit in stoned public contentment listening to Pink Floyd before boarding the Magic Bus from an office off Dam Square to ride the Hippie Trail to India and other points east. By the 1980s the city contained somewhere around fifteen hundred coffee shops. You could buy (and still can) Super Palm, Honey Yellow, Orange Bud, Black Bombay, Indian Cream, Burmese Kush, and a hundred other varieties, as well as Dutch brownies and space cake.

Prostitution followed a similar trajectory, with the difference that the perception of it as inevitable and thus to be tolerated goes back practically to the city's founding. In the case of prostitution the containment idea centered on two fronts: isolating it to specific neighborhoods (there are a couple of small red light districts in addition to the main one, De Wallen) and moving it off the streets and behind windows. The first prostitute windows—in which women displayed themselves to the public—appeared in De Wallen in the 1960s. There are several hundred windows today, as well as prostitutes who work in brothels. By the 1980s prostitutes had organized themselves. An advocacy group, called the Red Thread, came into being. Prostitutes wanted legalization of the trade. They wanted to change the mind-set that saw them as fallen women in need of reform and to be thought of simply as workers doing a job.

The year 2000 was a watershed for the kind of liberalization for which Amsterdam in its recent guise has become famous. It came about as a result of another of the Dutch convergences of social and economic liberalism. The governing coalition of parties included the main social liberal party, Labor, as well as two economic liberal parties, D66 and Liberal. Working together, and operating from different philosophical perspectives, they passed a slate of laws that extended civil liberties in several directions. Prostitution, gay marriage, and euthanasia were all legalized. This particular series of legalizations runs against the argument that Dutch tolerance is simply passive acceptance, for these decisions were made expressly to advance freedoms and rights. Same-sex marriage was a recognition of the equal rights of homosexuals, euthanasia of the right to die with dignity. Economic liberals argued for the legalization of prostitution on the grounds that citizens should have the right to practice a trade for which there is a market. Social liberals believed that legalization of prostitution would bring regulation, which would protect the prostitutes and their clients.

The business of prostitution did indeed become more normal. Some prostitutes are members of the FNV, one of the largest Dutch trade unions. The Red Thread offers advice on its Web site to sex workers, including tax help: "As a freelancer you may deduct the cost of condoms and transportation. Unfortunately, clothing and personal care costs are not deductible."

Many of the problems that plagued the business for centuries remained, some of them exacerbated by legalization. Amsterdam became a center of human trafficking. Likewise, the advent of coffee shops and the decriminalization of marijuana didn't erase problems associated with drugs. In a number of ways, the Dutch in the late twentieth and early twenty-first centuries have served as a scientific test case for the possibilities of radical liberalization of laws related to social behavior. One conclusion is that it's difficult to legalize something that the rest of the world does not allow without becoming a front for organized crime. As a result, Dutch politicians began to retreat from the liberal excesses. The numbers of coffee shops and prostitute windows were cut back, and Amsterdam and other municipalities began to take firmer steps to regulate the businesses.

Yet you didn't hear many Amsterdammers demanding that these businesses be stopped altogether. Job Cohen, who was mayor of Amsterdam from 2001 to 2010, told me that the answer to the problems caused by legalizing or officially tolerating the sex and drug trades was to better regulate. "In Amsterdam freedom is an ultimate value," he said. "People come here because they have the feeling that they can do anything they want. That is our history, and we have to protect it." As a result, you could find, in the wake of the city's 2008 prohibition on cigarette smoking in public places, signs such as this in coffee shops: "In compliance with new Dutch laws we have disallowed tobacco smoking in our bar. Cigarettes, blunts, and joints mixed with tobacco must be smoked outside. Pure marijuana joints can still be smoked indoors, as can pipes and bongs that do not contain any tobacco."

The curious flip side to Amsterdam's famously liberal approach to soft drugs is worth mentioning. The Dutch have one of the most restrictive attitudes in the world when it comes to prescription drugs. There is an innate mistrust of the pharmaceutical industry; the Dutch are deeply conservative when it comes to surgery. Doctors, amazingly, are disinclined to prescribe medicine. Prescription rates for antidepressants for young people, for example, are about one-third what they are in the United States. Several times I've gone to my doctor with physical complaints, only to have her write me a prescription for aspirin.

Something similar—a conservatism lurking beneath the infamous liberalism—applies in the approach to sex. The society that once brandished a prudishness that Aletta Jacobs, Bernard Premsela, and Benno Premsela fought against has not only legalized prostitution but developed one of the frankest of perspectives on all matters sexual. Birth control is presented to teenagers as a matter of course; the famous "double Dutch" method—girls taking birth control pills and boys using condoms—has resulted in one of the world's lowest rates of teen pregnancy and one of the lowest rates of abortion. The conservatism comes in in this way: sex is viewed as a matter not of secrecy but of health and normalcy. You see the same view reflected at the movies, where films that have R ratings in the United States for sexual content are open for all ages in Amsterdam. The flip side: a PG-13 film in the United States might be rated for adults only in the Netherlands, where movie violence that Americans think unexceptional is considered something to shield children from.

In January of 2000, the Dutch writer Paul Scheffer, a prominent member of the Labor Party, published an article in the NRC Handelsblad, the country's leading newspaper, called "The Multicultural Drama." Beginning in the 1980s, multiculturalism—meaning an effort both to promote more diversity in society and to support the distinctness of different subgroups—had become the new incarnation of the tolerance the Dutch had shown, and in some sense invented, in the seventeenth century. Multiculturalism—which was prevalent throughout Europe—had led, beginning in the 1970s, to a broad open-door immigration policy. The Dutch had built attractive processing centers for refugees, with swimming pools, tennis courts, and laundry services.

But Scheffer pointed out that multiculturalism was not building a new Dutch society, enriched by immigrants who blended in and added their talents to the whole. Instead, it had created an immigrant underclass that was becoming an unsupportable economic burden, whose members had little awareness of the values of the society that was sponsoring them and in some cases were openly abusive of the very values that had allowed them to settle there. Part of the problem was ideology. Multiculturalism, in this definition of the term, holds that all cultures are equal and should be treated equally; therefore it would be wrong to give preference to one language or way of doing things, even if it was that of the culture in which newcomers had chosen to live. But there was also a distinctly nonideological reason for the failure of multiculturalism. Newcomers were encouraged to keep their language and traditions not necessarily out of a pie-eyed sense of equality of cultures but because officials considered them "guest workers" who would eventually return to their home countries. The failure was also due to lack of follow-through. There was no master plan for integrating new arrivals. In its absence, the outdated pillar system, in which different groups had their own schools, neighborhoods, and media, reassserted itself. Immigrants moved into ghettos. Their children went to what were unashamedly called "black schools." With little to encourage or force them to learn the Dutch language or culture, they became second-class citizens.

Scheffer's article hit a nerve because these were things that were much on people's minds, but multiculturalism had been considered too politically correct to challenge. Now that it was in the open, a national conversation began. When the 9/11 attacks occurred in the United States, the conversation became a furious debate about immigration, Islam, and Dutch identity.

One of the many people who had come through the refugee processing centers was a young Somali woman named Ayaan Hirsi Magan. She had had a hard life in Somalia and Kenya, was subjected to female circumcision at age five, and eventually fled an arranged marriage—it was to hide from her husband that she changed her name to Ayaan Hirsi Ali. The Netherlands struck her as a bewildering paradise. She learned Dutch, enrolled as a student at Leiden University, and became entranced by her study of the Enlightenment. "I came to realize how deeply the Dutch are attached to freedom, and why," she wrote. "Holland was in many ways the capital of the European Enlightenment. Four hundred years ago, when European thinkers severed the hard bands of church dogma that had constrained people's minds, Holland was the center of free thought."

On Amsterdam's Leidseplein, opposite many of the bars and clubs that make up the city's nightlife district, is a debate center called De Balie. Hirsi Ali went there one night in November 2001, just after the 9/11 attacks, to hear a panel debate the question "The West or Islam: Who Needs a Voltaire?" The Dutch speakers took the position that the West, with its gaze narrowly focused on satisfying its consumerist cravings while vital issues were at stake, needed a new Voltaire, a new Enlightenment prophet. Hirsi Ali stood up and took the opposite position. "Look at how many Voltaires the West has," she said. "Don't deny us the right to have our Voltaire, too. Look at our women, and look at our countries. Look at how we are all fleeing and asking for refuge here, and how people are now flying planes into buildings in their madness. Allow us a Voltaire, because we are truly in the Dark Ages."

Within two years, Hirsi Ali had risen to become a member of the Dutch parliament and a fixture on television, as Amsterdam, and the world, debated the issues of immigration and Islam. She highlighted outrageous features of Dutch multiculturalism, such as the fact that while well-intentioned liberal Dutch observers criticized African countries for allowing female circumcision, the same barbaric practice was being conducted in immigrant communities in Dutch cities. As she drew ire—from Dutch liberals and from some Muslims—she was emboldened, becoming a critic of Islam as a religion and way of life and of the West for not standing up to what she said were threats to liberal culture inherent in Islam.

Hirsi Ali found an unlikely ally in Theo van Gogh, great-grandson of the brother of Vincent van Gogh, a filmmaker and artist whose mission, like Robert Jasper Grootveld's, was to provoke the establishment (but with the distinction that Van Gogh declared that chain-smoking was healthy). Van Gogh wanted to attack multiculturalism. He and Hirsi Ali collaborated on a ten-minute film, *Submission: Part 1.* It shows a young Muslim woman in the act of prayer. She is dressed head to toe in traditional costume, except that the middle of her body is exposed and covered with verses from the Quran. As she prays, we hear a series of stories told by different women who have suffered rape and other forms of outrage from men and yet, under Islamic law, must remain submissive.

The film was meant to be provocative, but when it aired on Dutch television it didn't get much immediate attention. Then on November 2, 2004, Van Gogh was shot to death as he was bicycling down the street near his home just off the Oosterpark. After firing eight bullets into him, Mohammed Bouyeri, a twenty-six-year-old Dutch Moroccan who had grown up in Amsterdam, slashed Van Gogh's throat, then stuck a five-page letter to his chest with the knife. It was a death threat directed at Hirsi Ali and an Islamist rant directed at the relativist, godless West.

Hirsi Ali went into hiding and became an international sensation. *60 Minutes* profiled her; *Time* named her one of the hundred most influential people in the world. Salman Rushdie and Christopher Hitchens lionized her as a champion of the Enlightenment arisen from the darkest regions of Islamist Africa. In the Netherlands, where she didn't shrink from the attention but used it to further her strident attacks on Islam, she became too controversial to be endured. In 2006, Rita Verdonk, then the minister for integration, revoked her passport, on the grounds that she had lied about her refugee status when she sought admission to the country. She was no longer a Dutch citizen. The furor over her actually brought down the Dutch government. Meanwhile, Hirsi Ali accepted an offer to become a fellow at the American Enterprise Institute in Washington and promptly stepped away from the aftermath of the explosion she had touched off.

Not long after, I had lunch with Hirsi Ali in New York, in order to interview her for a magazine article. She was every bit the poised, arresting fashionista she had been made out to be. And she was in a sense a near-perfect advocate for Amsterdam and its liberal tradition. You could feel the strength of the grasp that her outsider's perspective gave her on the worth and meaning of the liberal tradition. She insisted that the commitment to reason and individual freedom that Amsterdam had fostered is more vital than ever as a weapon against religious superstition. "The West was saved by the fact that it succeeded in separating faith and reason," she told me. "The only way to stand up to radical Islam is to revive the message of the Enlightenment, to make Europeans and Americans remember that their modern society didn't just fall out of the sky. There is a long history of struggle that led to this complex functioning society. And religion, including Christianity, has most of the time hindered that."

I found myself agreeing with her in large part. Religious absolutism *has* been a huge force for ill. I agreed that the separation of church and state is fundamentally important. I think we all need as many Voltaires—and Spinozas—as we can get. But Hirsi Ali's attack on Islam itself, and on all who practice it, was too much for me. And it was too much for the little world of Dutch politics through which she rose to fame. She seemed to long for a culture clash, on a biblical scale, as it were.

Amsterdam, meanwhile, reeled from the Van Gogh murder. People wondered if militant Islamism was about to break out into mass violence. If multiculturalism was wrong, what, people suddenly needed to know, was the right way to integrate, to adapt Western society to an ever more interconnected world? The city was so shaken, down to the level of individual households, that on the very evening of the assassination Mayor Job Cohen called for a mass gathering on Dam Square. At first he had thought to hold a silent vigil, but on learning that Van Gogh had detested silent vigils he made it a "noise vigil" and asked people to bring noisemakers.

Thousands streamed into the place that was the site of the medieval dam that gave the city its name. Many carried not only noisemakers but signs disparaging Cohen for not having foreseen the rise of militant Islam. In fact, in its multicultural heyday, the city had fostered the ghettoization of Muslims and subsidized Islamist organizations, which taught that women were naturally inferior and that Jews were enemies. People said you could almost feel the collective consciousness changing during the vigil, as people woke up to realize the scope of the failure of multiculturalism.

After the demonstration, a fascinating two-man team went to work: Cohen, the Jewish mayor, and Ahmed Aboutaleb, a city alderman who had been born and raised in a Berber village in Morocco. Aboutaleb was the son of an imam; he had emigrated to the Netherlands at age fifteen. Together, the Amsterdam Jew and the Amsterdam Muslim conducted a series of gatherings, sounding out the city neighborhood by neighborhood. "We operated as a kind of couple," Aboutaleb later told me. "It was a kind of city therapy." To neighborhood groups and the media, the two men offered different but complementary messages. Cohen stressed that non-Muslims had no reason to feel threatened by Muslims: investigations indicated that the young man who had killed Van Gogh had acted alone. In a way that Cohen himself couldn't have gotten away with, Aboutaleb used the occasion to push the city's Muslims to do more to integrate. Speaking at a mosque, Aboutaleb declared, "Whoever doesn't want to go along with Dutch society and its achievements can pack his bags."

At some point, Cohen, when asked to define his strategy, used the phrase *de boel bij elkaar houden*, which translates roughly as "keeping things together." Some ridiculed him for what sounded like a wishy-washy philosophy of governing. It fed into the rhetoric of Geert Wilders, the far-right politician who was using the furor over the murder to push his anti-immigrant, anti-Muslim agenda. After it became known that Cohen and Aboutaleb had drunk tea in mosques with groups of Muslims, Wilders turned "tea drinking" into an epithet: Cohen personified the ever-weakening West, kowtowing to an ascendant, aggressive Islam.

But Maarten Hajer, a political scientist at the University of Amsterdam, put it in a different context for me. "Tea drinking is the form of socializing in these communities," he said. "And while Cohen was doing that, he was also standing up for gay rights. In that sense, 'keeping things together' becomes a very meaningful phrase."

In the aftermath of the Van Gogh killing, *Time* named Cohen a "European hero," and in 2006 he came in second in a World Mayor contest. Both Cohen and Hirsi Ali, then, were lauded internationally for their very different ways of answering questions about immigration and integration, in particular the question of Islam in the West. In the years after the furor over the death of Theo van Gogh, even as immigration receded from the agenda in many places as the cutting issue of the day, and as Cohen ran for prime minister, lost, and retired from politics, people in Amsterdam continued to puzzle over the conflicting approaches that Cohen, the conciliator, and Hirsi Ali, the Enlightenment firebrand, personified. Which was the better path? More broadly, what—for those who believe in liberalism, not just in terms of immigration but in all respects—is the way forward?

Maybe the best response to such a serious question is to begin at the level of the ridiculous. Every city has its bad art. In Amsterdam and other Dutch cities, up until 1987 bad art held privileged status: it was funded by the public. Through the Beeldende Kunstenaars Regeling (BKR), or Fine Arts Subsidy, the government paid virtually anyone who applied and said he or she was an artist—three thousand people at the program's height—a living wage, which totaled $70 million a year in public funds. In exchange, the artist had to produce three works per year for the government. Most of the works—hundreds of thousands of them—were stored in warehouses, for an additional curiosity of the BKR was that the artworks submitted could not be sold. Since generally speaking artists are not keen to have their work sit in storage but also since some of the individuals partaking of the system were not so much dedicated artists as scammers, many pieces were mockeries of the process: people sent in items of household trash and called them sculpture.

The BKR is an example of the socialism-gone-wild comedy that set in in Amsterdam and other Dutch cities as the lowercase-l liberalism of the late twentieth century reached its absurdist low point. With the laudable intent to spread rights and freedoms as far as possible, to see just how far their commitment to liberal ideals could go, the Dutch created some systems that were truly worthy of parody. Maybe most ridiculous was the phenomenon of *kraken*, or squatting. In 1971 it became legal to break into an empty building and take up residence in it, and by the 1980s it was a rite of passage for groups of young people to take over a building and set up a neolithic existence in it (without electricity or running water). The squatting phenomenon, combined with the declawing of the police after the Provo period, produced absurdist street theater performances, in which a battalion of officers, in full riot gear, would show up outside a squatted building (its windows festooned with anarchic messages), making noise and brandishing their shields, while the kids inside would sneer from the windows. Then the police would go home.

Squatting was finally declared illegal in 2010, as part of the general official retreat from the lunatic horizon of liberal policy. By then, of course, the image of the city was well entrenched. A 2008 piece on Fox News's *O'Reilly Factor* that became a minor cult classic in Amsterdam used the city as a warning to the United States, in the aftermath of Barack Obama's first election victory, of what liberalism portends. Conservative commentator Monica Crowley, in conversation with host Bill O'Reilly, declared that the Dutch were engaged in "experimentation with social tolerance, free love, free drugs" and concluded: "Amsterdam is a cesspool of corruption, crime, everything's out of control—it's anarchy!" O'Reilly agreed, saying, "Every questionable person in Europe heads to Amsterdam because it's all there!" A twenty-five-year-old Dutchman named Robbert Nieuwenhuijs responded with a video that swept the Internet, putting the lurid claims of the commentators over images of ordinary life on the city's streets: people cycling, riding boats on the canals, kids playing. And he added some statistics for perspective: 40.3 percent of Americans have used cannabis, while only 22.6 percent of Dutch people have; drug-related deaths in the United States are 38 per million people, in the Netherlands 2.4 per million.

In fact, people in Amsterdam had long been aware of the truth embedded in the surreal exaggerations of the Fox News report. What the report ignored—what gets lost in the hippie-hazy image that the city has in the outside world—is the other side of its liberal tradition. In many ways Amsterdam still stands at the forefront of the advance of civil rights. In 2001, Job Cohen, shortly after becoming mayor, performed the world's first same-sex marriage—or actually four marriages, since he had arranged to have four couples standing ready at the moment the law went into effect, to make sure his city maintained its position at the vanguard of civil rights.

The social welfare system similarly reflects a real commitment to individual rights, one that may not be well understood elsewhere. Like the Fine Arts Subsidy, it was in the past subject to widespread abuse, with people making fake claims for sick leave and the like.

But it has had several overhauls, and it works. Even through the economic crises of the early twenty-first century, Amsterdam has found ways to manage its blend of economic and social liberalisms. As an outsider, I was at first bewildered by the social welfare system, then slowly I became a fan. I will never forget my confusion on first receiving a payment for *kinderbijslag*, a quarterly child subsidy, simply because I had children. Or *vakantiegeld*: vacation money, 8 percent of one's annual salary, which every working person receives in the spring, to help finance the cost of holiday travel. Again, such forms of assistance take place within the context of a capitalist culture; they are meant not to dissolve individualism but to give individuals some solid ground beneath their feet. I have found that, mostly, the idea works: you run your own life yet you feel that you are not entirely alone; you are a part of something. Sitting one chilly afternoon in the pleasantly dark recesses of Café Scheltema, a journalists' hangout since the days of the Nazi occupation, the Dutch writer Geert Mak contrasted for me the American and Dutch approaches to freedom. "My American friends say they live in the best country in the world, and in a lot of ways they are right," he said. "But they always have to worry: 'What happens to my family if I have a heart attack? What happens when I turn sixty-five or seventy?' America is the land of the free. But I think we are freer."

Freer . . . because you're not alone. That is the story that Amsterdam tells. Working together, we win land from the sea. Individually, we own it; individually, we prosper, so that collectively we do. Together, we maintain a society of individuals. For an American, raised on a diet of raw individualism, it remains a bit of a challenge to parse that logic. Another Dutch friend, who happens to be an expert on water management, drove home the differing sensibilities when he told me that the fable of Hans Brinker, the little Dutch boy who sticks his finger in the leaking dike to save the city and is rewarded for his heroism, is completely incomprehensible to the Dutch themselves. As it happens, it's not a Dutch tale at all but was written by an American in the nineteenth century. Carving their city out of the effluvial medieval muck necessitated a high level of cooperation among individuals, a communal sensibility that is evident today in the social welfare system. This is why, according to my friend, the fable doesn't work for the Dutch. "The heroism in the story," he said, "is purely American." Dike building and dike repair are communal enterprises; were the Dutch to construct such a fairy tale, the "hero" would probably be the town water board.

And yet, Amsterdam also goes far in the other direction, farther than any other place on earth. If maintaining individual freedom means treading a line between chaos and control, Amsterdam has shown a strong preference for erring on the side of chaos.

Amsterdam's history is so specific, so bound up with water, that its approach to individual freedom is different from that of most of the rest of the Western world. Still, many of us have long believed that the basic elements of liberalism are universal, and necessary for the future. But the future is shifting. Western democracies make up only a small portion of the world, and experiences with "nation building" have not had great success in transplanting democracy, for example, to regions that have never known it. And the political scientist Francis Fukuyama has argued that societies that have the concept of preserving individual liberties as part of their foundation are now at a crippling disadvantage. Fukuyama points to China and Singapore as examples of governments that operate without checks on power or accountability to the people—two hallmarks of liberal government—and whose orientation is not toward preserving individual freedoms but rather toward pushing the nation forward. Such countries are able to act faster to adapt to changing global situations, while Western democracies engage in congressional debates, parliamentary procedures, and media investigations, slowed by institutions whose noble founding goal was to ensure liberal values.

If liberalism is under threat in some places, then surely testing grounds for expanding individual freedoms are all the more vital. By the standards of world cities today—New York, London, Istanbul,

Paris, Mumbai—Amsterdam is a pokey place. It is small in population; in terms of geographic area you could tuck the whole of it into a corner of Shanghai or Karachi and it probably wouldn't be noticed. It has no skyscrapers. But the advantage of a modest skyline is the seemingly limitless horizon.

POSTSCRIPT

One gray, late-February morning, with a light mist in the air, I altered my weekly bicycle routine from my house in Amsterdam's Oud Zuid. Instead of taking my son, Anthony, to day care and then cycling to Frieda Menco's apartment to interview her about her experiences in the city before and after World War II, I brought him with me to see Frieda. She had called me the day before saying she had found a letter we had been talking about: a long letter her mother had written to a brother in New York in September 1945 summarizing all the suffering the family had been through, from the first appearance of Nazi uniforms on the streets of their neighborhood through the horror of Auschwitz. Since Frieda had been asking me lately about my little son, I told her I could come by her apartment on the way to day care and that way she could meet Anthony too. I had said we would be there between nine and nine thirty. She said, "So late for day care!" which seemed an odd comment. As it turned out, there had been a miscommunication. She thought I was coming after nine o'clock at night, after day care. She blamed the mistake on her age; I blamed it on my Dutch. At any rate, when I arrived at nine in the morning, Frieda was still in bed. I said I would come back another time, but she insisted we come in. We then had a little encounter in the hallway of her apartment that began with her apologizing for her appearance. Normally she was impeccably dressed and made up; now she wore a nightgown; without makeup, and having just roused herself from bed, her skin looked gray.

More to the point, there was a cloudy grayness in her eyes, a torment, almost. She said she had been thinking, since our last meeting, about one particular question I had brought up, something that truly bewildered me: how was it possible that, in choosing an apartment for herself in the early 1990s, she had settled on this one, which was located on the very block where her family had been brought after their hiding place had been discovered and where her Auschwitz nightmare began. How, I had asked Frieda the day before, could she have chosen to live in the very locus of her family suffering?

Then, she had answered me by saying she had simply liked this apartment, liked the light, felt happy here. "But since you brought it up I've been thinking about all of these things," she said now. "That building down the street, this letter, my mother . . . I just shake my head. How could I do that? I never saw my father again . . ."

And then this happened. I was holding Anthony in one arm. Frieda had clutched my other arm with both her hands as she recounted her recent tumble of emotions. She reached out and cupped the baby's cheek. "*Wat een schat!*" she said: such a sweetheart. He was a big, bright-faced toddler, and he stared at her with the seriousness he could sometimes summon. "He's thinking deeply," she said. "He's never seen someone so old." And for a moment she stared back at him. This woman who for me personified the history of Amsterdam—both its legacy of personal freedom and the betrayal of that legacy—locked her gaze onto my son, who was born here and so was the physical embodiment of my own involvement with the city. And she said, "You know what I've often said, ever since Auschwitz. Life is absurd. It has no meaning. But it has beauty, and wonder, and we have to enjoy that." Her hand was still on his cheek, her arm stretched out, revealing, beneath the almost silver surface of the skin, the watery blue numbers of the tattoo a Nazi clerk had pricked into it when it was still young and fresh. Then she looked from the boy to me and said, "I was wondering. Your book is about so many things: the whole history of the city. What are you going to end it with?"

"This," I said. "I'll end with this."

Acknowledgments

I would like to express my sincere gratitude to the following people for interviews, insights, facts and figures, lunches and dinners, canal strolls, corrections, and fruitful arguments: Ahmed Aboutaleb, Mayor of Rotterdam; Jaap-Evert Abrahamse; Buford Alexander; Kiki Amsberg and Joost Smiers; Randy Berry, U.S. Consul General in Amsterdam; Bas Bruijn; Eline Hopperus Buma; Tilly de Groot; Jan Donkers; Roel van Duijn; Didi van den Elsaker, Director of the Realtors' Association of Amsterdam; Carolien Gehrels, Deputy Mayor, City of Amsterdam; Martine Gosselink, Head of the Department of History, Rijksmuseum; Fred Feddes; Zef Hemel; Ayaan Hirsi Ali; Beth Johnson and Jan Kat; Virginia Keizer; Tim Killiam; Geert Mak; Dik van der Meulen; Iman Mreqqi; Lodewijk Petram; Alexander Rinnooy Kan; Julie Ruterbories; Marjan Scharloo, Director of the Teylers Museum in Haarlem; Paul Schuurman, Erasmus University Rotterdam; Deborah Scroggins and Colin Campbell; Jan Pieter Six; Jan Six X; Jan Six XI; and Paul Spies, Director of the Amsterdam Museum.

I am deeply grateful to Frieda Menco for her time, energy, willingness to endure my questions for long hours over many months, and most of all for her friendship.

In addition, I would like to thank Charles Gehring, Jaap Jacobs,

Robert Cwiklik, Gary Schwartz, Lodewijk Petram, Paul Spies, Dik van der Meulen, and Pamela Twigg for reading the manuscript. They improved the narrative with their comments and suggestions, and saved me from many errors, though naturally any errors that remain are my own doing.

Thanks, too, to the John Adams Institute board members and staff, past and present, for their help and for putting up with the writing of this book, including Maarten van Essen, Yara Deuss, Tracy Metz, Ruth Oldenziel, Marry de Gaay Fortman, Jeannette Saunders, Arie Westerlaken, Evert van den Berg, Pim Roest, David Vermijs, Chris Kijne, Carien van der Laan, Truus Valkering, Martine Bijkerk, Cobie Ivens, Anne Wertheim, and Monique Knapen.

Many Amsterdam institutions provided me with assistance and/ or inspiration, including the Rijksmuseum, Multatuli House, the Amsterdam Museum, the Anne Frank House, Stadsarchief Amsterdam, and the Rembrandt House. I would like to take special notice of the staff of the University of Amsterdam Library, an institution that lives up to Amsterdam's ideal of openness, which affords anyone who puts down the modest sum of thirty euros yearly membership and access to its vast holdings.

I would also like to express gratitude to Prime Minister Mark Rutte, Foreign Minister Frans Timmermans, former Prime Minister Jan Peter Balkenende, former U.S. Ambassadors to the Netherlands Clifford Sobel, Terry Dornbush, and Fay Hartog Levin, former Mayor Job Cohen, and their Royal Highnesses Willem-Alexander and Máxima for the courtesies they have extended me at various points over the past eight years.

My thanks to Miriam van der Meij for her outstanding work as researcher, translator, summarizer, and fact checker.

Thanks, as always, to my terrific editor, Bill Thomas, for his patented mixture of wisdom and calm, and for encouraging me with this project when it was just an idea. Thanks also to Coralie Hunter for her smart assistance. A thousand thanks to Anne Edelstein, my agent and friend. And thank you, Haye Koningsveld and Laurens Ubbink of Ambo/Anthos.

Lastly, I want to acknowledge the role that Friso Broeksma played in fostering this book. Once upon a time, he and his life partner, the renowned Dutch designer and gay rights activist Benno Premsela, built a remarkable house on Prinseneiland in Amsterdam. While enjoying a long stay in the guest apartment there, which also doubles as the travel library, I hit upon the idea of this book. Friso and I subsequently had many excellent chats about the city, its history, and its liberalisms. During one of those conversations, Friso told me he believed that his late partner's insistence that their house include a "refuge" for visiting friends was related to Benno's period in hiding during the Nazi occupation of Amsterdam—to his sensitivity to the concept of refuge. The thought that I was a beneficiary of such an impulse, which came out of the period when Amsterdam's liberalism faced its greatest threat, puts the mere task of writing a book in proper perspective.

Notes

CHAPTER 1: A BICYCLE TRIP

10   **"Now, where was I?"**: All quotes from Frieda Menco come from a series of personal interviews conducted in 2011 and 2012.

14   **"In Amsterdam, craziness"**: Personal interview, April 3, 2010.

15   **The city has between 5,000**: http://www.hetccv.nl/nieuws/2010/10/amsterdam-steunt-kwetsbare-prostituees.html.

16   **"No, I will speak"**: *Othello*, V, ii, 218.

17   **"In them I trust"**: *Henry VI*, Pt. 3, I, ii, 42.

17   **"her liberall brest"**: *OED*.

20   **"go down in history"**: Churchill, "The Truth about Hitler," *Strand*, Nov. 1935.

CHAPTER 2: THE WATER PROBLEM

24   **"anarchists, provos, beatniks"**: Roel Van Duijn, *Provo*, no. 1, July 12, 1965.

24   **"We were leftists"**: Personal interview, September 6, 2011.

26   **One day, while**: De Kruif, *Dagboek van broeder Wouter Jacobsz.*, 8.

26   **Or not quite all**: Koopman, "Huisvesting Universiteit van Amsterdam," 139.

31   **medieval phenomenon**: *Geschiedenis van Amsterdam*, 1:230, 263–66, 395.

32   **The Holy Place**: *Geschiedenis van Amsterdam*, 1:267.

34   **Dutch fishermen**: Unger, "Dutch Herring"; Unger, *Dutch Shipbuilding*; *Geschiedenis van Amsterdam*, 1:135–37.

35   **sailors, gutters**: Unger, "Dutch Herring," 257.

36   **200 million herring**: Unger, "Dutch Herring," 263.

38   **Whereupon he was given**: Tracy, *Erasmus*, 17, 18.
38   **"whipping boys to death"**: Tracy, *Erasmus*, 91–92.
39   **"superstition of ceremonies"**: Tracy, *Erasmus*, 136.
39   **He questioned the very**: Tracy, *Erasmus*, 93.
39   **"liberal studies"**: Israel, *Dutch Republic*, 49.
40   **"Luther is pestilential"**: Israel, *Dutch Republic*, 50.
41   **Two Amsterdam printers**: Visser, *Luther's Geschriften*, 10.
41   **"books made by"**: Visser, *Luther's Geschriften*, 9.
41   **"certain books of St. Paul's"**: Visser, *Luther's Geschriften*, 14–15.
41   **"My lords of the righteous"**: Visser, *Luther's Geschriften*, 12.
41   **"Alienation of a society"**: Israel, *Dutch Republic*, 148.
42   **Jan Goessens, a card maker**: Emeis, *Ons Amsterdam*, May 1975.
44   **In another sense, however**: De Vries, *Dutch Rural Economy*, chs. 2–4.
45   **Where land was controlled**: Israel, *Dutch Republic*, 108–9.
47   **There was a good deal**: Emeis, *Ons Amsterdam*, May 1975, quoting
         Wagenaar.
48   **Sheriff Dobbenszoon arrested**: *Geschiedenis van Amsterdam*, 1:328–50;
         Emeis, *Ons Amsterdam*, May 1975.
50   **They removed the local**: Israel, *Dutch Republic*, 127.
50   **A printed appeal**: Kossmann, *Low Countries*, 86–88.

CHAPTER 3: THE ALTERATION

53   **Later, he would attempt**: Thomas, *Golden Age*, 18, 20.
57   **Income from taxes totaled**: Parker, *Dutch Revolt*, 39.
57   **"maintain friends and informants"**: Parker, *Grand Strategy*, 78.
57   **"Remember that the French"**: Thomas, *Golden Age*, 506.
57   **"As we have seen and discovered"**: Parker, *Grand Strategy*, 115.
58   **Where Charles had ordered**: Thomas, *Golden Age*, 506.
58   **After his marriage to Elizabeth of Valois**: Kamen, *Philip of Spain*, 89.
58   **At the end of his life**: Kamen, *Philip of Spain*, 189.
58   **"God's service and mine"**: Kamen, *Philip of Spain*, 233.
59   **"To think that a passion"**: Kamen, *Philip of Spain*, 233.
59   **He made two decisions**: Parker, *Dutch Revolt*, 46–50.
60   **He thought he had found her**: Lettenhove, *Relations politiques*, 2:257.
63   **Whereupon the king let**: Aubery, *Mémoires*, 9.
64   **The king should abandon**: Arblaster, *History of the Low Countries*, 54.
65   **Over the course of several years**: Israel, *Dutch Republic*, 99; Arblaster,
         History of the Low Countries, 74–75.
65   **"Alias Tyranny"**: Arblaster, *History of the Low Countries*, 75.
66   **But there was also a strong**: Arblaster, *History of the Low Countries*,
         78–80.
66   **"to imagine—even"**: Arblaster, *History of the Low Countries*, 82.
67   **events in the south**: Arnade, "Beggars, Iconoclasts," 84.
67   **He was a vigorous**: Quoted in Motley, *The Rise of the Dutch Republic*,
         289.

68   **But the Calvinists had**: Emeis, *Ons Amsterdam*, May 1975.
68   **Within three days**: Emeis, *Ons Amsterdam*, May 1975.
68   **For proof, they had**: *Geschiedenis van Amsterdam*, 1:455.
69   **"You priests, stop"**: Emeis, *Ons Amsterdam*, May 1975, 137.
69   **"In the Old Church"**: Emeis, *Ons Amsterdam*, May 1975, 137.
69   **"Stand up against"**: Emeis, *Ons Amsterdam*, May 1975, 137.
71   **"distrust, bias, and"**: *Geschiedenis van Amsterdam*, 1:463.
72   **Alba hanged every**: Kamen, *Alba*, 46.
73   **"I'm here in the kitchen"**: Wedgwood, *William the Silent*, 90.
73   **"Cousin, if you take"**: Kamen, *Alba*, 87.
74   **"I have satisfied myself"**: Kamen, *Alba*, 87.
74   **"No one dares to"**: Kamen, *Alba*, 83.
75   **"Our Devil, who art"**: Kamen, *Alba*, 106.
76   **"freedoms, rights, customs"**: Kossmann, *Low Countries*, 84–86.
77   **"the Originals of the two"**: J. Adams, *Collection of State Papers*.
79   **"cut the throats"**: Kamen, *Alba*, 112.
79   **"slit the throats"**: Kamen, *Alba*, 113.
80   **"Making me come here"**: Kamen, *Alba*, 107–8.
80   **"If you strike camp"**: Kamen, *Alba*, 115.
81   **"care not whether"**: De Kruif, *Dagboek*, 18.
81   **One night he saw**: De Kruif, *Dagboek*, 43–44.
82   **"The whole of Amsterdam"**: De Kruif, *Dagboek*, 47.
82   **"On December 4, with"**: De Kruif, *Dagboek*, 47–48.
83   **He couldn't make the nuns**: De Kruif, *Dagboek*, 7–10.
83   **"Everywhere they go"**: De Kruif, *Dagboek*, 133.
83   **"O Lord, I have sinned"**: De Kruif, *Dagboek*, 20–21.
83   **"the 26th of May in the year"**: Mak, *Kleine geschiedenis*, 95.
84   **"as if the beer were water"**: De Kruif, *Dagboek*, 319.
84   **In March of 1580**: Arblaster, *History of the Low Countries*, 295–97.

CHAPTER 4: THE COMPANY

89   **They were nearly two months**: My sources for the voyage of De Houtman's fleet are Roeper and Wildeman, *Om de Zuid*; Hakluyt, *Principal Navigations*; Swart, "Lambert Biesman"; Gaastra, *De geschiedenis van de VOC*; Rouffaer and Ijzerman, *De eerste schipvaart*.

89   **"Our flesh and fishe"**: The quotation is from the first English-language account of the voyage, published in 1598, which is supposedly a translation of the Dutch but seems to be a composite, since it includes many details, such as this quotation, not found in the original journal.

93   **Schumpeter said that**: Lesger, *Rise of the Amsterdam Market*, 139–41.

99   **While in the Indies**: Knobel, "Frederick de Houtman's Catalogue"; http://www.ianridpath.com/startales/startales1c.htm#houtman.

100   **"Getting rich became"**: Fruin, *Tien jaren*, 267.

100   **"So long as Holland"**: The quotation is in Boxer, *Dutch Seaborne Empire*, 22–23, without attribution. It is also in Bastin, "Changing Balance," 25.

100   **More sails bent toward**: Israel, *Dutch Primacy*, 68.

102   **One area was helpfully**: Keyes, *Pieter Bast*.

102   **"a unique politico-commercial"**: Israel, *Dutch Primacy*, 71.

103   **Its surviving archives**: Van Boven, "Towards a New Age."

105   **The expansion of Dutch shipping**: Israel, *Dutch Primacy*, 407, passim; Van Boven, "Towards a New Age," passim.

105   **"Tea rejuvenates the very old"**: Schama, *Embarrassment*, 172.

107   **His street-level rooms**: Petram, "World's First Stock Exchange," introduction and ch. 1.

108   **Indeed, one of the oldest**: http://stadsarchief.amsterdam.nl/presentaties/amsterdamse_schatten/geld/voc_aandeel_van_een_wees/index.nl.html.

110   **Within days of Dirck van Os's**: Van Dillen, Poitras, and Majithia, "Isaac Le Maire," 54–55.

111   **This in itself was not problematic**: Details of the Le Maire scandal come from Van Dillen, Poitras, and Majithia, "Isaac Le Maire."

112   **So, for example, in April 1610**: I calculated the quantity of mace using figures from Klerk de Reus, *Geschichtlicher Überblick*, appendix 4.

113   **within a decade or so**: Israel, *Dutch Primacy*, 74.

114   **NYSE Euronext, as the**: http://www.nyx.com/who-we-are/history/amsterdam.

116   **"In such condition there"**: Hobbes, *Leviathan*, 95–96.

116   **The year after, thanks to especially**: Bastin, "Changing Balance," 287.

117   **"Greater trade is done"**: Sutton, *Jan van der Heyden*, 12.

118   **The city needed to expand**: My telling of the story of land speculation and the expansion of Amsterdam's canals is based on, among other sources, Elias, *De vroedschap van Amsterdam*, liv–lxxvi; Abrahamse, *De Grote Uitleg van Amsterdam*, 42–88; Lesger, *Rise of the Amsterdam Market*, 174–80; Brugmans, *Geschiedenis van Amsterdam*, 207–10.

119   **One example, cited by Clé Lesger**: Lesger, *Rise of the Amsterdam Market*, 175.

121   **Hoe heeft hem**: http://www.dbnl.org/tekst/vond001dewe03_01/vond-001dewe03_01_0038.php.

121   **"How did Amsterdam know"**: Thanks to Jaap Jacobs for the translation.

121   **Once Hooft saw what was going on**: Abrahamse, *De Grote Uitleg van Amsterdam*, 86.

122   **Six miles of canal**: Figures come from calculations made by architect Tim Killiam in the 1970s.

122   **Twelve miles of canal-side land**: Canal houses, pile driving, and figures for canals, bridges, etc.: Killiam and van der Ziejden, *Amsterdam Canal Guide*, 344, passim; Janse, *Building Amsterdam*, 34.

124   **Peter the Great set himself**: http://whc.unesco.org/en/list/1349.

125   **"When they constructed"**: Personal interview, March 12, 2012.

CHAPTER 5: THE LIBERAL CITY

127 **"the people who live"**: Jarrell, *A Sad Heart at the Supermarket*, 16.
128 **We know that she had**: Wijnman, "Een episode."
129 **When Willem of Orange rode**: Kuijpers, *Migrantenstad*.
130 **And the inhabitants**: Israel, *Dutch Republic*, 328.
130 **At least a third were**: Israel, *Dutch Republic*, 309.
130 **There were people who only**: Barnes, *The Butcher*, passim.
130 **Among the canals you could find**: Cook, *Matters of Exchange*, 142.
132 **Claes Pieterszoon was born**: My sources on Dr. Tulp include Dudok van Heel, *Nicolaes Tulp*; Afek, Friedman, et al., "Dr. Tulp's Anatomy Lesson"; Rogge; Schama, *Rembrandt's Eyes*.
133 **He even made a joke**: Sources on Harvey and Tulp are Dudok van Heel, *Nicolaes Tulp*, 165; Shorto, *Island*, 98; Shorto, *Descartes*, 10.
134 **"like our locks"**: Dudok van Heel, *Nicolaes Tulp*, 201.
136 **"Speculation . . . comes when"**: Galbraith, *Short History*, 28.
137 **More than a few people**: Dudok van Heel, *Nicolaes Tulp*, 196.
138 **the son of a miller**: My main sources on Rembrandt are Schwartz, *Rembrandt's Universe*; Chapman, *Rembrandt's Self-Portraits*; Schama, *Rembrandt's Eyes*; Bailey, *Rembrandt's House*; Hughes, "God of Realism"; Fuchs, *Rembrandt en Amsterdam*.
138 **"the greatest and most"**: Chapman, *Rembrandt's Self-Portraits*, 17.
140 **"In their extraordinary"**: Chapman, *Rembrandt's Self-Portraits*, 10.
141 **"gives himself wholly"**: Quoted in Chapman, *Rembrandt's Self-Portraits*, 17.
141 **"the supreme depictor"**: Hughes, "God of Realism," 10.
143 **The art historian Ann**: Adams, *Public Faces*, 4, 21–23.
144 **The Blaeu family of**: Bailey, *Rembrandt's House*, 140.
144 **"ships arriving laden"**: Descartes, *Philosophical Writings*, III:31–32.
149 **Seven years after Saskia's**: Most of what follows comes from Wijnman, "Een episode."
150 **"Rembrandt's face is lit"**: Schama, *Rembrandt's Eyes*, 680.
151 **The Dutch author Fred Feddes**: Feddes, *Millennium of Amsterdam*, 133–34.
152 **Van der Heyden also invented**: My sources on Van der Heyden include Sutton, *Jan van der Heyden*; Van der Heyden, *Description of Fire Engines*; Feddes, *Millennium of Amsterdam*.
154 **The writer Witold**: Rybczynski, *Home*, 51–75.

CHAPTER 6: "THE RARE HAPPINESS OF LIVING IN A REPUBLIC"

164 **"the noblest and most lovable"**: Russell, *History of Western Philosophy*, 569.
164 **"a free man's"**: Feuer, *Spinoza*, 198.
166 **The city struck a**: *Geschiedenis van Amsterdam*, 2:278.
167 **"The women mixed their"**: *Geschiedenis van Amsterdam*, 2:281.
170 **It was a city**: Spinoza, *Tractatus*, 1:264.

171   **"by decree of the angels"**: Nadler, *Spinoza*, 120.
172   **"acme of absurdity"**: Spinoza, *Tractatus*, 38–39.
172   **"Whatever is, is in God"**: Feuer, *Spinoza*, 55, from *Ethics*.
172   **"I believe in Spinoza's"**: "Einstein Believes in 'Spinoza's God,'" *New York Times*, April 25, 1929.
174   **"Instead, Spinoza was to"**: Goldstein, *Betraying Spinoza*, 121.
175   **As De Witt saw it**: Quoted in Feuer, *Spinoza*, 79.
175   **"neither in France nor"**: De la Court, *True Interest*.
176   **"Now seeing that we have"**: Spinoza, *Tractatus*.
176   **The herring fleet was decimated**: Israel, *Dutch Republic*, 716.
177   **Thus, Holland's republican**: Israel, *Dutch Republic*, 721–30.
178   **The city's per capita income**: http://whc.unesco.org/en/list/1349/.
178   **"scarce deserves the name"**: Marvell, "The Character of Holland," 1653.
179   **All the arenas of life**: Verwey, "Seventeenth Century," 29; also cited in Sprunger, *Trumpets from the Tower*, 29. Statistics also come from Deinema, "Amsterdam's Re-emergence," 5.
179   **Propagandists staged a play**: Israel, *Dutch Republic*, 765.
180   **The basis of politics**: Spinoza, *Tractatus*, as quoted in Israel, *Dutch Republic*, 787.
180   **"The city of Amsterdam"**: Spinoza, *Tractatus*, 64–65.
181   **"laws dealing with"**: Spinoza, *Tractatus*, 67.
181   **A spontaneous chorus**: Nadler, *Book Forged*, 224.
181   **Gottfried Wilhelm Leibniz, the great**: Quoted in Nadler, *Book Forged*, 231.
184   **"He told me that on"**: Feuer, *Spinoza*, 138.
184   **"Men are of necessity"**: Spinoza, *Tractatus*, 289.

CHAPTER 7: SEEDS OF INFLUENCE

187   **"the 13th of January 1624"**: Stadsarchief Amsterdam, Ondertrouwregister, archive 5001, inv. no. 428. My thanks to Jaap Jacobs, Charles Gehring, and Janny Venema for help with this passage. I also relied on Zabriskie, "Founding Families," and Koenig and Nieuwenhuis, "Catalina Trico," as well as the New Netherland Historical Manuscripts and New Netherland Documents series, in piecing together the story of Catalina Trico and Joris Rapalje.
189   **In particular, a large number**: My sources on New Amsterdam and New Netherland include Shorto, *Island*; J. Jacobs, *New Netherland*; Gehring et al., *New Netherland Documents*; Van Laer, *New York Historical Manuscripts*.
193   **They start modestly**: Van Laer, *New York Historical Manuscripts*, 1:11, 286.
194   **In 1637, Joris buys**: O'Callaghan, *Calendar*, 221, 364.
197   **In particular, they wanted**: Fernow, *Records of New Amsterdam*, 1:144.
197   **The Amsterdam chamber**: Van Laer, *New York Historical Manuscripts*, 11:149.

198   **In 1674, ten years**: J. Jacobs, *New Netherland*, 420.
202   **An Amsterdam basketmaker**: Henri Krop, "Radical Cartesianism in Holland: Spinoza and Deurhoff," in Van Bunge and Klever, *Disguised and Overt Spinozism*.
202   **Lodewijk Meijer, an**: Israel, *Radical Enlightenment*, 197–205; Mijnhardt, "Urbanization, Culture, and the Dutch Origins," 160–61.
204   **"the undisputed focus"**: Mijnhardt, "Urbanization, Culture, and the Dutch Origins," 167.
205   **"May this Town ever"**: Rosalie Colie, "John Locke in the Republic of Letters," in Bromley and Kossmann, *Britain and the Netherlands*, 119.
206   **Jean Frederic Bernard was born**: Sources on Bernard are Hunt, Jacob, and Mijnhardt, *Book That Changed Europe*, 90–111; Mijnhardt, "Urbanization, Culture, and the Dutch Origins," 171–72.
206   **One of Bernard's more**: Sources on *La Vie et l'esprit* are Silvia Berti, "The First Edition of the *Traité des trois imposteurs*, and Its Debt to Spinoza's *Ethics*," in Hunter and Wootton, *Atheism from the Reformation*; Hunt, Jacob, and Mijnhardt, *Book That Changed Europe*, 26–27; Mijnhardt, "Urbanization, Culture, and the Dutch Origins," 171.
207   **"to construct and disseminate"**: Berti, "First Edition," in Hunter and Wootton, *Atheism from the Reformation*, 186.
208   **In France the book**: Israel, *Radical Enlightenment*, 303.
208   **"I went over and over"**: Rudiger Otto, "Johann Christian Edelmann's Criticism of the Bible and Its Relation to Spinoza," in Van Bunge and Klever, *Disguised and Overt Spinozism*, 172.
209   **"There is no other philosophy"**: Israel, *Revolution of the Mind*, 71.
209   **"his whole philosophy is"**: Russell, 592.
209   **"Conservatism, Liberalism, Materialism"**: Melamed, *Spinoza's "Theological-Political Treatise,"* 2.
209   **In September of 1683**: My sources on Locke and his time in the Netherlands include Woolhouse, *Locke*; Colie, "John Locke in the Republic of Letters," in Bromley and Kossmann, *Britain and the Netherlands*; Schuurman, "Locke and the Dutch"; Cranston, *John Locke*.
210   **They exactly suited**: Woolhouse, *Locke*, 249.
212   **Locke dismantled this**: Locke, *Two Treatises*, 2.54, 2.96, 2.104.
213   **" 'Tis necessary that they"**: Van Limborch, *Compleat System*, 2:998.
215   **Locke may have helped**: Woolhouse, *Locke*, 219.
215   **"in the vigorous"**: Colie, "John Locke in the Republic of Letters," in Bromley and Kossmann, *Britain and the Netherlands*, 129.
216   **"In this city of Amsterdam is"**: Temple, *Observations*, 56.
217   **My favorite of these**: Shorto, *Island*, 319.
217   **This, according to one**: My sources on 1688 include Claydon, *William III*; Jardine, *Going Dutch*; Israel's *Dutch Republic* and *Anglo-Dutch Moment*.
219   **But in October the English**: Jardine, *Going Dutch*, 4.
219   **Those who saw the spectacle**: Israel, *Dutch Republic*, 850; Jardine, *Going Dutch*, 8.
220   **"By 1688 England and Holland"**: Jardine, *Going Dutch*, 349.

221 **"It is both certain and"**: History of Parliament Trust, *Journal of the House of Commons* 10 (1802).

CHAPTER 8: THE TWO LIBERALISMS

225 **An example: one official gave**: Mak, *Kleine geschiedenis*, 168.

225 **"A rude female"**: Mak, *Kleine geschiedenis*, 173.

226 **Four days of rioting**: Van Gelder and Kistemaker, *Amsterdam*, 199; http://stadsarchief.amsterdam.nl/presentaties/amsterdamse_schatten/oproer/pachtersoproer/index.html.

227 **"Our dear Orange"**: Van der Capellen, *Aan het Volk van Nederland*.

231 **It is also just steps**: My account of Dekker/Multatuli is based on Van der Meulen, *Multatuli*; King, "Multatuli's Max Havelaar"; King, *Multatuli*; Fasseur, "Purse or Principle"; Toer, "The Book That Killed Colonialism"; the Multatuli House Museum; and conversation with Dik van der Meulen.

232 **"He has heard such"**: Multatuli, *Max Havelaar*, Introd., 2.

234 **And Dekker's "self-portrait"**: Multatuli, *Max Havelaar*, 93.

234 **"There has been of late"**: Van der Meulen, *Multatuli*, 418.

236 **Echoing Spinoza, he**: Multatuli, *Ideën*, vol. 1, 166; vol. 7, 1233.

236 **Once, as socialists were**: *Rotterdamsch Nieuwsblad*, Nov. 15, 1886.

237 **"The Indonesian revolution not"**: Toer, "The Book That Killed Colonialism."

240 **Wilders infamously compared the Koran**: http://www.elsevier.nl/Politiek/nieuws/2007/8/Wilders-wil-verbod-op-islamitische-Mein-Kampf-ELSEVIER132670W/.

240 **The group of thirty**: Amsterdam Stadsarchief, http://stadsarchief.amsterdam.nl/presentaties/amsterdamse_schatten/beroemd/karl_marx_geschaduwd/index.html.

241 **"In the eighteenth century, the kings"**: Published in *La Liberté*, Sept. 15, 1872.

242 **It had involved years**: "The North Sea Canal," *New York Times*, Nov. 12, 1876.

243 **A sermon he heard**: Van Gogh, letter 120, http://vangoghletters.org. I infer the lesson from Van Gogh's description.

243 **"It's a beautiful city"**: Van Gogh, letter 120.

243 **It was in a cemetery**: Van Gogh, letter 126.

243 **He saw it as he walked**: Van Gogh, letter 131.

243 **It was in "the people"**: Van Gogh, letter 116.

244 **In the last letter he**: Van Gogh, letter 144.

246 **"As a child I was"**: A. Jacobs, *Memories*, 53.

247 **Her office in the Jordaan**: Harriet Pass Freidenreich, "Aletta Jacobs in Historical Perspective," in A. Jacobs, *Memories*, 179.

248 **The court argued first**: A. Jacobs, *Memories*, 55.

249 **The discovery of oil**: http://www.forbes.com/global2250/.

250 **The Dutch moved faster**: Arblaster, *History of the Low Countries*, 192.

250   **One of the leaders of the orthodox**: My sources on Gorter include http://
       www.iisg.nl/bwsa/bios/gorter.html; http://www.marxists.org/archive/gorter/
       index.htm; and http://www.dbnl.org/auteurs/auteur.php?id=gort004.

251   **On the other side**: My sources on Polak include Bloemgarten, *Henri
       Polak*; Montagne and Winkler, *Doctor Henri Polak*; and Historici.nl.

251   **keep the family together**: Montagne and Winkler, *Doctor Henri Polak*,
       26–29.

254   **"The point of departure"**: Feddes, *Millennium of Amsterdam*, 226.

255   **In all, thirty thousand dwellings**: Levy-Vroelant, Reinprecht, and Was-
       senberg, "Learning from History," 36.

255   **Private developers did the**: T. Schaap, in Schnabel, Rijnboutt, Koek,
       and Schaap, *Design of Urban Public Space*, 41.

256   **The building was all**: My sources on the Beurs van Berlage include Van
       der Werf and Derwig, *Beurs van Berlage*, and Bank and Van Buuren,
       1900.

256   **"Our self-esteem"**: Quoted in Kossmann, *Low Countries*, 545.

258   **He believed that equality**: Brandhorst, "From Neo-Malthusianism," 56.

258   **He wrote a series**: *Sexuele moeilijkheden: Huwelijks- en liefdeproblemen in
       brieven die ik ontving.*

259   **"We may have been Jews"**: HP/De Tijd, Dec. 24, 1993. Quoted in www
       .hennyble.dds.nl/engels/chapt_02.htm.

260   **According to one story**: Müller, *Anne Frank*, 49.

CHAPTER 9: *"WE INFORM YOU OF THE ACTION OF A POWERFUL
GERMAN FORCE"*

263   **"Nobody will question"**: Maass, *Netherlands at War*, 19.

263   **Even after numerous**: Mak, *Kleine geschiedenis*, 249.

264   **"We inform you of the"**: Maass, *Netherlands at War*, 31.

265   **The story goes that the Luftwaffe**: Stigter, *Bezette stad*, passim. The
       bullet story comes from a tour of the Stadsarchief.

265   **Mass executions of Jews**: Operation Tannenberg began in August 1939.

266   **"an indispensable aid"**: *"Een onmisbaar hulpmiddel voor het vervolgings-
       beleid van de Duitse bezetter."*

267   **Of approximately 80,000 Jews**: Croes and Tammes, *Gif laten wij niet
       voortbestaan*, 39.

267   **"The path of collaboration"**: De Jong, *Netherlands and Nazi Germany*, 11.

268   **"the first and only antipogrom"**: De Jong, *Netherlands and Nazi Ger-
       many*, 8.

270   **The most daring and**: For the Van Halls during the war I have relied
       on E. Schaap, *Walraven van Hall*, esp. 50–100, and http://www.verzets
       museum.org/museum/nl/exposities/tijdelijk,geweest/wally-van-hall.

271   **In 2010, the city of Amsterdam**: The monument is in front of the cur-
       rent headquarters of the Dutch National Bank. At the time of the rob-
       bery, the bank was housed in a building on the Rokin.

271   **"Nations of heroes do"**: De Jong, *Netherlands and Nazi Germany*, 49.

272   **in today's money**: http://www.iisg.nl/hpw/calculate.php.
273   **"She's not a mother"**: Frank, *Diary*, 141, 185.
273   **"Night after night, green"**: Frank, *Diary*, 69.
273   **"It's funny, but I can"**: Frank, *Diary*, 167.
273   **Both the Brommets and the Franks**: In reconstructing this episode I
       have relied on Middelburg, *Jeanne de Leugenaarster*, and Van Liempt,
       Frieda: Verslag van een gelijmd leven, in addition to interviews with Frieda
       Menco.
277   **You can see the thousands**: http://stadsarchief.amsterdam.nl/english/
       amsterdam_treasures/second_world_war/doden_op_7_mei_1945/index
       .en.html.
283   **It later became the Cultuur**: http://www.coc.nl/over-ons.
284   **"The problem of homosexuality"**: Boelaars, *Benno Premsela*, 50–51.

CHAPTER 10: THE MAGIC CENTER

288   **In 1960, on learning that**: My account of Amsterdam's counterculture
       movement is based on Righart, *De eindeloze jaren zestig*; Kempton, *Provo*;
       Van Duijn, *Diepvriesfiguur*; Kennedy, "Building New Babylon"; Voeten,
       "Dutch Provos"; as well as interviews.
288   **"I thought, we just finished"**: Personal interview, December 14, 2012.
295   **Beatles fans started to**: My take on the bed-in relies on Brugge, Van
       Galen, and Van den Hanenberg, *In Bed met John en Yoko*; Sheff, *Playboy
       Interviews*; Wiener, *Come Together*; Righart, *De eindeloze jaren zestig*; and
       interviews.
296   **"That's a good idea"**: http://vorige.nrc.nl/international/article2185207
       .ece/Amsterdam_remembers_John_and_Yokos_bed-in.
296   **"If people are invited to"**: Wiener, *Come Together*, 88.
296   **"We told them"**: Personal interview, December 18, 2012.
297   **Lennon held himself back**: http://weblogs.vpro.nl/radioarchief/2008/
       12/08/sterfdag-john-lennon/.
299   **In 1900, more than 45 percent**: http://www.os.amsterdam.nl/pdf/2001_
       factsheets_5.pdf
300   **The Dutch American historian**: Kennedy, "Building New Babylon."
300   **In 1973, three political parties**: De Kort, *Tussen patiënt en delinquent*,
       224.
301   **"clear and fair trade"**: http://www.onsamsterdam.nl/tijdschrift/jaargang
       2008/252-nummer-11-12-november-december-2008?start=6.
303   **"As a freelancer you may"**: http://rodedraad.nl/index.php?id=1720.
304   **Prescription rates for antidepressants**: http://www.capmh.com/content/
       2/1/26.
306   **"I came to realize"**: Hirsi Ali, *Infidel*, 238.
306   **"Look at how many Voltaires"**: Hirsi Ali, *Infidel*, 275. Note that I am
       relying on Hirsi Ali's own recollection of what she said.
314   **And the political scientist Francis**: Fukuyama, *Origins of Political Order*,
       19–22.

Bibliography

Abrahamse, Jaap Evert. *De Grote Uitleg van Amsterdam*. Bussum: Uitgeverij Thoth, 2010.

Adams, Ann Jensen. *Public Faces and Private Identities in Seventeenth-Century Holland: Portraiture and the Production of Community*. Cambridge: Cambridge University Press, 2009.

Adams, John. *A Collection of State-Papers Relative to the First Acknowledgment of the Sovereignty of the United States of America, And the Reception of their Minister Plenipotentiary, by their High Mightinesses the States General of the United Netherlands*. London: 1782.

Afek, Arnon, Tal Friedman, et al. "Dr. Tulp's Anatomy Lesson by Rembrandt: The Third Day Hypothesis." *IMAJ* 11 (July 2009): 389–92.

Arblaster, Paul. *A History of the Low Countries*. Basingstoke: Palgrave, 2006.

Arnade, Peter. *Beggars, Iconoclasts, and Civic Patriots: The Political Culture of the Dutch Revolt*. Ithaca: Cornell University Press, 2008.

Asaert, Gustaaf. *1585: De val van Antwerpen en de uittocht van Vlamingen en Brabanders*. Tielt: Lannoo, 2004.

Aubery, Louis du Maurier. *Mémoires pour servir à l'histoire de Hollande et des autres provinces unies*. Paris: 1680.

Augustijn, Cornelis. *Erasmus: His Life, Works, and Influence*. Toronto: University of Toronto Press, 1991.

Bailey, Anthony. *Rembrandt's House*. Boston: Houghton Mifflin, 1978.

Bakker, Boudewijn, Maria van Berge-Gerbaud, Erik Schmitz, and Jan Peeters. *Landscapes of Rembrandt: His Favorite Walks*. Bussum: Uitgeverij Thoth, 1998.

Bank, Jan, and Maarten van Buuren. *1900: Hoogtij van burgerlijke cultuur*. The Hague: Sdu, 2000.

Barnes, Donna. *The Butcher, the Baker, the Candlestick Maker: Jan Luyken's Mirrors of 17th-Century Dutch Daily Life*. Hempstead: Hofstra Museum, 1995.

Bastin, John. "The Changing Balance of the Southeast Asian Pepper Trade." *Spices in the Indian Ocean World*. Ed. M. N. Pearson. Aldershot: Variorum, 1996.

Beemon, Fred Edwin. "The Ideology of Rebellion: Philippe de Marnix, Sieur de Sainte Aldegonde, and the Dutch Revolt." PhD diss., University of Tennessee, 1988.

Benedict, Philip, Guido Marnef, Henk van Nierop, and Marc Venard, eds. *Reformation, Revolt, and Civil War in France and the Netherlands, 1555–1585*. Amsterdam: Royal Netherlands Academy of Arts and Sciences, 1999.

Bloemgarten, Salvador. *Henri Polak: Social democraat*. The Hague: Koninginnegracht, 1993.

Boelaars, Bert. *Benno Premsela: Voorvechter van homo-emancipatie*. Bussum: Uitgeverij Thoth, 2008.

Bøgh Rønberg, Lene, and Eva de la Fuente Pedersen. *Rembrandt: The Master and His Workshop*. Copenhagen: Statens Museum for Kunst, 2006.

Bosman, Machiel. *De polsslag van de stad: De Amsterdamse stadskroniek van Jacob Bicker Raije (1732–1772)*. Amsterdam: Athenaeum, 2009.

Boxer, C. R. *The Dutch Seaborne Empire, 1600–1800*. London: Penguin, 1990.

Brandhorst, Henny. "From Neo-Malthusianism to Sexual Reform: The Dutch Section of the World League for Sexual Reform." *Journal of the History of Sexuality* 12 (Jan. 2003): 38–67.

Brants, Chrisje. "The Fine Art of Regulated Tolerance: Prostitution in Amsterdam." *Journal of Law and Society* 25 (Dec. 1998): 621–35.

Bromley, J. S., and E. H. Kossmann, eds. *Britain and the Netherlands: Papers Delivered to the Oxford-Netherlands Historical Conference, 1959*. London: Chatto and Windus, 1960.

Brugge, Jan-Cees ter, Jan van Galen, and Patrick van den Hanenberg. *In Bed met John en Yoko: Acht Geruchtmakende Dagen in het Hilton Hotel Amsterdam*. Amsterdam: Nijgh and Van Ditmar, 2009.

Bruggeman, J. G. *Geschiedenis van het Nederlandse liberalisme*. Assen: Van Gorcum, 1982.

Brugmans, H. *Geschiedenis van Amsterdam*. Utrecht: Het Spectrum, 1973.

Buchanan, Allen E. *Marx and Justice: The Radical Critique of Liberalism*. Totowa: Rowman and Littlefield, 1982.

Buruma, Ian. *Murder in Amsterdam: The Death of Theo van Gogh and the Limits of Tolerance*. New York: Penguin, 2006.

Chapman, H. Perry. *Rembrandt's Self-Portraits: A Study in Seventeenth-Century Identity*. Princeton: Princeton University Press, 1990.

Claydon, Tony. *William III and the Godly Revolution*. Cambridge: Cambridge University Press, 2004.

Cohen, P., and A. Sas. *Cannabis Use in Amsterdam*. Amsterdam: Centrum voor Drugsonderzoek, 1998.

Cook, Harold J. *Matters of Exchange: Commerce, Medicine, and Science in the Dutch Golden Age*. New Haven: Yale University Press, 2007.

Cranston, Maurice. *John Locke: A Biography*. London: Longmans, 1957.

Croes, Marnix. "The Holocaust in the Netherlands and the Rate of Jewish Survival." *Holocaust and Genocide Studies* 20 (Winter 2006): 474–99.

Croes, Marnix, and Peter Tammes, *"Gif laten wij niet voortbestaan"*: *Een onderzoek naar de overlevingskansen van Joden in de Nederlandse gemeenten, 1940–1945.* Amsterdam: Aksant, 2006.

De Haan, Ido. "Imperialism, Colonialism, and Genocide: The Dutch Case for an International History of the Holocaust." *BMGN/LCHR* 125 (July 2010): 301–27.

Deinema, M., and M. B. Aalbers. "A Global Red Light City? Prostitution in Amsterdam as a Real-and-Imagined Place." *Imagining Global Amsterdam: History, Culture, and Geography in a World City.* Ed. M. de Waard. Amsterdam: Amsterdam University Press, 2012.

Deinema, Michaël. "Amsterdam's Re-emergence as a Major Publishing Hub in a Changing International Context." Paper presented at the IXth International Conference on Urban History, Lyon, Aug. 29, 2008.

De Jong, Loe. *The Netherlands and Nazi Germany.* Cambridge: Harvard, 1990.

De Kort, Marcel. *Tussen patiënt en delinquent: geschiedenis van het Nederlandse drugsbeleid.* Hilversum: Uitgeverij Verloren, 1995.

De Kruif, H. *Dagboek van broeder Wouter Jacobsz., 1572–1579.* Soesterberg: Aspekt, 2008.

De la Bruhèze, A. A. Albert, and F. C. A. Veraart. *Fietsverkeer in praktijk en beleid in de twintigste eeuw.* Eindhoven: Stichting Historie der Techniek, 1999.

De la Court, Pieter. *The True Interest and Political Maxims of the Republic of Holland.* London, 1746.

De Rooy, Piet, and Emma Los, eds. *De canon van Amsterdam.* Amsterdam: Boom, 2008.

Descartes, René. *The Philosophical Writings: Volume 3: The Correspondence.* Cambridge: Cambridge University, 1991.

De Vries, Jan. *The Dutch Rural Economy in the Golden Age, 1500–1700.* New Haven: Yale University Press, 1974.

Draper, Hal. *The Marx-Engels Chronicle.* New York: Schocken, 1985.

Dudok van Heel, S. A. C. *Nicolaes Tulp: The Life and Work of an Amsterdam Physician and Magistrate in the 17th Century.* Amsterdam: Six Art Promotion, 1998.

Duyvendak, J. W., and P. W. A. Scholten. "Beyond the Dutch 'Multicultural Model': The Coproduction of Integration Policy Frames in the Netherlands." *The Journal of International Migration and Immigration* 12 (2011): 331–48.

Elenbaas, Peter, and Lambiek Berends. *Amsterdam Onbewolkt.* Amsterdam: Uitgeverij Bas Lubberhuizen, 2005.

Elias, Joh. E. *De vroedschap van Amsterdam, 1578–1795.* Haarlem, 1903.

———. *Geschiedenis van het Amsterdamsche Regentenpatriciaat.* The Hague, 1923.

Emeis Jr., M. G. Series of articles on the history of Amsterdam appearing in *Ons Amsterdam*, February, March, May, June, November, December 1975.

Faculty of Architecture, Technical University Delft. *Architecture in the Netherlands, 1900–2000*. Rotterdam: NAi, 1999.

Fasseur, C. "Purse or Principle: Dutch Colonial Policy in the 1860s and the Decline of the Cultivation System." *Modern Asian Studies* 25 (1991): 33–52.

Feddes, Fred. *A Millennium of Amsterdam: Spatial History of a Marvelous City*. Bussum: Thoth, 2012.

Fernow, B., ed. *The Records of New Amsterdam from 1653 to 1674*. Trans. E. B. O'Callaghan. 7 vols. New York, 1897.

Feuer, Lewis S. *Spinoza and the Rise of Dutch Liberalism*. New Brunswick: Transaction, 1987.

Frank, Anne. *The Diary of a Young Girl*. New York: Penguin, 2001.

Fruin, Robert. *Tien jaren uit den Tachtigjarigen Oorlog, 1588–1598*. The Hague: Nijhoff, 1899.

Fuchs, R. H. *Rembrandt en Amsterdam*. Rotterdam: Lemniscaat Rotterdam, 1968.

Fukuyama, Francis. *The Origins of Political Order: From Prehuman Times to the French Revolution*. New York: Farrar, Straus & Giroux, 2011.

Gaastra, Femme S. *De geschiedenis van de VOC*. Zutphen: Walburg Pers, 1991.

Galbraith, John Kenneth. *A Short History of Financial Euphoria*. New York: Penguin, 1994.

Gehring, Charles, et al., trans. and eds. *New Netherland Documents Series*. 5 vols. Syracuse: Syracuse University Press, 1987–2003.

Gelderblom, Oscar. *Zuid-Nederlandse kooplieden en de opkomst van de Amsterdamse stapelmarkt (1578–1630)*. Hilversum: Verloren, 2000.

Geschiedenis van Amsterdam. Ed. Marijke Carasso-Kok, Willem Frijhoff, R. A. M. Aerts, and Piet de Rooy. 4 vols. Amsterdam: Sun, 2004–07.

Goldstein, Rebecca Newberger. *Betraying Spinoza: The Renegade Jew Who Gave Us Modernity*. New York: Schocken, 2006.

Guicciardini, Ludovico. *The Description of the Low Countreys*. London, 1593. Amsterdam: Theatrum Orbis Terrarum, 1976.

Hakluyt, Richard. *The Principal Navigations, Voyages, Traffiques, and Discoveries of the English Nation*. Vol. 10. Glasgow, 1903–05.

Haley, K. H. D. *The Dutch in the Seventeenth Century*. London: Harcourt Brace Jovanovich, 1972.

Haverkamp-Begemann, E. *Rembrandt: The Nightwatch*. Princeton: Princeton University Press, 1982.

Hirsi Ali, Ayaan. *Infidel*. New York: Free Press, 2007.

Hobbes, Thomas. *Hobbes's Leviathan: Reprinted from the Edition of 1651*. Oxford: Clarendon, 1929.

Homza, Lu Ann. *The Spanish Inquisition, 1478–1614: An Anthology of Sources*. Indianapolis: Hackett, 2006.

Hoogenboom, Annemieke, Bert Gerlagh, and Jan Stroop. *De wereld van Chrstiaan Andriessen: Amsterdamse dagboektekeningen, 1805–1808*. Bussum: Thoth, 2008.

Hughes, Robert. "The God of Realism." *New York Review of Books*, April 6, 2006.

Huizinga, J. H. *Dutch Civilization in the Seventeenth Century*. New York: Harper and Row, 1968.

Hunt, Lynn, Margaret C. Jacob, and Wijnand Mijnhardt. *The Book That Changed Europe: Picart & Bernard's Religious Ceremonies of the World.* Cambridge: Belknap Press, 2010.

Hunter, Michael, and David Wootton, eds. *Atheism from the Reformation to the Enlightenment.* Oxford: Clarendon, 1992.

Israel, Jonathan. *Dutch Primacy in World Trade: 1585–1740.* Oxford: Clarendon, 1989.

———. *The Dutch Republic: Its Rise, Greatness, and Fall.* Oxford: Clarendon, 1995.

———. *Radical Enlightenment: Philosophy and the Making of Modernity, 1650–1750.* Oxford: Oxford University Press, 2001.

———. *A Revolution of the Mind: Radical Enlightenment and the Intellectual Origins of Modern Democracy.* Princeton: Princeton University Press, 2010.

———, ed. *The Anglo-Dutch Moment: Essays on the Glorious Revolution and Its World Impact.* Cambridge: Cambridge University Press, 1991.

Jacobs, Aletta. *Memories: My Life as an International Leader in Health, Suffrage, and Peace.* New York: Feminist Press, 1996.

Jacobs, Jaap. *New Netherland: A Dutch Colony in Seventeenth-Century America.* Leiden: Brill, 2005.

Janse, Herman. *Building Amsterdam.* Amsterdam: de Brink, n.d.

Jansen, A. C. M. *Cannabis in Amsterdam: Een geografie van hashish en marijuana.* Amsterdam: Coutinho, 1989.

———. "The Development of a 'Legal' Consumers' Market for Cannabis: The 'Coffee Shop' Phenomenon." *Between Prohibition and Legalization: The Dutch Experiment in Drug Policy.* Ed. Ed Leuw and Ineka Haen Marshall. Amsterdam and New York: Kugler, 1994.

Jansen, Leo, Hans Luijten, and Nienke Bakker, eds. *Vincent van Gogh: The Letters.* Amsterdam and The Hague: Van Gogh Museum and Huygens ING, 2010. http://vangoghletters.org.

Jardine, Lisa. *Going Dutch: How England Plundered Holland's Glory.* London: HarperCollins, 2008.

Jarrell, Randall. *A Sad Heart at the Supermarket: Essays & Fables.* New York: Atheneum, 1962.

Jonker, Joost. *Merchants, Bankers, Middlemen: The Amsterdam Money Market during the First Half of the 19th Century.* Amsterdam: Neha, 1996.

Kamen, Henry. *Philip of Spain.* New Haven: Yale University Press, 1997.

———. *The Duke of Alba.* New Haven: Yale University Press, 2004.

Kempton, Richard. *Provo: Amsterdam's Anarchist Revolt.* New York: Autonomedia, 2008.

Kennedy, James. "Building New Babylon: Cultural Change in the Netherlands during the Sixties." PhD diss., University of Iowa, 1995.

Keyes, George. *Pieter Bast.* Alphen aan den Rijn: Canaletto, 1981.

Killiam, Tim, and Marieke van der Ziejden. *Amsterdam Canal Guide.* Utrecht: Het Spectrum, 1978.

King, Peter. *Multatuli.* New York: Twayne, 1972.

———. "Multatuli's Max Havelaar, Fact and Fiction." Bibliography and Literature Series, Paper No. 4. Hull: University of Hull Centre for South-East Asian Studies, 1987.

Klerk de Reus, G. C. *Geschichtlicher Überblick der administrativen, rechtlichen und finanziellen Entwicklung der Niederländischen-Ostindischen Compagnie*. The Hague, 1894.

Klomp, Aranka, and John Kroon, eds. *The Netherlands 2006: The Mood after the Hysteria*. Amsterdam: Prometheus/NRC Handelsblad, 2005.

Knobel. E. B. "On Frederick de Houtman's Catalogue of Southern Stars, and the Origin of the Southern Constellations." *Monthly Notices of the Royal Astronomical Society* 77 (1917): 414–32.

Koenig, Dorothy A., and Pim Nieuwenhuis. "Catalina Trico from Namur (1605–1689) and Her Nephew, Arnoldus de la Grange." *New Netherland Connections* 1 (1996): 55–63. Also "Further Information about Catalina Trico." *New Netherland Connections* 1 (1996): 89–93.

Koopman, José. "Huisvesting Universiteit van Amsterdam: van Agnietenkapel tot Bullewijk 1." *Ons Amsterdam* 27 (5), 1975.

Kossmann, E. H. *The Low Countries: 1780–1940*. Oxford: Clarendon, 1978.

Kossmann, E. H., and A. F. Mellink, eds. *Texts concerning the Revolt of the Netherlands*. London: Cambridge University Press, 1974.

Kuijpers, Erika. *Migrantenstad: Immigratie en sociale verhoudingen in 17e-eeuws Amsterdam*. Hilversum: Verloren, 2005.

Lamster, Mark. *Master of Shadows: The Secret Diplomatic Career of the Painter Peter Paul Rubens*. New York: Doubleday, 2009.

Lendering, Jona, and Arjen Bosman. *De ran van het Rijk: De Romeinen en de Laghe Landen*. Amsterdam: Athenaeum, 2010.

Lesger, Clé. *The Rise of the Amsterdam Market and Information Exchange*. Hants: Ashgate, 2006.

Lettenhove, Kervyn de. *Relations politiques des Pays-Bas et de l'Angleterre sous le règne de Philippe II*. 11 vols. Brussels, 1882–1900.

Levy-Vroelant, Clair, Christoph Reinprecht, and Frank Wassenberg. "Learning from History: Changes and Path Dependency in the Social Housing Sector in Austria, France, and the Netherlands (1889–2008)." *Social Housing in Europe II: A Review of Policies and Outcomes*. Ed. Kathleen Scanlon and Christine Whitehead. London: LSE London, 2008.

Locke, John. *A Letter concerning Toleration*. London, 1689.

———. *An Essay concerning Human Understanding*. New York: Meridian, 1964.

Logtenberg, Hugo, and Marcel Wiegman. *Job Cohen: Burgemeester van Nederland*. Amsterdam: Nieuw Amsterdam, 2010.

Maass, Walter B. *The Netherlands at War: 1940–1945*. London: Abelard-Schuman, 1970.

Mak, Geert. *Amsterdam: A Brief Life of the City*. Amsterdam: Olympus, 1994.

Maltby, William. *The Reign of Charles V*. New York: Palgrave, 2002.

Manent, Pierre. *An Intellectual History of Liberalism*. Princeton: Princeton University Press, 1994.

Melamed, Yitzhak, and Michael Rosenthal, eds. *Spinoza's "Theological-Political Treatise": A Critical Guide*. Cambridge: Cambridge University Press, 2010.

Middelburg, Bart. *Jeanne de Leugenaarster: Adriana Valkenburg: hoerenmadam, verraadster, femme fatale*. Amsterdam: Nieuw Amsterdam, 2009.

Mijnhardt, Wijnand. "Urbanization, Culture, and the Dutch Origins of the European Enlightenment." *Low Countries Historical Review* 125 (2010): 139–77.

Mijnhardt, Wijnand. "Tolerantie als politiek probleem." *Rekenschap* 43 (1996): 121–28.

Molhuysen, P. C., and P. J. Block, eds. *Nieuw Nederlandsch biografisch woordenboek*. Leiden: Sijthoff, 1933.

Montagne, O., and Johan Winkler. *Doctor Henri Polak: Van het vuur dat in hem brandde*. Amsterdam: Kuurstra, 1948.

Moryson, Fyne. *An Itinerary: Containing His Ten Yeeres Travell through the Twelve Dominions of Germany, Bohmerland, Sweitzerland, Netherland, Denmarke, Poland, Italy, Turky, France, England, Scotland, & Ireland*. Glasgow: University Press, 1907.

Motley, John Lothrop. *The Rise of the Dutch Republic*. New York: Thomas Crowell, 1901.

Müller, Melissa. *Anne Frank: The Biography*. New York: Metropolitan, 1998.

Multatuli [Eduard Douwes Dekker]. *Max Havelaar: Or the Coffee Auctions of a Dutch Trading Company*. New York: Penguin, 1987.

Multatuli [Eduard Douwes Dekker]. *Ideën*. 7 vols. Amsterdam, 1862–77.

Nadler, Steven. *Spinoza: A Life*. Cambridge: Cambridge University Press, 1999.

———. *A Book Forged in Hell: Spinoza's Scandalous Treatise and the Birth of the Secular Age*. Princeton: Princeton University Press, 2011.

Naifeh, Steven, and Gregory White Smith. *Van Gogh: The Life*. London: Profile, 2011.

O'Callaghan, Edmund. *Calendar of Dutch Historical Manuscripts in the Office of the Secretary of State, Albany, New York, 1630–1664*. Ridgewood, N.J.: Gregg, 1968.

Outshoorn, Joyce. "Pragmatism in the Polder: Changing Prostitution Policy in the Netherlands." *Journal of Contemporary European Studies* 12 (Aug. 2004): 165–76.

———, ed. *The Politics of Prostitution: Women's Movements, Democratic States, and the Globalisation of Sex Commerce*. Cambridge: Cambridge University Press, 2004.

Pakes, Francis. "Globalisation and the Governance of Dutch Coffee Shops." *European Journal of Crime, Criminal Law, and Criminal Justice* 17 (2009): 243–57.

Parker, Geoffrey. *The Grand Strategy of Philip II*. New Haven: Yale University Press, 1998.

———. *The Dutch Revolt*. London: Penguin, 2002.

Parthesius, Robert. *Dutch Ships in Tropical Waters: The Development of the Dutch East India Company Shipping Network in Asia, 1595–1660*. Amsterdam: Amsterdam University Press, 2010.

Petram, Lodewijk. "The World's First Stock Exchange: How the Amsterdam Market for Dutch East India Company Shares Became a Modern Securities Market, 1602–1700." Doctoral diss., University of Amsterdam, 2011.

Pontanus, Johannes. *Historische beschrijvinghe der seer wijt beroemde coop-stadt Amsterdam: Waer inne benevens de eerste beginselen ende opcomsten der stadt, verscheyden privilegien, ordonnantien, ende andere ghedenckweerdighe gheschiedenissen met het ghene de nieuwe vergrootinghen der stadt, als oock de handel ende verre reysen ende de politie betreffende is, tot desen teghenwoordighen tijt.* Amsterdam, 1614.

Presser, Jacob. *Ashes in the Wind: The Destruction of Dutch Jewry.* London: Souvenir Press, 1968.

Price, Richard. *Observations on the Nature of Civil Liberty, the Principles of Government, and the Justice and Policy of the War with America.* 1776.

Raico, Ralph. "Liberalism, Marxism, and the State." *Cato Journal* 11 (Winter 1992): 391–404.

Ricklefs, M. C. *A History of Modern Indonesia since c. 1300.* London: Macmillan, 2009.

Righart, Hans. *De eindeloze jaren zestig: Geschiedenis van een generatieconflict.* Amsterdam: Arbeiderspers, 1995.

Roeper, Vibeke, and Diederick Wildeman. *Om de Zuid: De Eerste Schipvaart naar Oost-Indië onder Cornelis de Houtman, 1595–1597, opgetekend door Willem Lodewycksz.* Nijmegen: Uitgeverij Sun, 1997.

Röling, Hugo. "Bernard Premsela, pionier van de seksuologie." *Ons Amsterdam,* Sept. 1994.

Rouffaer, Gerrit, and Jan Willem Ijzerman. *De eerste scheepvaart der Nederlanders naar Oost-Indië onder Cornelis de Houtman, 1595–1597.* The Hague: Nijhoff, 1915.

Russell, Bertrand. *A History of Western Philosophy.* London: Allen & Unwin, 1946.

Rybczynski, Witold. *Home: A Short History of an Idea.* New York: Penguin, 1986.

Schaap, Erik. *Walraven van Hall: Premier van het verzet.* Wormer: Stichting Uitgeverij Noord-Holland, 2006.

Schaap, Ton. *Amsterdam.* Rotterdam: Forum, 2008.

Schama, Simon. *The Embarrassment of Riches.* Berkeley: University of California, 1988.

Schnabel, Paul, Kees Rijnboutt, Richard Koek, and Ton Schaap. *The Design of Urban Public Space.* Amsterdam: Praemium Erasmianum Foundation, 2011.

Schuurman, Paul. "Locke and the Dutch: A Preliminary Survey." *Geschiedenis van de Wijsbegeerte in Nederland. Documentatieblad van de Werkgroep Sassen* 11 (2000): 119–40.

Schwartz, Gary. *Rembrandt's Universe: His Art, His Life, His World.* London: Thames and Hudson, 2006.

Schwartz, Gary. *The Night Watch.* Amsterdam: Rijksmuseum, n.d.

Sheff, David. *The Playboy Interviews with John Lennon and Yoko Ono.* Sevenoaks: New English Library, 1981.

Shorto, Russell. *The Island at the Center of the World.* New York: Doubleday, 2004.

———. *Descartes' Bones.* New York: Doubleday, 2008.

Sigmond, Robert, and Cees van den Bosch. *Escape across the Rhine: Operations*

"Pegasus" I and II, October/November 1944. Oosterbeek: Airborne Museum, 1999.

Spierenburg, Pieter. *Written in Blood: Fatal Attraction in Enlightenment Amsterdam.* Columbus: Ohio State University Press, 2004.

Spies, Paul, et al., eds. *The Canals of Amsterdam.* The Hague: SDU Uitgeverij Koninginnegracht, 1991.

——, eds. *Het Grachtenboek.* The Hague: SDU Uitgeverij Koninginnegracht, 1992.

Spinoza, Baruch. *Tractatus Theologico-Politicus. The Chief Works of Benedict de Spinoza.* Ed. R. H. M. Elwes. Rev. ed. Vols. 1 and 2. London, 1919.

Sprunger, Keith. *Trumpets from the Tower: English Puritan Printing in the Netherlands, 1600–1640.* New York: Brill, 1994.

Stigter, Bianca. *De bezette stad: Plattegrond van Amsterdam 1940–1945.* Amsterdam: Athenaeum, 2005.

Sutton, Peter C. *Jan van der Heyden (1637–1712).* New Haven: Yale University Press, 2006.

Swart, Fred. "Lambert Biesman (1573–1601) of the Company of Trader-Adventurers, the Dutch Route to the East Indies, and Olivier van Noort's Circumnavigation of the Globe." *Journal of the Hakluyt Society* (Dec. 2007).

Temple, William. *Observations upon the United Provinces of the Netherlands.* Oxford: Clarendon, 1972.

Thomas, Hugh. *The Golden Age: The Spanish Empire of Charles V.* London: Allen Lane, 2010.

Threlfall, Tim. *Piet Mondrian: His Life's Work and Evolution, 1872–1944.* New York: Garland, 1988.

Toer, Pramoedya Ananta. "The Book That Killed Colonialism." *New York Times Magazine,* April 18, 1999.

Tracy, James D. *Erasmus of the Low Countries.* Berkeley: University of California Press, 1996.

Unger, Richard. "Dutch Herring: Technology and International Trade in the Seventeenth Century." *The Journal of Economic History* 40 (June 1980): 253–80.

——. *Dutch Shipbuilding Before 1800.* Assen: Van Gorcum, 1978.

Van Boven, M. W. "Towards a New Age of Partnership: An Ambitious World Heritage Project." UNESCO "Memory of the World" application, 2002.

Van Bunge, Wiep, and Wim Klever, eds. *Disguised and Overt Spinozism around 1700.* Leiden: Brill, 1996.

Van de Pol, Lotte. *The Burgher and the Whore: Prostitution in Early Modern Amsterdam.* Oxford: Oxford University Press, 2011.

Van der Capellen tot den Pol, Joan Derk. *Aan het Volk van Nederland.* Weesp: Heureka, 1981.

Van der Heyden, Jan. *A Description of Fire Engines with Water Hoses and the Method of Fighting Fires Now Used in Amsterdam.* Trans. and introd. Lettie Stibbe Multhauf. Canton: Science History Publications, 1996.

Van der Meulen, Dik. *Multatuli: Leven en werk van Eduard Douwes Dekker.* Amsterdam: Sun, 2002.

Van der Werf, Jouke, and Jan Derwig. *Beurs van Berlage*. Amsterdam: Architectura & Natura, 1994.

Van Deursen, A. Th. *Plain Lives in a Golden Age*. New York: Cambridge University Press, 2003.

Van Dillen, J. G. "Nieuwe Gegevens Omtrent de Amsterdamsche Compagnieën Van Verre." *Tijdschrift voor Geschiedenis* 45 (1930): 350–59.

Van Dillen, J. G., Geoffrey Poitras, and Asha Majithia. "Isaac Le Maire and the Early Trading in Dutch East India Company Shares." *Pioneers of Financial Economics*. Ed. Geoffrey Poitras. Vol. 1. Cheltenham: Edward Elgar, 2006.

Van Duijn, Roel. *Diepvriesfiguur: Autobiografie van PD106043 in samenwerking met de AIVD*. Amsterdam: Van Praag, 2012.

Van Gelder, R., and R. Kistemaker. *Amsterdam 1275–1795: De ontwikkeling van een handelsmetropool*. Amsterdam: Amsterdams Historisch Museum, 1982.

Van Gogh, Vincent. *The Letters*. Ed. Leo Jansen, Hans Luijten, and Nienke Bakker. Van Gogh Museum. www.vangoghletters.org.

Van Laer, A. J. F. *New York Historical Manuscripts: Dutch*. 4 vols. Baltimore: Genealogical Publishing, 1974.

Van Liempt, Ad. *Frieda—verslag van een gelijmd leven*. Westerbork: Herinneringscentrum Kamp Westerbork, 2007.

Van Limborch, Phillipus. *A Compleat System, or Body of Divinity: Both Speculative and Practical, Founded on Scripture and Reason Written Originally in Latin, by Philip Limborch; with Improvements, from Bishop Wilkins, Doctor Scott, and Several Other Divines of the Church of England*. Trans. William Jones. 2 vols. 1702.

Van Rijn, Elmer. "Patriotic Propaganda and the Development of the Calvinist Party in the Netherlands, 1576–1581." PhD diss., University of Michigan, 1955.

Van Tulder, Roland, et al., eds. *Het XYZ van Amsterdam*. Amsterdam: Selexyz Scheltema, 2008.

Verwey, H. de la Fontaine. "The Seventeenth Century." *Copy and Print in the Netherlands: An Atlas of Historical Bibliography*. Ed. Wytze Hellinga. Amsterdam: North Holland Publishing, 1962.

Visser, C. *Luther's Geschriften in de Nederlanden tot 1546*. Assen: Van Gorcum, 1969.

Voeten, Teun. "Dutch Provos." *High Times*, Jan. 1990.

Wedgwood, C. V. *William the Silent*. London: Jonathan Cape, 1944.

Welsh, Robert P. *Piet Mondrian's Early Career*. New York: Garland, 1977.

Welsh, Robert, Boudewijn Bakker, and Marty Bax. *Mondriaan aan de Amstel, 1892–1912*. Bussum: Thoth, 1994.

Wennekes, Emile. *Het Paleis voor Volksvlijt (1864–1929)*. The Hague: Sdu Uitgevers, 1999.

Wibaut, F. M. *Levensbouw*. Amsterdam: Querido, 1936.

Wiener, Jon. *Come Together: John Lennon in His Time*. London: Faber and Faber, 1984.

Wijnman, H. F. "Een episode uit het leven van Rembrandt: De Geschiedenis van Geertje Dircks." *Jaarboek Amstelodamum* (1968): 106–19.

Williams, Julia Lloyd. *Rembrandt's Women*. Munich: Prestel, 2001.
Woolhouse, Roger. *Locke: A Biography*. Cambridge: Cambridge University Press, 2007.
Zabriskie, George Olin. "The Founding Families of New Netherland, No. 4: The Rapalje-Rapelje Family." *De Halve Maen*, Jan.–July 1972.

Index

ABOUT THE AUTHOR

Russell Shorto is the bestselling author of *The Island at the Center of the World* and *Descartes' Bones*. He is the director of the John Adams Institute in Amsterdam and a contributing writer at *The New York Times Magazine*.